£12.99.

SPEAK
TO THE
HILLS

SPEAK
TO THE
HILLS

An anthology of
twentieth century British and
Irish mountain poetry

Edited by
HAMISH BROWN
and
MARTYN BERRY

Foreword by
NORMAN NICHOLSON

ABERDEEN UNIVERSITY PRESS

First published 1985
Aberdeen University Press
A member of the Pergamon Group

© This collection Hamish Brown and Martyn Berry 1985

The publisher acknowledges subsidy from the
Scottish Arts Council towards the publication
of this volume

British Library Cataloguing in Publication Data

Speak to the hills: an anthology of 20th century
   British and Irish mountain poetry
   1. Mountain—Poetry. 2. English Poetry
I. Brown, Hamish M. II. Berry, Martyn
821'.008'036   PR1195.M6/

ISBN 0 08 030406 0

PRINTED IN GREAT BRITAIN
THE UNIVERSITY PRESS
ABERDEEN

FOREWORD

Today, for many people, the hills are an escape, a place to 'get away from it all'. The reason for this is obvious yet, for me, it is at most a half-truth. I live within three miles of Black Combe — not the highest but the most conspicuous of all the Lake District hills, the most clearly visible and recognisable from as far away as Scotland or Wales. Yet I have not climbed Black Combe since 1930 when I was sixteen years old. From then onwards a slope with a vertical rise of a hundred feet has been as much as I can manage and two miles on the level is the fullest extent of a walk. From the point of view of most of the contributors to this anthology I just don't know what I'm talking about.

Yet, with the aid of buses or a car and much patience and some gumption, I have been able to visit many of the loneliest places in Britain, from Unst to Dartmoor, from the South Downs to Harris. I have sat for hours on the slopes of Black Combe, among bilberries and butterwort and Grass of Parnassus, in uninterrupted solitude, on days when the main roads of the Lake District were as busy as Oxford Circus. Until quite recently I could claim I was among the hills, two or three days a week, in almost any month of the year.

For all this, I have never felt that the hills were an 'escape'. They were the normal background to my everyday life, always on the close horizon. Even less familiar hills (Suilven, Ben Loyal, Cader Idris or the Malverns) were, as it were, a widening of that horizon but still, in essentials, the same kind of horizon. Though I was born and have lived all my life in Cumberland it was not in rural Cumberland. As a boy I did not think of myself as living in the country. Millom, in those days, had its iron-ore mines and its blast furnaces and, though its population was only ten thousand, it still seemed to me to be in all respects a town. The country was where the farmers lived; Millom and London were towns.

Strange as it may seem, many townspeople, perhaps even the majority, in Great Britain, live not far from and often in sight of the hills. London and the West Midlands are the exceptions and the attitudes of Londoners have been accepted as the norm for the English. The people of Manchester, Leeds and Newcastle can all look out to the hills from their taller buildings. Practically the whole of industrial Yorkshire and Lancashire is huddled round the foothills or tucked into the clefts of the Pennines. The Iron-and-Steel Age of the Twentieth Century had its beginnings, two hundred years ago, beside the becks of Southern Lakeland; the factory system evolved in the moorland valleys of East Lancashire.

The hills in fact remind us of what we come from. They are not, of course, nature entirely untouched by man. The Cumbrian fells are very different today from what they were before man arrived there. Tree-felling, the clearance of scrub, sheep farming, the silting up of tarns, the draining of mosses, the building of walls and, more recently, the planting of coniferous forests, all these have made great changes in the landscape. But only on the surface. The underlying shapes are still the same, there is still the feeling that this is rock-bottom nature, this what we have got to live on and with. This is the basic stuff of our world and, here, the elemental forces of sun, wind, rain, frost and ice are still at work. The slow process of geological change, the grinding down and building up of the landscape, is still going relentlessly on as it did millions of years before we came, and will continue after we have gone.

In the city and the suburb, in the farming factories of Lowland England, we can easily imagine that we now have nature well under control, that we can manipulate it in whatever way we may wish. It could be our fatal mistake. Muck about with the earth and we get denudation, sterility, famine; muck about with the atom, and we may be done for. If the hills are an escape at all, they are surely an escape back to reality.

Norman Nicholson

CONTENTS

THE HUMAN ANIMAL ON THE HILL

HABITATION AND HABITAT

HILLS TO THE NORTH

WAYMARKS OF THE ELEMENTAL

FELLS OF LAKELAND

THE HEART HAS ITS FEELINGS

SCOTTISH BENS AND GLENS

IN LIGHTER MOOD

INTRODUCTION

Most anthologies of poetry range widely in time, space and mood. This collection is confined to the interactions of men and women with our own home mountains and wild countryside. It is limited to twentieth century writing without being restricted by any date-line. In keeping to the present century we think there is a gain. Wordsworth and the Romantics have been anthologised enough, and our harsher world has moved so far and fast that a sparser verse is now more satisfying. There are plenty of poems included which are written in standard forms with 'good old-fashioned' rhyme and rhythm — but without the *thees* and *thous* that so marked the century gone.

The limitation of subject matter enables, paradoxically, a wide diversity of treatment. The approaches and styles are as varied as the hillgoers themselves. Some are frankly descriptive, others introspective to the point of near-obscurity, others take a new look at the eternal WHY, others simply look again at this natural world with clearer, fresher vision, some take sweeping views, others look at the detail, some preach, some weep, some are even prepared to laugh (we make no apology for the more frivolous penultimate section); many of the poems are Easy, some are Difficult, a few are Severe and there are the odd Extremes; but all can be enjoyed with little aid, art being greater than artificiality, as in climbing itself.

The collection is a mixture of work by 'professional' poets, who have happened to touch on mountains as a theme, and those who are essentially walkers and climbers who have simply, in irrational moments, broken into verse about their irrational pastime. We all head for the hills for enjoyment, for enrichment, whether they be there as Harrison's Rocks or Ben Nevis or spread as English Downs, Welsh Valleys, or the Macgillycuddy Reeks. We hope this collection mirrors the range of our moods and feelings on the heights as we have lived through a century of ups and downs. Within the century the emphasis is on contemporary work; thus while there are single poems by Kipling, W H Davies and John Masefield, there are more poems by Edward Thomas, Michael Roberts or Robert Graves — and a full measure from Patric Dickinson, Norman MacCaig, Ted Hughes and other writers of today. But this is, as indicated above, far more than a collection by well-known names; and one of the great joys for the editors has been the 'discovery' of many talented poets whose work deserves an audience wider than the specialist magazines and presses.

The poems have been laid out in alternating thematic and geographical groupings though there are overlapping ideas. An occasional minor theme pops up now and then and sometimes there are surprising conjunctions of style and personality. Some poets write almost entirely of one area (Norman Nicholson or R S Thomas spring to mind) while others (Andrew Young is the supreme example) range from end to end of the countries. Climbers may be surprised to see such a succession of names as Winthrop Young, Menlove Edwards, Wilf Noyce and Ed Drummond; they have written more than new routes on time's pages. Whatever our interests in hills, or poetry, this collection should provide a guide to summits new and old.

This is a big collection but we feel the subject merits it. There were many hundreds of poems we reluctantly left out; very little of the material from *Poems of the Scottish Hills*, for instance, has been repeated. (We feel that that book is a companion volume to this one — though it draws on all periods and includes dialect poems). Simply for reasons of space and to keep an overall evenness *all* dialects and languages other than English have been avoided in this collection. Balance, contrast, geographical needs, as well as quality, influenced which poems were used. In a few cases ridiculous copyright fees meant leaving out a work — which is tough on the poet.

Some hundreds of people have been involved; well over a thousand letters have been written in working towards the final poems we have selected. We would like to thank all our contacts, the helpful editors of magazines, the patient publishers, willing librarians, the gifted team of photographers, the two artists, the two cartoonists (for new pieces) and, of course, the contributing poets: to all these enthusiasts we sincerely dedicate this book.

A special thanks we reserve for Norman Nicholson for his Foreword.

We have tried to trace all sources of poems used, but it is possible that an occasional poem may inadvertently have appeared without the permission of a copyright holder. We apologise for any such and hope their appearance will be welcome. The Acknowledgements/Index of Authors has been laid out to act almost as a bibliography — and thus a spur to further reading. Mountains are after all only one (rather esoteric) aspect of our twentieth-century world. Most of the works quoted will be found in the following specialised libraries: The

Arts Council Poetry Library, 105 Piccadilly, London, WIV OAU, the Northern Arts Poetry Library, Central Library, The Willows, Morpeth, Northumberland, NE61 1TA, and the Scottish Poetry Library, Tweeddale Court, 14 High Street, Edinburgh EH1 1TE. (All publish useful catalogues.) We also made grateful use of the libraries of Trinity College, Dublin.

An author's spelling of names has normally been left unaltered. Descriptions of the subjects of the illustrations are given in the Acknowledgements/Index at the back of the book. This alphabetical list of contributors should assist in finding any person's poems and give enough bibliographical information to encourage 'further reading'.

January 1985

Hamish Brown
Martyn Berry

Go speak to the hills
Or shout on the sea,
Echoes will bring you
A brief liberty.

The Restless Compulsion

ALEX GILLESPIE

HIGH HILLS

There is much comfort in high hills,
and a great easing of the heart.
We look upon them, and our nature fills
with loftier images from their life apart.
They set our feet on curves of freedom, bent
to snap the circles of our discontent.

Mountains are moods; of larger rhythm and line,
moving between the eternal mode and mine.
Moments in thought, of which I too am part,
I lose in them my instant of brief ills. —
There is great easing of the heart,
and cumulance of comfort on high hills.

Geoffrey Winthrop Young

THE VALLEY

The valley,
dark arms of silent sleep,
will wait in vain for me.
I shall not come,
no, I cannot come,
for the hills have captured me.

I wrap my heart
on the starlight stair
and rest my feet by the silver stream.
I lay my head
By the overhang.
I watch the hills
and I dream.

Dave Gingell

ESCAPE

It is necessary
every once in a while
to escape
from the oppressive closeness
of the city;
to take a bus
away from the city
to a small village
up on the moor's edge
from where
I can walk up
into the hills
where there is
no roar of traffic
but the rippling of a stream
Though the city
is but a mere
bus ride away
it could be a million miles
for here is not the solitude
of the city,
which is loneliness,
but the solitude
of the country,
which is freedom

Gerald England

EVEREST OVER LONDON

Between new blocks of glass and steel
Rebuilt to deal with stocks and shares
A wide expanse of sky was seen,
Pale smokeless blue shading to green;
And high upon horizon's rim
An unseen hand began to limn
Great clouds with Everest their peak,
And sister mountains men still seek.
The summit's snowy plume was there,
Ethereal pink in sunset air,

While Lhotse, Nuptse reared nearby
On that unearthly blue-green sky.

They were so far, they were so near,
Yet no one seemed to see those clear
Uncommon spearpoints rising high.
Oh, buy and sell, and sell and buy,
No economic wares decry,
But let men see the dreaming once:
Their Everest before they die.

Odette Tchernine

from PROCESSIONAL

I must be rising and I must be going
On the roads of magic that stretch afar,
By the random rivers so finely flowing
And under the restless star . . .

Neil Munro

THE COMFORT OF THE HILLS

Heart! If you've a sorrow
    Take it to the hills!
Lay it where the sunshine
    Cups of colour spills!
Hide it in the shadow
    Of the folding fern;
Bathe it in the coolness
    Of the brown hill burn;
Give it to the west wind
    Blowing where it wills;
Heart! If you've a sorrow
    Take it to the hills!

Heart! If you've a sorrow
   Take it to the hills!
Where pity crowns the silence
   And love the loneness fills!
Bury it in bracken
   Waving green and high;
O'er it let the heather's
   Peaceful purple lie!
Trust it to the healing
   Heaven itself distils;
Heart! If you've a sorrow
   Take it to the hills!

Will H Ogilvie

THERMODYNAMICS

I saw beyond the blackboard and the bare wall,
Beyond the abstract, confining symbols
A rough and simple cliff, ascending in steep tiers
To fade in mist-bound mystery.

I travelled time and space to feel again
The grip of Vibram soles on weathered rock,
The trustful uplift of the body
On holds made safe by balance
Held in fingertip subjection;
I heard rope-rustle on the shelving slabs,
Friends' laughter and the headstrong wind;
I smelt the dew-damp heather, and
The gentle scent of turf and moss;
I saw the elemental rock,
Flecked with colour, scarped and wrinkled,
Cheerfully give way to skill;
Sudden sunshine on the crags,
And other ranges, distance-blue,
Guarding shadowed valleys;
I tasted joy, more wholesome sweet
Than pleasure and not cloying.

I knew the freedom of fellowship
Knit with stronger bonds than nylon.

I offered humble thanks, and quietly
Came back to the Lecture Room.

Martyn Berry

CHOICE

It is on etched hills and lithoed seas
That the stars appear to spin free
About the sky. Freedom is a glance
At the wheeling stars and we
Find that sight by choice, not chance.

Hamish Brown

SPACE

Give me a lake
Long enough to wind
Into the sunset.
Give me a wood
Vast enough to screen from me
A ruin or a rill
Even after years of searching.
Give me a wilderness,
Hill upon hill upon hill of it,
Stretching to I know not where;
Nor does the shepherd know;
Nor does the deer.
Nor ever will.

Thora Orton

ROCKS

'Look, mum — lovely rocks — there in that garden!
Are they real rocks, mum, like on mountains?'

Come, boy on the London bus — come!
Come to the mountains whence rocks come,
Come to the mountains that are their home.

The rocks in the garden are dead as fish
Slapped on the slab, served on the dish,
Corpses of rock, piteous mock,
Foolish, futile, forlorn.

Come to the crags where the rocks are born!
Come where the rocks are old as earth,
Young as at birth.
Come where they live, and never die,
Come where they sing, and cry.

Come, feel the granite grip the steel,
Stretch your knee, spring your heel.
Hear the wind yell in the heart of the fell
Booming around Helvellyn's bowl.
See the clouds race at Helvellyn's face,
Swirl and swoop and over loop
In an oceanic roll.

Come at night when the moon's alight
And the crags are black and the tarn is bright,
And lonely and lost you will see by chance
The great rocks stately dance.

Guy Ragland Phillips

8

OUTWARD BOUND

There's a waterfall I'm leaving
Running down the rocks in foam,
There's a pool for which I'm grieving
Near the water-ouzel's home,
And it's there that I'd be lying
With the heather close at hand,
And the curlews faintly crying
Mid the wastes of Cumberland.

While the midnight watch is winging
Thoughts of other days arise,
I can hear the river singing
Like the Saints in Paradise;
I can see the water winking
Like the merry eyes of Pan,
And the slow half-pounder sinking
By the bridge's granite span.

Ah! to win them back and clamber
Braced anew with winds I love,
From the river's stainless amber
To the morning mist above,
See through cloud-rifts rent asunder
Like a painted scroll unfurled,
Ridge and hollow rolling under
To the fringes of the world.

Now the weary guard are sleeping,
Now the great propellers churn,
Now the harbour lights are creeping
Into emptiness astern.
While the sentry wakes and watches
Plunging triangles of light
Where the water leaps and catches
At our escort in the night.

Great their happiness who seeing
Still with unbenighted eyes
Kin of theirs who gave them being,
Sun and earth that made them wise,

Die and feel their embers quicken
Year by year in summer time,
When the cotton grasses thicken
On the hills they used to climb.

Shall we also be as they be,
Mingled with our mother clay,
Or return no more it may be?
Who has knowledge, who shall say?
Yet we hope that from the bosom
Of our shaggy father Pan,
When the earth breaks into blossom
Richer from the dust of man,

Though the high Gods smite and slay us,
Though we come not whence we go,
As the host of Menelaus
Came there many years ago;
Yet the self-same wind shall bear us
From the same departing place
Out across the Gulf of Saros
And the peaks of Samothrace;

We shall pass in summer weather,
We shall come at eventide,
When the fells stand up together
And all quiet things abide;
Mixed with cloud and wind and river,
Sun-distilled in dew and rain,
One with Cumberland for ever
We shall go not forth again.

Nowell Oxland
(Killed in action, Gallipoli 1915)

'GO, HIDE AMONG THE HILLS'

Go, hide among the hills.
    Here is no place for you, men know you not.
Their passionate clamour fills
    Roadways and rooms. You walk unseen, forgot.

Why have you left your hills?
    Was it for those who brought to you their youth
And vowed to you their wills
    And loved the silences that harbour truth?

Far lie those mystic hills
    Behind us now; we face a conquering sea.
Storm follows storm and spills
    Its wreckage at our feet. These things must be.

You, with whispering of hills
    And faint reproach for tenderness betrayed,
Against these huger ills
    What strength, what hope have you, what barricade?

Is there talk in the hills
    Of crowds enmeshed in vast perplexities?
Or, were it so, what skills
    Mere truth amongst our fierce insanities?

Geoffrey Faber

UNITY

All the jewelled islands ride
firm on this moon-haunted tide,
blue Atlantic Hebrides,
bright Aegean Cyclades.

The cloud that on Olympus rests
will clothe the Cordillera crests
and snow on Monte Rosa turn
to Lakeland beck and Scottish burn.

And we shall turn from war's disgust,
and this dark prison of mistrust,
find life again on Lochnagar,
on Scafell and on Finsteraar:

Not slaves to time's dictatorship,
but free and kind relationship;
with mountain chains to span
the brotherhood of man.

Majorie Milsom

DAY DREAM

Strong winds blow loud from southward
   On the wide Jullundur plain,
And black clouds sweep the heavens
   With the burthen of their rain.

I am striding over Snilesworth
   Through the bracken and the heather,
Beating up along the headland
   In the wild and stormy weather,

With Black Hambledon before me,
   Ryedale Head upon the right,
Rain above and bog beneath me
   And a gale upon the height.

I breast the open moorland,
   To the summit I have fought —
And an orderly is standing
   At the entrance of my court.

Bill Cowley
(Rawalpindi 1942)

MOUNTAIN AIR

Give me a song of rushing streams
And the scent of mountain air,
To clean my lungs of the city grime,
And my mind of drab despair.

Let me tramp the hills when hope is dim,
When faith and courage falter;
With the sun and wind and the song of birds,
And the spray of tumbling water.

Then let me walk where the heather grows,
Far from the homes of men,
Where the tangled thread Life's pattern shows,
And the colour gleams again.

L H Cox

FROM THE PLAINS

I cannot bear the overbearing sky
That crushes down these sad and slavish lands
And swings unending round the weary eye
In everlasting circles. Nature stands
Stock-still in sulky idleness, and I
Upbraid her with unreasoning demands.

Oh for the torrents and the tall brave peaks,
The grey rock and the heather and the rain,
The mountains where the deeper music speaks
And, answering, the tired heart sings again!
Their distant calling seeks, forever seeks
Me out, and henceforth shall not seek in vain.

I will turn northwards from this lifeless place
Where the land wearies and the straight road kills
The spirit. I will turn, and set my face
Towards greener vales where purer water spills
In roaring joy and plenitude of grace,
And I may feel befriended of the hills.

Showell Styles

LAKESLOVE

Drunk with water —
Three sheets in the wind
With lake and pond.
With pool and beck,
With tarn and mere I am merry.
No vino or vodka here and all but sunk;
I am half seas over with Lakeland,
Drunk
With water.

Tipsy with trees —
Long-stemmed eyes crane up
Through curtained larch;
Through birch and fir,
Chestnut and rowanberry.
I am charged with joy as a child or a whirling gypsy,
As a dizzy spinning top I am
Tipsy
With trees.

High on mountains —
Intoxicated, flushed
With crag and clough,
With brackened fell,
Headland and tor and skerry.
I stride in the heady air to the sharp sky
Gasping a grin,
Inebriated,
High —
On mountains.

Olive Culshaw

WHY

Do I climb to find words?

In the sheer face, tracing
faults and intrusions, guttural scribbles
of quartz, diorite, serpentine and churt,

to an inn of language out of the wind,
where fingers scrape for a penny of holds
in the thin lips of cracks.

To brush
on the hills' anvils,
the crumbling breasts of feeling,
clasp the madonnas of nothing on wind-washed ledges,
reach for the fresh
enchiladas of fear.

To hear
in the breathless dictionary of the sky,
among the volumes of limestone,
old shell of brains and blood
that I have dragged up all these years,

the silent sea.

Edwin Drummond

MOUNTAIN LOVER

And if I shout
and cry it is because I find you fair,
rocks, ice and snow,
and having you in this brief sunset hour
with peachblossom for clouds, nectar, suave drink, for air,
too well I know
that you are senseless, chemical stuff — why, soon
you'll leave me; in a month, two weeks or four
you'll slip from my memory,
yes, go.
Therefore I'm mad the more.

Wilfrid Noyce

I LEAVE TONIGHT FROM EUSTON

I shall leave tonight from Euston
By the seven-thirty train,
And from Perth in the early morning
I shall see the hills again.
From the top of Ben Macdhui
I shall watch the gathering storm,
And see the crisp snow lying
At the back of Cairngorm.
I shall feel the mist from Bhrotain
And pass by Lairig Ghru
To look on dark Loch Einich
From the heights of Sgoran Dubh.
From the broken Barns of Bynack
I shall see the sunrise gleam
On the forehead of Ben Rinnes
And Strathspey awake from dream.
And again in the dusk of evening
I shall find once more alone
The dark water of the Green Loch,
And the pass beyond Ryvoan.
For tonight I leave from Euston
And leave the world behind;
Who has the hills as a lover
Will find them wondrous kind.

Anon.
(Written on the door of Ryvoan Bothy
and fortunately copied before it was burnt)

GUARD'S VAN TO WALES

Via Euston, via the Friday rush,
Via starting-time arrears
I landed in the guard's van with
A scree of mountaineers.

All corduroyed and confident
They cluttered up the floor
With rucksacks, ropes and one-man tents
And climbing-gear galore.

Sprawled careless on the oil-soaked boards
  Basic to all guard's vans
They spread their multi-coloured maps
  Discussing craggy plans.

And I, still dressed in City rig,
  Nostalgic and *de trop*,
Eavesdropped along the rocky routes
  I'd scrambled long ago,

As, bumping through the gusty dark
  We followed mountain trails
With foothold and belaying point
  From Euston up to Wales.

By Ogwen and her guardian heights
  Their talking carried me
To Idwal's nail-scarred slabs and past
  The cauldron of Twll Du.

Till Bangor's gloomy station yard,
  Gale-swept and slatey-wet,
Reminded me what different ways
  Our compasses were set.

Robert Chaloner

THE TREASURE OF HEIGHTS

Seek them, ye strong,
  The cold of morning and the mountain wind.
    Through sun and whispering spray
    There lies one open way
  For manhood still to find
The lamp of vision and the river of song:
Seek them for truth, ye strong.

Feel them, ye feet,
  The spring of heather and the shrinking snow.
    Cloud and the dews of night
    Leave them for your delight

17

That ye may gladly go
Through the grim city and the cobbled street:
Feel them for hope, light feet.

Hold them, ye hands,
  The rough of granite and the stinging rain.
    Earth stores them on hill-slope,
    Cleansing and clasp of hope,
  To cheer your age again.
Groping in darkness through the last grey lands:
Hold them for strength, sure hands.

Take them, O heart,
  The joy of comrades and the thrill of strife.
    Who has the hills for friend
    Has a God-speed to end
  His path of lonely life,
And wings of golden memory to depart:
Take them for love, true heart.

Geoffrey Winthrop Young

THE SECRET SPRINGS

Where are the secret springs, and where
The hidden source of sudden joy?
Whence is the laughter, like the torrent, falling? Whence
The tears, the rainbow-scattered sunlight, overhead?

Over the pinewood and the pasture and the pathway
Rises the rockface where the bootnails scratch
Smooth mossy walls, and the blind fingers reach
Damp ferns in crevices, and icy pools,

Water on brant and slape; the little streams
Rise in the gullies and the squelching moss:
Somewhere above the chockstone springs
Joy, and the sudden halt of tiny grief.

Summer will dry the rock-pool; winter bind
These, and the immortelles will bloom
In memory, and in memory only, these
Slow drops will fall.

Somewhere above the rockroses and the lichen,
Even in summer, or midwinter, moves
The powder-snow, the changing counterpart
Of changing, and unchanging, sea.

Somewhere above the step, the springs of action
Rise, and the snow falls, and the séracs; and the green
    glacier-ice
Moves down like history, or like the huge
Slow movement of a nation's mind.

Somewhere above the ice, unwitnessed storms
Break in the darkness on the summit ridge
And the white whirling avalanche
Blends with the storm, the night, the driven snow;

And sunlight, and the dark, and gravitation,
These are all: these are the hidden springs, simplicity,
And darkness is
The epitome of light, and darkness, and all lonely places.

Michael Roberts

THE WANDERER

I will return again to the hills that were once my prison;
The hills that shut me in from the great wide world so free;
I shall feel the calm of the night in the glen when the moon
    has risen
And it shines, like a pale white ghost, on the pools of Dee.

I will return again to the hills of my early dreaming,
The hills I trod in grief when my feet would be faring forth.
Till I took the road at last, in my youth and my pride not
    deeming
That I left the half of my heart back there in the north.

I put the brogues on my feet and the bundle over my
    shoulder;
I whistled a piper's tune as I took the mountain track;
And the hills looked down and seemed to say to me: 'You'll
    be older
And you'll be wiser too — and you'll come back'.

And it's true; for the roads lead far where garish lights are
    thronging,
And the sound of the city comes like the surge of a wintry
    shore.
And I pause at times in the crowd and think with sudden
    longing:
'Oh, to be back in the peace of the glen once more'.

I will return again to the hills that were once my prison;
The sheltering pines shall whisper their benison to me.
I shall feel the calm of the night in the glen when the moon
    has risen
And it shines, like a pale white ghost, on the pools of Dee.

W D Cocker

ROCK PILGRIM

Let the damned ride their earwigs to Hell, but let
    me not join them.
For why should I covet the tide, or in meanness
    purloin them?
They are sick, they have chosen the path of their
    apple-green folly,
I will turn to my mountains of light, and my mauve
    melancholy.

Let their hands get the primrose — God wreathe
    me! — of lowland and lagland;
For me the small yellow tormentil of heath-hill
    and crag-land.
Man's days are as grass, his thought but as thistle-
    seed wind-sown;
I will plod up the pass, and nourish the turf with
    my shin bone.

I should stay for a day, I should seek in high faith
   to reclaim them!
But the threadbare beat straw, and the hole in my
   shirt will inflame them.
They are blinder than moles, for they see but the
   flies in God's honey;
And they eat off their soles; and they kneel to the
   Moloch of money.

They have squeezed my mouth dumb; their clutch
   for a year yet may rankle.
I wil tie Robin Death to my side, with his claw
   on my ankle.
Let them come, stick and drum, and assail me
   across the grey boulders,
I will flutter my toes, and rattle the screes on their
   shoulders.

Let the damned get to Hell and be quick, while
   decision is early.
I will tie a red rose to my stick, and plant my feet
   squarely.
My back shall be blind on their spite, and my rump
   on their folly;
I will plod up the ridge to the right, past the
   crimson-green holly.

Herbert E Palmer

On Southern Slopes

MARK RICHARDS

SKYSCAPE

Norfolk, they say, is flat. Well, have it so:
These undulations never rise so high
They reach the dignity of hills — but, oh,
Range upon range, the mountains of the sky!

F Pratt Green

UP ON THE DOWNS

Up on the Downs the red-eyed kestrels hover,
Eying the grass.
The field-mouse flits like a shadow into cover
As their shadows pass.

Men are burning the gorse on the down's shoulder;
A drift of smoke
Glitters with fire and hangs, and the skies smoulder
And the lungs choke.

Once the tribe did thus on the downs, on these downs burning
Men in the flame,
Crying to the gods of the downs till their brains were turning
And the gods came.

And today on the downs, in the wind, the hawks, the grasses
In blood and air,
Something passes me and cries as it passes,
On the chalk downland bare.

John Masefield

THE RUN OF THE DOWNS

The Weald is good, the Downs are best --
I'll give you the run of 'em, East to West.
Beachy Head and Winddoor Hill,
They were once and they are still.
Firle, Mount Caburn and Mount Harry

Go back as far as sums'll carry.
Ditchling Beacon and Chanctonbury Ring,
They have looked on many a thing,
And what those two have missed between 'em,
I reckon Truleigh Hill has seen 'em.
Highden, Bignor and Duncton Down
Knew Old England before the Crown.
Linch Down, Treyford and Sunwood
Knew Old England before the Flood;
And when you end on the Hampshire side —
Butser's old as Time and Tide.
The Downs are sheep, the Weald is corn,
You be glad you are Sussex born!

Rudyard Kipling

DOWNLAND

The sea laid down this land. Chalk track and thorn
Over the swell and fall of downland tell
More truth than upstart orchards, orderly,
Man-mustered to stiff rule. Unmastered still,
A land of flint and scrub with a sea roll
Under its stubby churches, this can slip
Further than memory. Look where it lifts
Its cottage ships towards the sky's long rim
Surely to swallow them, yet is so slow
Oaks grow and crumble on the sloping waves
That never break, dry roothold for the whin.
Many lie drowned here in the shape of sea
Whom no tide moves. The mole tunnels in sand,
The plough's keel bucks on stones, a wake of gulls
Streams white behind the firm wave-walking plod
That bears a man across pre-Domesday depths
Unreckoning what wreckage clarts his heels.
He will not hear the grinding undertow
When waves run through the corn. A mouldered oar
Shall sprout him harvest bread. Whose threadbare sails
Break into surf of blossom he'll not know.

Sydney Tremayne

MOLE-HILLS ON THE DOWNS

Here earth in her abundance spills
Hills on her hills,
Till every hill is overgrown
With small hills of its own;
Some old with moss and scorpion-grass,
Some new and bare and brown,
And one where I can watch the earth
Like a volcano at its birth
Still rise by falling down;
And as by these small hills I pass
And take them in my stride
I swell with pride,
Till the great hills to which I lift my eyes
Restore my size.

Andrew Young

RECOLLECTION, GORING HILL

Follow the map and you may mark it still:
The old way where he walked, the tangled brook
Riddled with weed, the stile long since forsook
And the slow suave upreaches of the hill.
Here he would climb on idle holidays
When the sun spilled a lusty afterglow
Mellow and bland, and where — far, far below —
The Thames moved like a lizard through the haze.
Now, where he pricked a copse, a forest grows
Fifty years strong, and woodpeckers are heard
Noisy about their business, where stirred
Once but the foxglove and the wild dog-rose;
But when the mist falls, grey and large and chill,
Time tells no tales at all on Goring Hill.

Jean Kenward

SMOOTH LANDSCAPE

The long, low hills, the sky, the little fields:
A boneless country founded on no rock,
A moulded country offering no holds
To take the eyes up slowly. Without check
The eye sweeps over it along the sky
And almost naturally is taught to fly.

Smooth landscape, filled as much with flint as flowers,
Opened by sunlight, narrowed by the rain,
Those who have learned how brilliance disappears
Wait best for change to bring it back again
Out of the mist that settles in for days,
Consumes the sky and makes a smoke of trees.

Sydney Tremayne

from UP IN THE WIND

                    ... While I drank
I might have mused of coaches and highwaymen,
Charcoal-burners and life that loves the wild.
For who now used these roads except myself,
A market waggon every other Wednesday,
A solitary tramp, some very fresh one
Ignorant of these eleven houseless miles,
A motorist from a distance slowing down
To taste whatever luxury he can
In having North Downs clear behind, South clear before,
And being midway between two railway lines
Far out of sight or sound of them? There are
Some houses — down the by-lanes; and a few
Are visible — when their damsons are in bloom.
But the land is wild, and there's a spirit of wildness
Much older, crying when the stone-curlew yodels
His sea and mountain cry, high up in Spring.

Edward Thomas

LAST RITES AND COUNTRY REMEDIES

Edward Thomas wrote of that Other whom he followed into the
    heart of this green country;
I have a map that no Ordnance men ever surveyed,
For to me this is no discovered country until I see it for myself,
And bury my wanderlust in the green heart of its innocence;
When this map is drawn, then I also shall be shaded in.

The track (when you find it)
is like a green river
branch river
disappearing as you approach
over the horizon,
taking its unmetalled pace
through a quiet country,
among peaceful men.

I know that Other, too, he's a hard, sarcastic man.
He waits for me at stiles along the way, shredding the red sorrel
And brushing himself down fastidiously. He jeers:
'Still seeking the same old remedy for the same old sorrow,
    are we?
'It makes no difference, it all comes to the same in the end.'
I do not seek him. Maybe one day I will kill him.

Summer rusts into Autumn
along the empty trackbed.
A farmer celebrates the Harvest Home,
buying a pint for his contractor.
At sunset a fox, red as blood,
lifts his dripping mask from a trough
and follows the levelling shadows
deep into the weathered hills.
Birds grow melodious
in the hedgerows where history lies
silent as night.
An owl
loosens his grip
on the flesh
of an oak
to cut the fields
with his chainsaw cry.
Things are not what they seem, nor are the seasons

approachable in verse.
We gain no more comfort from their appearance,
feeling them diminished year by year.
Could be we owe these scenes a country death;
That Other will be my sacrifice, for as it is
he blocks the stiles, yawns in my face,
like blue sky over prairie fields, fills in my map for me
telling me that someone else has been that way —
'Nothing new under the sun' — except what's old.
He'll burn like rotten sticks, the black earth shall have his ashes,
And mulch his memory to triumphant green Spring.

Envoi:

Thomas walked for miles along the unmapped roads,
and at each crossroads wondered why he was unhappy.
Now he strides a deeper hollow lane, his head tricked out
    with stars.
Every now and then he stops to look through a flower,
Then shakes his head and strides on, ever faster.

J H Earl

CHILTERN

I do not like
harmless hills
they are cautious
freeing sides
to Welsh wind

winter
knows how
to waylay
a landscape
with strangeness

knows how
to recall
a hill
from oblivion

winter allows
cloud
to come between
gods and prey.

David J Morley

STORM OVER THE CHILTERNS

Will no one lift the weight of sullen day?
A load of thunder clipped between the hills
Shuffles and fumbles — yearns to break away
But is held captive. Still the dark sky fills
Its laden pouches with excessive rain
That will not, cannot, fall or find release.
Parching, the dry beads of sun-ripened grain
Look for a sensitive and subtle ease,
But nothing comes. Only beyond the far
Keel of the Chilterns, arrows pale as bone
Tell where refreshed and scented counties are,
And the green lizard leaves his watered stone,
And limes drip golden pleasure, and the small
Grasses are jewelled for a festival.

Jean Kenward

WESSEX HEIGHTS

There are some heights in Wessex, shaped as if by a kindly hand
For thinking, dreaming, dying on, and at crises when I stand,
Say, on Ingpen Beacon eastward, or on Wylls-Neck westwardly,
I seem where I was before my birth, and after death may be.

In the lowlands I have no comrade, not even the lone man's
    friend —
Her who suffereth long and is kind; accepts what he is too weak
    to mend:

Down there they are dubious and askance; there nobody thinks
   as I,
But mind-chains do not clank where one's neighbour is the sky.

In the towns I am tracked by phantoms having weird detective
   ways —
Shadows of being who fellowed with myself of earlier days:
They hang about at places, and they say harsh heavy things —
Men with a wintry sneer, and women with tart disparagings.

Down there I seem to be false to myself, my simple self that was,
And is not now, and I see him watching, wondering what crass
   cause
Can have merged him into such a strange continuator as this,
Who yet has something in common with himself, my chrysalis.

I cannot go to the great grey Plain; there's a figure against the
   moon,
Nobody sees it but I, and it makes my heart beat out of tune;
I cannot go to the tall-spired town, being barred by the forms
   now passed
For everybody but me, in whose long vision they stand there fast.

There's a ghost at Yell'ham Bottom chiding loud at the fall of
   the night,
There's a ghost in Froom-side Vale, thin-lipped and vague, in a
   shroud of white,
There is one in the railway train whenever I do not want it near,
I see its profile against the pane, saying what I would not hear.

As for one rare fair woman, I am now but a thought of hers,
I enter her mind and another thought succeeds me that she
   prefers;
Yet my love for her in its fulness she herself even did not know;
Well, time cures hearts of tenderness, and now I can let her go.

So I am found on Ingpen Beacon, or on Wylls-Neck to the west,
Or else on homely Bulbarrow, or little Pilsdon Crest,
Where men have never cared to haunt, nor women have walked
   with me,
And ghosts then keep their distance; and I know some liberty.

Thomas Hardy

WILTSHIRE DOWNS

The cuckoo's double note
Loosened like bubbles from a drowning throat
Floats through the air
In mockery of pipit, lark and stare.

The stable-boys thud by
Their horses slinging divots at the sky
And with bright hooves
Printing the sodden turf with lucky grooves.

As still as a windhover
A shepherd in his flapping coat leans over
His tall sheep-crook
And shearlings, tegs and yoes cons like a book.

And one tree-crowned long barrow
Stretched like a sow that has brought forth her farrow
Hides a king's bones
Lying like broken sticks among the stones.

Andrew Young

ON CLIMBING BELAS KNAP

Under hawthorn heat, spiking wood and barleyfield
With thorns of flame, we climbed;
No skylark but the wind close turning in the trees:
Quiet eddying of time that does not change.

The summer's noonday runs its sleep, swift-fingered,
Through oak and sycamore; a steel-shot web of greenness
Racked tight to the hill's shoulder, pushing bone skywards
In silent aim — all enmeshed are cloud and tussock,
Lilac valley and the poppies, blood-red,
That trace our pathway through the hushing corn.

This is a place of death; grass dips into a long slug of stone
Where darkened orifices still breathe pomp
And blur the windless faces of the grave.
I feel the shadow where my own flesh lies, long-outlawed.

Vanished the rings, the funereal unguents, and gold coin to
    bring
Safe passage into centuries of dreams —
I will make no voyage out across the valley into mist.

My figureheads are broken, split to their powdery core,
While Bela tends his whitening fires and broods:
None come to worship but three alien walkers, and the
    teeming flies.

Hilary Davies

ON WENLOCK EDGE

On Wenlock Edge the wood's in trouble;
    His forest fleece the Wrekin heaves;
The gale, it plies the saplings double,
    And thick on Severn snow the leaves.

'Twould blow like this through holt and hanger
    When Uricon the city stood:
'Tis the old wind in the old anger,
    But then it threshed another wood.

Then, 'twas before my time, the Roman
    At yonder heaving hill would stare:
The blood that warms an English yeoman,
    The thoughts that hurt him, they were there.

There, like the wind through woods in riot,
    Through him the gale of life blew high;
The tree of man was never quiet:
    Then 'twas the Roman, now 'tis I.

The gale, it plies the saplings double,
    It blows so hard, 'twill soon be gone:
To-day the Roman and his trouble
    Are ashes under Uricon.

A E Housman

SPRING DAY ON THE MALVERN HILLS

Down the dust-ridden highroads go
    The windy turmoils of the spring,
Tossed back and forth and to and fro,
    Tempestuously echoing.

High, high above the smooth swept hills
    Cloud following cloud from the clear north
Borne onward silent, stately, still,
    Fares out and forth, fares out and forth.

Here in a sun-warmed sheltered place
    I lie midway of gods and men,
Above their blind and furious race,
    Beneath their universal ken.

Geoffrey Faber

from the chorus of
NOAH AND THE WATERS

Stand with us here
On the south-western cliff of the great Jurassic escarpment,
A common for rare wood-larks, a place where wind-pumps veer
Constant as your necessity, drinking that reservoir
Free to all: invisible the veins it is life to open,
The lake only your death may look on.

Stand with us now and hear
Only the wood-lark's irrelevant song, the shepherd's whistle,
And seven-league footfall of wind striding through dry grasses.
For as yet the torrents to come are but a roaring in the ear
Of prophets, or the raving fancy of one delirious with thirst
Pacific the sky, a delight for shepherds and hikers; though a seer
Might behold over the cities to north and north-east spreading
A stain, clouds not white, the coaling-up of wrath.

Stand with us here.
Feel underfoot the linked vertebrae of your land
Stretching north to the far fells, the head of rivers.

Prehistory sleeps below in many beds. Before
Man set a value on his thoughts or made a prison for fear,
These hills were grown up, to the sky happily married,
That now are wrinkled with the rains of more than mortal years,
Old enough to remember the first birds and the great reptiles.

Stand with us. Far and near
See history unfolded in the scrolled hills, her secret
Indelible as hieroglyphs stamped on their stone, clear
To the eye but hard for you to interpret. The green barrows
Of Britons. The high camps where Roman eagles kept watch
On Wales unblinking. The manors, cosy in combes. Dear
The dewponds, and still black the circles of Jubilee bonfires.

Stand with us here,
The past at your feet, your fingers nervous like the lark's wing
To be up and doing. And now, for to-day's sun goes higher,
Let your hearts grow warm as wax to take note of the future:
Let him step forward, if one there be wise to weather,
From behaviour of martens or altered tones of the smooth-
    voiced weir
Able to learn and to beware.

C Day Lewis

SHROPSHIRE HILLS

The floor of an ancient sea
is thrust into
waves embedded with shells
and fossils
of water-creatures.

Flowers are shepherded
in gardens neat
as pens.
Streams walk out
from the hills with visions
of hidden waterfalls,
clambering sky.

The town is filled with
ash of sunset,
dusk moves through the bracken
like a cat,
Long Mynd is showered
in stars.

We stuff our pockets;
everyone needs a hoard of light.

Isobel Thrilling

CLIMBERS: AVON GORGE

Beyond the blurred traffic's opposite insistence
discover a lawn, a tent,
and a great grey cliff. The dark lorries blind by
and between them your eye
glimpses impossible distance:

serious rock, wind, the classical ascent,
worry and laughing anger
above a high tarn's stillness. Discontinuity
colours the city
fast colours of fixed intent.

Here on the bevelled holds what messages we exchange
are shouted against your wind
of work; against the highway's logical violence
we reckon to balance
this unnecessary danger.

Taking such purchase as intelligence can find
we make the reach into doubt
towards firmness; across fear, past fear; or, shuffling, leaning,
test out a meaning
above a blurred traffic of mind

— the acceptance of pluralism : this is the keenest route,
the line of most resistance,
the city-cliff's crux : to balance humanity's
opposite energies
is just what the climbing's about.

Jim Hunter

A BARROW ON THE QUANTOCKS

Each night I pass the dead man's mound
I keep on turning round;
I almost stumble on the track
With looking back.

Although that mound of ling and stones
May hide his brittle bones,
I do not think that there he sleeps
Or wakes and peeps.

He is too intimately near
To see or touch or hear;
I only feel my blood is crossed
By his chill ghost.

It may be that all things are made
Of substance and of shade
And such a hill as I walk here
He walks elsewhere.

I know not which the substance is,
This hill of mine or his,
Nor which of us is the true ghost
In shadows lost.

Andrew Young

ON SELWORTHY BEACON

Behind, a land bright with gorse, dark with a last castle.
To the limit of sight its squared cultivation
Is cast on the cushioned hills like a deck of spilt cards.
Below glitters the small town, pincered
Between black coombes, and held among larks
And marshes with its feet in the channel.
Around me sing legends older than Doone or pirate
But out to sea at the foot of Llewelyn's mountains,
Porthcawl's factories glimmer white into moving mist
And sun, and still water;
The making of a legend for those who will stand
Watching for the bright towers of a new Lyonesse.

Teresa L Gray

MOOR IN WINTER

Down from the treacherous tussocks of bog grass
Streamed white by melted snow I find shelter
In old workings where thorns bend their man-shapes
Over stone and wind-bleached moss moves like white hair.
Wind blatting at the man-made safe of stone
Where the tinner kept his tools and the days' bread.
Rested I leave them — not to be alone,
Pockets of resistant snow occupy
The landscape, bivouacked on the cold side
Of hill and wood and wall.
Arrogantly they flash their steel in blown sun,
And wait, confident of reinforcements.

Teresa L Gray

DIAMOND SOLITAIRE, LUNDY ISLAND

Again that sensation of the tide rising,
Alone on a wave-cut platform
Watching the surge and suck
With retreat already awash.

Again I'd wanted it all,
The climb of the week,
And the island event of the week —
Driving dumb calves down the cliff path
To the waiting jaws of a landing craft
Made faintly hospitable with hay.
On the bouldered beach the ring
Of helpers had become the quiet patience
Of the wizened farmer at their centre.

So, late starting, I was now a frowning gargoyle
At the base of this great flying buttress
Watching long waves roll through the ring
While a rope nest was being woven
In the dark cleft above me.
A thin crack tempted hands
Into its quartz bite while feet
Tip-toed on diamonds above the sparkling sea
To break clear onto the spine
And belay astride the back
Of the wind plucked harp.

To dare from here to step out
Above the strung rhythms
Is to find toothed finger slots
Across the flying wall to another crystal crack
That plucks me up to a cushion of sea pink.

Charged, and changed a little,
I look down at sucking sea
Crashing white and green
Where I had been.

Terry Gifford

THE SEASONS IN NORTH CORNWALL

O spring has set off her green fuses
    Down by the Tamar today,
And careless, like tidemarks, the hedges
    Are bursting with almond and may.

Here lie I, waiting for old summer,
    A red face and straw-coloured hair has he:
I shall meet him on the road from Marazion
    And the Mediterranean Sea.

September has flung a spray of rooks
    On the sea-chart of the sky,
The tall shipmasts crack in the forest
    And the banners of autumn fly.

My room is a bright glass cabin,
    All Cornwall thunders at my door,
And the white ships of winter lie
    In the sea-roads of the moor.

Charles Causley

SUICIDE WALL, BOSIGRAN

I am thinking, *mortal*
and none of this full-stretch holds much appeal.
    (Being too vain and covenanting even,
    for the mild-extremes of chalk.)
Thus, I dry one soused hand,
hung out in the steeped and honeyed air of Cornwall.
The other, meanwhile, white-knuckled on the flakes
of *Suicide's* grained and perfect granite,
extravasates ... (Sweats blood!)
That's it — Forget the euphony,
Rock-climbing does not lend itself to song
and in this heat,
even a cool, pragmatic syntax sounds all wrong.

Des Hannigan

THE KNOLLS

The village where I was young lay strung
As frill at the base of a high chalk hill,
And when of level life we'd had our fill
There were always adventures to be wrung
From those many-pitted slopes, pursuers
And pursued, grand battles, brave deed doers,
We roamed these slopes in actions still unsung.
In winter snow we had our Cresta Run,
Acres of snow for novice and daredevil
On battered tea trays, fun for everyone.
No doubt we took our hill for granted,
Never thought how fortunate we were,
And yet the seeds of later fruit were planted,
Insensibly the love of hills had grown
Within us as we played; now I prefer
Above all other to be close to hills,
But of all hills that one remains my own.

Michael Dundrow

WEST PENWITH

A neck of land that stretches toward the West
Where Zennor Hill stands up to take the breeze
That sets its myriad bracken fronds a-quiver
From the twin gateways of the Channel Seas;
Its granite has the strength that granite gives,
A moorland and a harsh land that breed men
Who seek their fortune at the world's far end
And never rest till they come back again.

A W Andrews

The Seasons Through

DONALD BENNET

WINTER SOLSTICE

I watched the sun
a golden sperm
drop cold
upon the hills' immaculate snow
to fertilize the earth.

In tonight's darkness
a conception will take place
that will bring life
to the brooding land.

A slow growth
has already started
sprung from that solstice-seed's
miracle.

And from winter's womb
shall come a joy-child
and men shall call his name
Summer.

Christopher Rush

WINNATT'S PASS

Wind grew that hawk perched
on the peak's brooding shoulder;
wind strokes its stone feathers . . .
and the shirt off the sweating walker's back,
the cusped harebell, slopes of lovers.

Wind moves today warm
as blood through gorge it christened,
through crags sharp as frost flowers
on the sky's blue-brilliant pane —
that stay with the heart, just where they should.

Geoffrey Holloway

WINTER MOUNTAIN

Colder than ranges that my heart has crossed
pain steals into earth as winter frost;
and on this summit uninhabited I hear
a seashell murmuring like a star in space,
or silence pressing closely on the ear
in windy patterns traced on clouded lace.

But what was once so musical and warm
bereaves the senses with a dumb alarm.
So many flowers clothed the mountainside,
impossible to count the petals crushed,
torn leaf and calyx pulverised,
and wasted sap cemented in the dust.

Echo turns inward, for they all have sped
who made contentment on a day now dead;
in loaded thunderbolts have gone abroad
armed with blind anonymity, and so
bid them farewell. Now from the raven's hoard
fool retribution draws his cloak of snow;

and winter covers all, and present pain
tries to prolong December; all insane
he comes, clanging his copper-throated gong,
cries, like the raven, all is lost and late.

Remembering the summer and the song,
I hold the seashell closer still, and wait.

Marjorie Milsom

THE MOUNTAIN IN SPRING

All that survived is convalescent now,
Content to live.
The mountain rears above, inscrutable,
And from its bony shoulders and its brow
The distant streams
Hang like pale ribbons. On its sparse-clad ribs
Sheep, tired, with trailing fleeces, seek their lambs.

Below, the valley stretches like a cat,
Lazy and striped and warm and full of dreams.
The bent trees stir. The ragged birds respond
With a thin sweetness, forgetful of their dead.
Far down, upon the coloured stamp-like fields
The farm is but a toy,
A sugar-cube, white as remembered snow.
Lean cows are creeping dots of cream and red —
And man too small to see.

The mountain rears above, inflexible.
The mountain, stern, unmoved by death or life,
Or grief or joy,
Had done with pain these million years ago.

Phyllis Lyth

EARTH-MOTHER LOVE

I like to lie and laze
And gaze at the sky
On a fine spring day
In the firm warm grip
Of a grassy valley
And listen to the loud
Drip, drip, dripping
Of time as it slips
Down a slate-green waterfall
To the distant, silent sea.
My pulse quickens with
The feel of fresh sharp air;
I am earth-bound, earth-born.

Joanne M Weeks

WARM DAY

This is the year's first warmth,
fragile yet, harried by a shrewd wind.
A yellow bulldozer, high on a new farm-road,
adds another line to the hill.
The roar of its brown churning
fills the valley. Wind slackens
and the sound fails, drops to a secretive mutter
behind the sharp calling of lambs.

Here in the churchyard
three children idle, on their way anywhere,
scuffing shoes on grass-grown tiles
of what was once a nave.
Across the field, a hopeful pony whinnies.
Suddenly purposeful, the children are gone.
Grass on grave-mounds sifts and sifts
all that is left of the wind.

The far-off bulldozer grinds on
along Rhiw Gareg Lwyd, cutting across
the monks' road, the sheep-paths and the drovers' tracks.
This year, lorries will carry lime to the high slopes.
Long-abandoned hill will be re-seeded.

The children and the pony
have found each other.

Air nuzzles the yew-trees.
The day's warmth strengthens.
Its only promise — of summer — seems enough.

Ruth Bidgood

48

NORTHERN MIDSUMMER

It's never really dark
Here in the Hebrides
In June;
The bird has hardly lost its tune
Than it sings again.

Two a.m.
Daylight fades
But see — a strange glow
Hovers hawk-winged
Behind those hills waiting —
Watching the silver throw of moonlight
Move over seal-rocked sea loch,
Heron-homed islets.

Three a.m.
A blackbird, re-entering the fray,
Gathering dawn together,
Carols day.

Margaret Gillies

RESTING

at the top of the hill
the old man stops to lean
against this mountain oak
which was an ancient tree
when his grandfather was a boy
and gathered acorns here

now where a patch of bark
is stripped away
his fingers idly trace
the tangled labyrinth that reveals
an insect's secret wanderings
through the brief summer that was
                all its life

Alec Smith

AUTUMN

A barbed fence
Tufted with wet wool
As boy and tyke
Climb through the mists
His pockets like
A hamster's cheeks
Stuffed full.

Alec Smith

AFTER THE SUMMER

At long last. Now and now
the fields are flailed
with rain.
The high-flying sky
is shut out
by anvils of thunderheads
spiralling soundlessly
over the hills.

In all the villages,
wet-slated, sloping,
the dripping eaves percuss
the pavements,
stippling shining patterns
on the roads.

Becks run, brown-footed.

The welcome water
falls
with a high-stepping,
hopscotch bounce,
greening the yellow grass.
Now and now.

Judith Smallshaw

OCTOBER

Honey for the eye.

Wind floods the valley,
great shoals of time
breaking summer's dam.

I drove my boots
up Mellbreak and Red Pike,
dragging my lungs like a dog.

Up on the top
you had to squat
or be budged

and punched out
over the edge. A cloud
like a whale sailed

suddenly over a peak
almost within hand's reach,
then shredded as it went.

Down, down those hunched
and muscled shoulders, toy legs
aghast at the flung eye.

Old oak trees brittle up
from seas of moss. My mind's
a simple hod now,

heaving me home like stone.

William Scammell

THE GOLDEN HILL

She watched the light fade from the golden fleece
Of silver birches in October leaf
That shawled the slopes and shoulders of the ben —
She watched the light fade slowly that with brief
Glory of rainy gold had filled the glen
And filled her tempest-troubled heart with peace —

A shining peace that failed not as the light
Faded from crag and corrie, peace that still
Would soar, a glowing presence, in her mind,
A golden-peaked inviolable hill
Of refuge when the valley-ways were blind
Beneath the roaring cataract of night.

Wilfrid W Gibson

BRACKEN HILLS IN AUTUMN

These beds of bracken, climax of the summer's growth,
Are elemental as the sky or sea.
In still and sunny weather they give back
The sun's glare with a fixed intensity
  As of steel or glass
  No other foliage has.

There is a menace in their indifference to man
As in tropical abundance. On gloomy days
They redouble the sombre heaviness of the sky
And nurse the thunder. Their dense growth shuts the
 narrow ways
  Between the hills and draws
  Closer the wide valleys' jaws.

This flinty verdure's vast effusion is the more
Remarkable for the shortness of its stay.
From November to May a brown stain on the slopes
Downbeaten by frost and rain, then in quick array
  The silvery crooks appear
  And the whole host is here.

Useless they may seem to men and go unused, but cast
Cartloads of them into a pool where the trout are few
And soon the swarming animalculae upon them
Will proportionately increase the fishes too.
        Miracles are never far away
        Save bringing new thought into play.

In summer islanded in these grey-green seas where the
    wind plucks
The pale underside of the fronds on gusty days
As a land breeze stirs the white caps in a roadstead
Glimpses of shy bog gardens surprise the gaze
        Or rough stuff keeping a ring
        Round a struggling water-spring.

Look closely. Even now bog asphodel spikes, still
    alight at the tips,
Sundew lifting white buds like those of the whitlow grass
On walls in spring over its little round leaves
Sparkling with gummy red hairs, and many a soft mass
        Of the curious moss that can clean
        A wound or poison a river, are seen.

Ah! well I know my tumultuous days now at their prime
Will be brief as the bracken too in their stay
Yet in them as the flowers of the hills 'mid the bracken
All that I treasure is needs hidden away
        And will also be dead
        When its rude cover is shed.

Hugh MacDiarmid

BURNING THE BRACKEN

When summer stopped, and the last
Lit cloud blazed tawny cumulus
Above the hills, it was the bracken

Answered; its still crests
Contained an autumn's burning.
Then, on an afternoon of promised

Cold, true flames ripped
The ferns. Hurrying fire, low
And pale in the sun, ran

Glittering through them. As
Night fell, the brindle
Flambeaux, full of chattering

We were too far to hear, leapt
To the children's singing.
'Fire on the mountain,' we

Chanted, who went to bed warmed
By joy. But I would know that fires
Die, that the cold sky holds

Uneasily the fronds and floating
Twigs of broken soot, letting
Them fall, fall now, soft

As darkness on this white page.

Leslie Norris

AUTUMN BLOWN, AMBLESIDE

The waiting man surprised
with his head in the clouds
gathers sycamore keys and dreams.
Autumn blown he stands firm
and mothers the bone
of his father's grave,
an oak within mountainsides.
He sees late blackberries,
like eyes of polished coal
fighting frosts,
mountains blinded by swirling mists
and bird clouds
that cannot wait for skies.

David Watkin Price

AUTUMN

A touch of cold in the autumn night —
I walked abroad,
And saw the ruddy moon lean over a hedge
Like a red-faced farmer.
I did not stop to speak, but nodded,
And round about were the wistful stars
With white faces like town children.

T E Hulme

from PRELUDE TO WINTER

Now the rowan's red again, the summer's fading,
the sun declines in long autumnal rays.
In a quiet glen I study the distant shading,
wondering why I so foolishly wasted my days.
The spring and the summer cannot be made to stay
but eternity can be caught in the silence here.
The prospect of winter is hardly a matter for fear.

William Neill

PLACE

The train's brakes lowing like a herd of cattle at sunset
As it draws up by Lesson's Stone, by mountains
Like deeply carved curtains, among small birds
Knapping at the stationmaster's crumbs, hopping-black
Like commas of wet ink: I could see their small eyes glisten.
I thought I must die in my sleep, I lay in my bunk
Like wet clothes soaking, the convulsions were the journey.
The bedroom bumped. I stepped off and the mountain
    landscape
Was like stone guests set round a still table
On which was set stone food, steaming
With the clouds caught on it; a plateau
Surrounded with peaks and set with cairns
And stone houses, and a causeway up to Giant's Table,

And the railway trailing like a bootlace. My house
Was hard by Lesson's Stone, near the sparkling Force
That tumbled off the cliff, that in summer
Left its dry spoor full of thornbush. Then the lizards
Flickered among the rocks, like shadows
Of flying things under a clear sky, or like
Bright enamelled painted rock on rock, until they swiftly
Shot sideways too fast to see. I arrived
On Lesson's Stone Stop platform a decade ago;
The place where I live is still like pieces
Of a shattered star, some parts shining
Too bright to look at, others dead
As old clinker. I am afraid to mention
The star's name. That would set it alight.

Peter Redgrove

WINTER MOUNTAINS

Cold sunlight gilds the fields.
Beyond, and brilliant
are the curving backs of whales,
grey in their perpetual
distant Iceland.

At the line's head
are mammoths with wrinkled flanks
lurching against the void,
frozen in their ranks
in undulant stampede.

They died steel and silver dead.

J D Marshall

COLOURS OF JANUARY

Colours of January,
Brown and white, bleak
Green and black, grey;
Here, walking by
The backend land
— Blencathra
Round as a bowl, and
A stonecut road
Hinged over a valley —
Here we meet winter.

Soft as water
So far, cloudwrecked
Skies and hurling
Air whirling leaves and
Wet boughs, the year;
Full beck, far roar
Of force and white falling
Plummets of water;
At night, rafter-creak,
Air squalling.

The first fallen
Snowline
Low on peat hills:
Brown water
Below the miner's road
Juggles, dividing
A half-bog, reed-green
Valley; appears
For no thing
A living.

A Honda's
Back wheel kicks turf paths,
Boy and engine
Buck over beck, up
A bouldered mountain,

And predator
Stoat, in white coat,
Ermine,
By Glenderaterra
Leaps for its snowline.

David Wright

WINTER

On snowy nights the mountains go away.
I do not hear them when I am asleep,
Stumbling down stony valleys to the sea.
But in the morning, when I look for them,
Great striped and streak'd beasts stand about the dale,
With furry heads and big, soft, quiet paws.

Edmund Casson

FOR WHAT ARE MOUNTAINS WAITING?

For what are mountains waiting?
All night they are expectant: heavy hoods
of hills rounding against the stars seem opening
about invisible eyes,
that watch within the darkness under brows
of darker precipice; up the still skies
fingers of shadow-height are threatening
to hush the impatient woods;
half fearfully, the waterfalls unclose
their drowsy lashes; and each wide-eyed lake
signals the sentinel moon. Nothing abating
their watch for the earth's darkening,
these mountains are awake!
The uneasy converse of their day is broken:
in listening ranks the intent hills are awaiting
some secret of the silence nearly spoken,
some moment almost nearing.
At night we feel mountains are hearkening,
and all but hearing.

Geoffrey Winthrop Young

AS SO OFTEN IN SCOTLAND

as so often in Scotland
the sun travelled
dyke over dyke, burning
dead grass golden and ending
after a wallow of foothills,
on one brown summit;
that flared its moment, too,
and was gone.

G J F Dutton

SUNSET

After a sullen day, windless and chill,
The west began to brighten, and the sun,
His course, concealed since dawn, soon to be done,
Blazed suddenly between cloud-fringe and hill,
Enormous, incandescent; all the west
Glowed like the wings of an archangel spread;
To gold and rose the clouds lit overhead
Till silent splendour earth and heaven possessed.
On the transfigured hills I walked alone
Grateful for benediction, and renewed
As though some reassurance was my own
From that triumphant hour by light endued.
Call it not the folly of a dreamer's brain
That from a sunset he takes heart again.

W K Holmes

THE DOWLY TREE

At dusk, the last night of the year, I climb
to reach the Dowly Tree. As startled sheep
skip further up the scree, I make my claim
gripping the lichened bark. How ice-winds nip

between my body and the squall-bent bole.
   Seeming oddly secure upon this Scar,
   weird, wild tree, seeded by some owl
that ripping crop or gizzard dropped you here;

or else the searing wind that chops the tarn.
   Maybe the broad-winged buzzard took some part.
Whatever origin, you stand alone

protesting life, stabilility, in turn.
   A poet is like you in his questing heart
redeeming words from harsh, eroded stone.

Michael Ffinch

UP THERE

I know that it is today, and that there was yesterday, and
   will be tomorrow;
But up there, where the hills are deep in snow, that is eternity:
That is out of all reckoning and telling.
You can't measure that proud white beauty,
But you can live with it for a little space,
That will not belong to today, or yesterday, or tomorrow,
But to the time beyond time.

Margaret Cropper

Wales of the West

LEONARD AND MARJORIE GAYTON

ARRIVAL

Not conscious
    that you have been seeking
      suddenly
    you come upon it

the village in the Welsh hills
      dust free
    with no road out
but the one you came in by.

    A bird chimes
    from a green tree
the hour that is no hour
    you know. The river dawdles
to hold a mirror for you
where you may see yourself
    as you are, a traveller
      with the moon's halo
    above him, who has arrived
    after long journeying where he
      began, catching this
    one truth by surprise
that there is everything to look forward to.

R S Thomas

ABOVE PENMAENMAWR

The upland farmers have all gone;
the lane they laid twists without purpose,
visiting broken gates and overgrown
gardens, to end in clumps of gorse.

Their unroofed houses, and fallen barns,
rich in nettles, lie dead in hiding
from the wind that howls off Talyfan's
saw-tooth ridge; their walls divide

63

bracken from bracken; their little church
of bare rock has outlasted use:
hikers' signatures in the porch,
'Keys obtainable at the Guesthouse'.

Yet, not to sentimentalize,
their faces turned from drudgery
when the chance showed itself. There is
hardly a sign of the husbandry

of even the last to leave — so slight
was their acceptance by the land.
They left for seaside towns, to get
easier jobs, and cash in hand.

Five miles of uplands, and beyond —
a thousand feet below — the coast,
its bright lights twinkling; freezing wind
dragging the cloud down like a frost

from Talyfan. Alone upon
these darkening, silent heights, my fears
stay stubbornly with the farmers, gone
after six hundred thankless years.

Tony Connor

THE HILL FARMER SPEAKS

I am the farmer, stripped of love
And thought and grace by the land's hardness;
But what I am saying over the fields'
Desolate acres, rough with dew,
Is, Listen, listen, I am a man like you.

The wind goes over the hill pastures
Year after year, and the ewes starve,
Milkless, for want of the new grass.
And I starve, too, for something the spring
Can never foster in veins run dry.

The pig is a friend, the cattle's breath
Mingles with mine in the still lanes;
I wear it willingly like a cloak
To shelter me from your curious gaze.

The hens go in and out at the door
From sun to shadow, as stray thoughts pass
Over the floor of my wide skull.
The dirt is under my cracked nails;
The tale of my life is smirched with dung;
The phlegm rattles. But what I am saying
Over the grasses rough with dew
Is, Listen, listen, I am a man like you.

R S Thomas

MARCHLYN

I no longer believe in Arthur.

I believed (like all loyal Arthurians
of the Arfon denomination) that
he was buried beneath Marchlyn,
the kingliest and most mysterious lake in Gwynedd.
I also believed he would rise again
and lead us (all Welsh-speaking
men of Gwynedd, that is) to victory.

But the ground, as it were, of my belief
has been shifted: McAlpines have drained the lake.
The steel monsters that have defiled his grave
have not dredged up one murmur of dissent
from Arthur.

Can he be frightened by a horde of Irishmen?
Or is it even worse than that? —
Perhaps he's actually in league with them:
for when the desecration is complete
they're going to replace the lake,
neatly landscaped,
and up McAlpines' new road will come
bright busloads of comfortable pilgrims
straight from the Dragon Routes.

But, try as I might, I can't accept
a King who's joined the Wales Tourist Board:
not *there* lies victory!

Of course, he may have left,
not quite having slept enough yet.
The last time I went to look for a sign,
The Blue Knight at the gate barred my way,
saying: 'We are empowered to stop anyone from
    coming in —
Though we can't stop anyone from going out'
and tapped, cunningly, the motto 'Securicor'
emblazoned on his helmet.
So Arthur may have slunk off,
disguised as a stray rambler,
his crown hidden in his rucksack.

Ian Hughes

STRANGER ON THE HILL

There is a stranger out upon the hill
My sheep run to the far corner
Of the enclosure — they huddle,
Watching, from triangular shadow.
He climbs the gate — not Jackie Isaf
Who knows the trick of that old latch.
Not Bryn-Owen-Hendre-With-The-Limp —
And no local ever walked the
Summer hills wearing a bright white shirt.
The man stands for a moment, resting.
His distant blob-face turns whitely
To the sky then he looks at the view.
He crosses my square of vision
Turns off down through the wood, and I know
He has taken the quarry path
When a cackle of rooks rise up and
The buzzard wheels on his current
Watching our stranger through the valley.
Jackie Isaf saw him, and so did
Bryn-Owen-Hendre; the sheep watched,
All farm dogs alerted themselves —

Would he call to enquire the way?
He will never know that watch was kept,
This stranger out upon our hill,
The man who thought himself alone with God.

Teresa L Gray

HIRAETH
(For Prof. Iolo Wyn Williams)

Y Drum was the first: a boy,
wide-eyed in the wilderness, wondered
at light and air and strangeness.
Tryfan was next: clutching the rock
he sought safety and found joy.
Then Crib Goch: growing terror
sublimed slowly into exaltation.
Yr Wyddfa, Elidir, Y Garn,
Tal y Fan, Arenig, Rhobell,
Moelwyn, Hebog, Yr Aran.
A lovely litany, familiars,
companions through lesson and lecture.
For thirty years they've graced boots,
uplifted body and soul.
Too rarely I return. Eryri teaches
the meaning of hiraeth and tagnefedd.

Martyn Berry

ON MYNYDD HIRAETHOG

High in a marshy hollow
On heather-hued Hiraethog
There stands marooned for ever
So it seems,
A massive monolith
Aborted from a melting glacier's womb
In ages long ago
When these great moorlands lay
In bondage to harsh dynasties of ice.

Now, here it looms
A stark, forbidding stone
Gigantic in the mists of early morning:
And riven from its kin,
Remote and solitary, deaf and mute,
Bereft of all authority,
It cannot hear
The credulous, croaking frogs
Who pledge their hoarse allegiances
Around the plashy feet
Of their imagined monarch.

It cannot see
The questing, hovering kestrel
Contracting to a speck
Before its plummet-swoop
On unsuspecting prey:
Or watch the calm, unhurried fox
Loping at ease to his lair
Beneath the dark dome
Of the pines.

Immune to all disease, immovable
Save by some huge catastrophe
Contrived by evil men,
Or by a freak
Of pitiless, unheeding nature,
It draws no breath, is warmed
By no one. Desolate and doomed
To endless solitude, it cannot feel
The fires of love, the poignant pain
And spear-thrusts of bereavement.
Alone through endless days
Of blind monotony,
It can never reach
The haven of old age,
Nor wait with calm assurance
To grasp the gentle, kindly hands
Of healing, all-revealing death.

A G Prys-Jones

ISGOLION DUON

Water falling
Sounds through the quiet that the wind allows,
Falling in icy trickles to the stones,
Each drop a cold, reluctant sacrifice,
Or crying down the blackness of the rocks,
Bitterly crying to the callous air.

Behind the mist
That shifts and stirs, to lap itself again
Round the enduring patience of the crag,
A sheep, somewhere amid old drifts of snow,
Wails out its wet and solitary grief
And gets no answer but the moss's drip.

A flap of wind,
The still air shattered by a noisy whirr,
And on the misty grey a blot of life
Splashed by the kestrel dropping to the plains,
And then again the stealthy quiet comes,
Kept close and cherished by the mist's soft door.

Water falling,
And lusty rush of wind that sinks to rest,
While heather tufts, looking to flow'ring time,
With now no other blossom but dead snow,
Scratch their bare stalks and listen for the Spring
And cry of shudd'ring lambs born in the rain.

E H Young

BY LLYN OGWEN

Two hours ago the mountains were blackcapped like
    a hanging judge,
and the winds wrestled in an aerial dogfight
tearing the low clouds in shreds flying and wheeling,
and the lower slopes were a backdrop of brown
over the slate-coloured lake.

But now the sun is a god of victory
exulting over his kingdom of immense
hills, and his paraclete blesses and illumines
their slopes in sharp light and deep shadows,
and the stream, earlier a lead-coloured cleft in the field,
sparkles like a glass necklace.

I can understand how simpler men in simpler ages
saw the sun as a great god charioting the heavens,
and I could easily believe at this moment
that God rode in a golden cart, shaping, reshaping
the whole of this vast valley in his hands.

Frederic Vanson

Y GARN

She sits in splendour, great against the sky,
And broods upon the little ways of men:
Her mighty knees reach down to meet the road
Where men and horses, sheep and barking dogs
Pass every day without a look for her
Who holds in the wide lap they cannot see
A secret tarn like the dim eye of God,
Wet for the sorrows of the world he made.

E H Young

A BOY GOES BLIND

The first sight of mountains, blue and far, reaches above
    the plain,
The nearer valleys, filled with blue streams and mossy dell,
The jagged triple crown of Tryfan soaring above Ogwen's
    flat.
The crests of solitude — the moaning wastes of the Carnedds,
The frightened curlew flying from a wrecked plane's wing.
The empty, perfect, peaceful top of Llewellyn.

Rock days high above Llydaw and Glaslyn,
The spiny ridge of Pinnacle Wall that may cause a shudder
   in the dark.
The fierce corners of the Cromlech, the twisted vegetation
And the steep rock of Cwm Glas, alpine blooms and peace
   and sunlit lakelets.
The last few feet of Y Wyddfa —
Gulls cry and drop like quartz,
Glinting, catching sunbeams, down, down, down.
Dark, dark, dark, black the lake below.
All sight gone; the blind boy's dream.
So many things he's seen but now
The burnished twigs by Afon Lâs,
The spewing waters over rocks
And leaning spires against fast mist —

All this is pictured, backward glanced.
Forward only dark and lightning glare.
But he is fortified by hill memories
And will always see the gold
Of that summer's slab, that icy arête of many years ago
When sight was a reality.
That first sight of mountains, blue and far, reach above
   the plain,
The dark, empty plain.

Roger A Redfern

TRYFAN

Surely some stormgathering god remains here!
Shrouded in steamy cloud the mountain frowns
Over the leaden lake, a god of anger,
A raingiver, drenching at times the floodplain,
Swelling at times the tithing streams that roar his fear
Where thunderous waters fall from the lake's end.

Rising steep as a wall his fastness dwarfs
The hardwon works of man. Unbeautiful
In a land of beautiful mountains, this giant, black,
Barren, bleak, cloudgathering point

Broods over the small water meadows, frowns
On the windlashed, cold llyn,
And, sinister even in summer, holds court
With the manysided winds.

Surely some hammerwielding god, older than man,
Remains here, rockbound but reverberating
In sudden thunder, prisoner of his own
Eight-winded kingdom, till darkness shall fall again
And the green hopes of man are finally humbled,
And the death of the sapraising sun
Leaves him his sway, unchallenged and eternal.

Frederic Vanson

NIK AT A CRUX
(Canopy Route, Milestone Buttress)

A red spot like a ladybird
on grey knuckles, a fixed gauntlet
the rock buttress: Nik's helmet,
and he then stretched on the stepless stair there
rain had begun to corrupt for me,
two hours away

and down, now, by the van selling tea
in the lay-by the rest of us, rain-dulled
lake on a level, the soft-edged canopy
closing in, erasing, scaling done, the slabs, the blocks
have scaled down all of us
to spots against grey,

'Do you take sugar?' and I think I hear him right,
'The best time, now, that summer, remember?
Before last? August, it rained a solid fortnight?
Three fishermen in the lake there up to their
waists, me in my van here and nothing else
but the sheep and the rain . . . '

I don't turn though, clamped, suddenly,
in a vigil to see you safe now, silly as touching
wood, knowing too though the burnished root-crook —

make out the matchstick tree of it — hand you home,
the long descent still, darkening now,
false paths, loose shale —

and you could trip on a molehill! This strange caring
jams the door wide though, till I should recognize
till magnified out of all definition another, nearing,
roadside stance for me, my own children
out on my known far trickier ground,
out of earshot, late,

when I must turn away, holding my plastic cup
with greater faith than for you, Nik.

Libby Houston

BETHESDA

Three things of slate in this village:
Work, home, and grave.
Golgotha, you called it,
Grim, biblical —

The joke was apt enough.
I lived above a graveyard
Thick sown with teeth of slate,
Gleaming a glaze of rain.

Slate dust in skin and lung
The dead from the quarry mountain —
A black half-loaf of slate
Sliced by a vicious God.

Dark-suited on a Sunday
In chapels with plain dim windows
They filled the ghost-town streets
With hymns of singing brass.

Brief rays of watery sunlight —
God's grudging smile — a Victorian
Engraving for the Bible,
Bound with coal black.

And the very air constricts.
You look across to the hills
On the same level, looming.
The clouds absorb the hymns.

Edward Larrissy

WE HAVE NO NEED TO DREAM

We have no need to dream of the mountains
Of home or the fall of water and its swirl
To the parting tides.

We are here, where the rock is sharp
Under our feet and the mat grass
Sways under the wind whirl.

We are here and may see hanging valleys
Gorge themselves on cloud and mist
And we listen everywhere to voices of water —
Now harped like glass strings over pebbles,
And then phrased, male-mouthed as a choir
For the shell trebled, skate-flown sea.

We can look with respect and easy affinity
Into the cooled magazine of the world,
Where Holly Fern and Rose-root and ice flowers
Hide in hollows (but not from us) and grip
Vice hard to ledges in the bracken gold of light
That tones this thunder-ripped bed of stone
Below the mew of buzzard.

We can stroke the slice of slate
And the temples of quartz,
Where the vixen's bark sends
The bleating through the ffridd
And the shallow soil drives flocks for miles
But, like us, they know the home ground
When the shepherd shrills a black flash
Of dog to the Crîb.

Stare through the streams where the sun
Hammers wedding rings on smooth anvils
And the hint of white water shapes
In the corner of your eye.

There are shells scalloped and spiralled
Into Snowdon, where the old folded seams
Heaved like sperm whales from the seabed,
And perched blocks rode limpet-back
To their salt cradles or stared as blind
Oriels and lancets in glazed minsters
Lurched to the monstrous cracking shore.

We of the mountains, streams and the Welsh sea
Of sunsets only leave them once — no more —
For we cannot bear the distant dreams.

T Ll Williams

TO A POET MET IN CWM DYLI

Grey goblets of clouds
not yet drunk by sun: gulls stitch
the sky together.

Under the mountain
a wanderer searches for
substance of his craft:

not metal or gems
or woods or furs but only
words to weave and bind,

words to cast and carve.
He tilts up flat stones to look
underneath for blind

burrowing earth-words.
He parts each stiff clump of grass
to see if quiet

winds, in carding it,
have left any words there. He
seeks words of white flame

to kindle his tongue,
and supple green fern-words, and
words of still water

to flow into the
shape of vessels. The sun and
the moon bring him words.

The clouds melt and drip
words on him: cold gulls cry words
into the morning.

Amory Lovins

ON CRIB GOCH

So high am I upon this lofty chair
The shouting mountain-torrent's thunderous boom
Sounds but a murmuring throb upon the air;
Along the grey-green levels of the cwm
A knotted silver thread I see it go,
Far below.

The great rocks stand together solemnly,
Bending their wrinkled brows in awful calm
Like judges, and Y Wyddfa's majesty
Stands at their head with stern uplifted arm,
Contemptuous of the easy lands I know
Far below.

Stripped of the things for which my hands have striven
I stand to hear the windy spaces speak;
Straightened and scoured by the blue blaze of heaven,
A naked soul upon a naked peak,
All cares and passions drained, like melted snow,
Far below.

Could I but hold this moment and this peace
Within my mind, renew my mental birth
With this high hour that is my soul's release,
Then were I god and mine were all the earth —
I that am pygmy Man, and now must go
Creeping along, exceeding small and slow,
Far below.

Showell Styles

THE SIGN

High on the hoary temple of the Skull
Between the nose and crown
A cold flame flared
Only when the wind blew.
The orange nylon tress of a jammed sling
Tugged and tussled at its anchor-hole
But the clench of the rock's jaw was everlasting.
As we fingered and toed
The ice that glassed the grooves of Crib y Ddysgl
Seven hundred feet above the road,
My eyes were drawn back high and sideways
To that forlorn flare.
It was as though I saw the climber cling
One-handed, desperate to place it there,
His second lunge to take it off, and fail,
Then spider upwards to security.
In little better order, charily,
We inched along the face, unnerved by ice.
Before we reached the snow I looked again,
Expecting that the sign
Might now have vanished in the cavernous dark.
Hard to be sure; but in this shuddering
Airstream seven winters later
I think its warning-flag will still be signalling.

David Craig

LLIDDAW

Old wrinkled gossip says
No bird dare fly across this craggy llyn,
Fearing the anger of that doom-led queen
Who to its black depth took her loneliness.
Today I saw the water in distress
For, harried before the gale, it beat the rock
With phantom-flying precipices of spray,
And moaning as it struck.

But when I looked back from the mountain side
The crags were softly dyed
With the last swoon of daylight, and below
The llyn shone with a quiet inward glow;
And then
I knew her spirit was at peace again.

Stanley Snaith

THE MINERS' TRACK

Up the stony pathway, splashing
Through Llyn Llydaw, deep below
The steep and barren flanks of Lliwedd
And the sword-edge of Crib Goch,

Up where Arthur's knights lie sleeping
Till the Celtic trumpets' summoning cry,
By Glaslyn's waters green, where deepening
Shadows linger, here will I

Ascend the slopes to old Y Wyddfa,
Climb its ancient cairn, then lie
And watch the ravens reel beneath me,
Tumbling down the sky.

Sue Smith

SNOWDON

The mountain. Nude,
not to be moved.

Carrying well-dressed men with quiet wives
and two children;
hugging couples in city shoes
they chess against the polished rocks;
striding, whippet-kneed climbers
with ropes on their shoulders,
and one or two elderly gentlemen,
sticked, piped, steady as clocks,

The wide path ambles, slowly rearing
at the sky . . .

Up there, flimsy in the wind,
I gangplank along.
Lakes,
ink in the shadows
hours below. Sheep
tinkering among the rocks.

Gulls hung
under the summit, witching out
at the lip of the precipice,
precise, sculpt
scavengers; I laboured
into the clouds,
pushing for the hotel.

The train lunks past,
Britain's last rack railway
— glassed-in faces, cameras
snapping at the sky
and sudden gulfs —
creaking in its grease.

Steaming teas, bad apples,
people gollopping the last of supper
before nightfall.

The black chain of the train chinks downward,
dark brandy windows gleaming
for a long time.

At the summit
the smithereening wind
was about its business of chilling and uplifting
detached objects,
licking clean the tops of Easter,
flinging rice grain rain at my up-turned face.

Aortas inside
the mountain,
bible-black
mine-shafts sigh all night.

I have to go down.

Edwin Drummond

EXULTATION

I, Williams —
   sing here a moon and a mountain song —
A soaring song tossed of the wine of this bottled air,
With its bouquet lightly traced for your eyes and ear;
A song along high places of hoar-frost,
Stored sweetly for far flighted meadows,
And slow-footed on ice.

He, Evans --
   will still for you the torrent sunlight
Crazed in the weather, with reeds poised heron-legged,
Heads raised dry, in patient shallows of Cwm Ffynnon;
And then, his gold is from the bracken — broken-backed,
Crown old in October — around the ragged milestones
Set foursquare in homesteads;
Buttressed in goatfields.

We'll invite
                for you, delight in stars and moonflash,
And in tremble of wind and in towers of clouds;
Moel Siabod darkly browed and lashed with skies;
All big-breasted hills buttonholed in yellow flowers;
And Y Lliwedd the apple of Llynnau Mymbyr eyes.

T Ll Williams

THE WELSH THREES

It's three in the morning — I grope for reality.
My companion needs shaking to join my almost-real world.
One hour to go before we start that lung-bursting attempt.
How long ago was it we first conceived this madness?
A year has gone by and we're still convinced we are men
enough to pit our minds, our bodies against this
magnificent permanence. We who are so transitory.

The tent's down. Light is lifted from behind the
darkened mountain ridges. It seems to rise from out of the
sea. Is it the chillness of the dawn that makes our hearts
beat fast? I think what lies ahead accelerates the pulse.
At Pen-y-Pass headlights stab at the receding gloom.
Others who share the madness are gathering.
We meet as the confluence of rivers — our purpose one.

We rise to the level of small-talk, not putting into
words our feelings of the effort that will be required
of our minds, our bodies. The pace is slow, heads down,
an occasional grunt to acknowledge that each exists.
The path steepens, hands are required to pull as well
as legs to push. We make a first contact with the rock —
and it is good.

Within the hour we stand on Crib-goch; we moved quicker
than we thought. The pace increases — but now we are
aware of the acceleration. Finely balanced on the Red
Ridge, we are mindful of our aerial walk and required
balance. We tread Crib-y-ddysgl through thickening
cloud. The party splits — those natural mountain
athletes zoom into the distance — we shall meet at the end.

81

Down the endless rack and pinion track, over the
edge and into the abyss behind Clogwyn station.
Nant Peris lies below, rest and refreshment.
The descent is steep, a careless foot would
plunge a fellsman into tragedy.
A person jogs across the car park, cup in hand,
eager to please. I drink the offering, my God, it's good.

Elidir Fawr, portentous massif.
My legs ache, my lungs clutch at a paucity of air.
The peak, the first is a false one, and so with the
second and with the third, is reached with thankfulness.
But I am on my own — others have forged ahead. Y Garn,
noble mountain, comes into view — no sooner seen than climbed.
Then down to the llyn below the Glyders. I stop to chat
with two whose chosen task it is to refresh us.

Voices from the thickening cloud. Two who moved ahead
talk their way out of the shroud. Their faces betray a
weariness, a despondency of the lost, and lost they had
been. We take to the Glyders. I hear Bob moan and be-
wail the fact that he spent himself ascending the wrong
mountain. Soon I am alone again. From Glyder Fach I
drop to Tryfan's bwlch. This mass of rock looms over me;
before I was the one who, from the Glyders, dominated.
'Christ, give me the strength to reach the summit.'

The climb is tortuous, my whole body almost surrendering
itself to the constant aches that leave no bone undisturbed.
Below, Ogwen beckons, and once more we know that refreshment
waits. I am too weary to take the food and drink — but
effort finally overcomes lassitude. Inside the hour
I am ready to push myself again. Six to go, and I know
that I have not reached my limits.

Penyrolewen, the mountain I feared. Its steepness
I know will drag the heart from out of me. I reach
its summit with surprising lack of effort.
And now the Carneddau. Dafydd looms above a swirling
mass of cloud. Evening is drawing in. Almost seven
o'clock. Llewelyn beckons us on. Beyond that Carnedd
lies Yr Elen, mountain out on a limb. It's there and back
to Llewelyn. My body fights to resist the paralysing
fatigue. Tiredness beyond what I thought possible claws

for power to make me accept defeat. Two to go — and I
feel at the point of death.

Foel-grach, and as I stumble across its flat-topped
summit I sink to the ground knowing that there is just
one more mountain between me and oblivion. There is
no steepness, just agonising distance. The trig point,
ages coming into view. Below, Llyn Anafon, and beyond,
a patch of blackness which is the end.

Darkness makes the gentle downhill a danger.
My legs are beyond the feelings of aches — they throw
themselves fitfully this way and that.
My eyes, red with sweat, sting as though a thousand
bees bored their way into my head. I tumble into a
waiting car -- it's all over. No glory, no sense of achieve-
ment — but that will come tomorrow; just a pleasant
succumbing to exhaustion.

Peter Travis

SHE'LL BE COMING ROUND THE MOUNTAIN

Space and time entangle in this
patchy world, almost at the top
of Wales, where blurred shades scramble
the horizons and winds fire
thorns into my face. Droplets
coalesce on the cold window pane
of my forehead, trickle
into my mouth. This wild womb
has taken me in and I exult
as the wind makes a drum of my hood.

The thorns have turned to arrows fired
from longbows in the valley
and their song rises to the pitch
of ice on glass. The streams become
a torrent and my tongue chills under
its flow. Your little girl is too fragile
for this mountain and you will have
turned. I open my hood to the wind
and rest on a green-skinned block of granite.

83

Strange, as I sit here, staring at my
boots against the scudding cloud, how the
wind plays tricks. Fragments of the human
voice flit by, cohere, and are
shuffled by my mind into an old
song. Then, like the Cheshire cat, a smile
congeals in the mist, linked loosely
to a pair of tennis shoes, light-footing, a slim
hand clasping a smaller one, jerkily swinging.

John Latham

ABOVE NANTLLE

The hills across the valley rigid
whale-backs, the clouds slow-running

waves that pour over them, the lake
completing a green world, with downside-

up image that for an instant
bewilders the eye;

the tips of slate-waste crude
reminders of human-waste,

hard-knuckled poverty, minds
made bare of all but the most

primitive belief. Ash-trees
quiver on a quiet breeze, hawthorns

remain impervious. It is all green,
grey, grey-green, except for the harsh-voiced

sheep . . . and rowan berries spattered
red against the cloud.

John Ashbrook

MYNYDD GILFACH

Along the mountain's haunch
The sheep track sidles, morsed
With droppings black and round
As olives. The boy inside

Stepped nimbly in the battered rut,
And winter breath sang stinging
Down my throat, my duffle coat
No poet's cloak to stream

Romantically behind. Old Huw
Walked here, imperious and gaunt,
Oblivious of the miners he passed by,
Remote in his utopian dreams.

And Bob the Runner trained his lurcher
Bounding up these steep ascents;
No fancied greyhound ever raised
A finer spray of morning dew.

Today the tangled brambles
Are random heaps of rusty wire,
Scabrous traps for freezing air
And tufts of wool, Gorgon manes.

Outcrops of sheep are still
And grey as stones. The boy beside
Is running to the low spilled wall,
Rolling its lichen-gilded lumps,

Watching them come to rest
As grey and still as sheep.
The farmer's wire is here,
So taut it cuts the wind

In tunes. The two boys feel
The hurt within, and turn
To see projected on the mist
The shadow of their mountain.

The cwm fills up with evening,
Clotting round the terraces,
Lapping at the crenellated
Ranks of chimneys row by row,
The loop of road, the central void.

Sam Adams

APRIL

Strange I will not see the mountain for three months and
  a little more
Since like January this Easter very cold is, very raw,
And it will be like wet ice in our cottage in Croesor,
Dampness seeping through and congealing on the grey slates
  of the floor
And the Welsh wind creeping through the windows and
  inaccurate door.
But it seems to see no buzzard, ravens, sheep — I do not care,
Since within my heart and my mind they are present ever-
  more.
With me on this April morning though they are not present
  here
In my being, near dawn, brooding, they could not be much
  closer,
Buzzard, curlew, raven, heron, in my mind's eye they are here.
And those mountains Cnicht, Moelwinian, could not be a jot
  nearer,
Perhaps it's because last zero summer, no walking, a cracked
  lumbar,
So I sat in the great heat taking in the fells' fauna.
Gleaning into my mind each detail, mountain bracken and
  heather,
So that now they are co-present where the streets of London
  are;
My forever salient Alpha and eternal Omega.

Thomas Blackburn

86

SLATE

Drawn from his fold on the mean mountain
the brittle man of Wales shuffles black dominoes
and builds, on the shards of his father's dreams,
this meaner mountain, where grieving winds

polish the grim sarcophagus at Blaenau Ffestiniog.
We watch — but from a decent distance — the dismembering
of another's way of life, hewn, sawn, split and split again
to a wafer thin, then leaving the man spitting the dust

of his own drear day, well entertained we drive away
past prim rhododendron mountains, to tea and toast
on a silver tray with damask cloth at Betws-y-Coed,
and ladies with trim white hair and brown moustaches.

Maurice Rutherford

SLEEPING OUT AT GALLT-Y-CEILIOG

Something, perhaps an idea, is again eluding me.
It belongs nowhere in particular but might
At any moment appear and surprise me.

It's not part of the usual epiphanies.
It has no colour, or even night-colour, since
Lying awake half the night will not fix it.

The trees are alive, the candle flame gusty
And flattened. We lie in our quilted chrysalises
With still heads, like ancient funeral masks.

The moon at our backs rises over the mountains:
An understudy, practising with silent lips,
Sharing the sky with one star above the holly tree.

Nothing is spoken. The precise text of leaf
And crag is not known, or has been quite forgotten.
We're happy with what is offered, like visitors.

Perhaps after all there is nothing to remember
But this simplicity. The grass is grey
At dawn. It is the earth awakes, not I.

John Fuller

AT TRE'R CEIRI

There were giants in Llŷn in those days, and they lived on
    this mountain
Behind these drystone walls piled high to keep secrets and
    hutch holy
Things from the god-searching singing wind off the sea twelve
    fields below.

The peak of Yr Eifl towered over them, more psalmist than
    guardian,
For it lifted their eyes to the fierce sun drowning beyond
    Ireland
And gave them scale, while the rubble trickling slowly down
    the scree slopes

Taught them comparative weight and the fragility of all flesh.
They were invincible in all other respects. So they stood gods
Among men, gods of power and hate, gods who looked down
    on their people

In purest contempt for that they were weak and small and
    subservient,
And for that they worshipped, and lifted up their mute eyes
    in their turn,
And for that they drew their water from deep St. Aelhaearn's
    well.

Up on Tre'r Ceiri water came from a spring which sang below
    ground
And emerged blinking. They never enclosed it, or put stones
    around it,
Or (*O fons Bandusiae*) cut any kid's throat on an altar.

There was no need, the stones were sufficient protection. The
    walls now

Are ruinously splayed, but the stream still flows, and the
  well is full,
And at the mountain's foot still swings the eternal eroding
  sea.

Brian Morris

GATHERERS

They taste of the uplands,
bilberries do; of
rain through the heather,
peat thin-scarfed
over acid rock. A small darkness,
nudging identity
like the smell of woodsmoke or the way
faces flickered
round the bonfire.
Eating them in winter from the deep freeze
resurrects the kindness
of that day we snatched
to go and look for them, climbing
out of sea-fog to discover
in its steep stone streets, Tre'r Ceiri held
an ancient clearness still. Only summits showed
in an ocean of drowned centuries;
the real sea was fathoms-deep, forgotten.
It was a world for women —
details stood out, safe.
The sky was a daylong yawn
of content, the smells all
moist earth we were part of,
just women gatherers. A kestrel
hovered close, a brood of choughs
screamed at the wheeling blur
beneath their wings, and all
afternoon we talked, were quiet,
and picked, our ease absolved
by being useful. The children found
harebells and tormentil, got wet feet,
drowsed in white heather
beside bones they thought a fox's kill.

'We must come again,' we said,
but with no conviction, knowing
the three-fold pivots of our lives
would swing us out of range again.

So, 'That's the last of them,'
I say, ' — this year's bilberries — '
but though the winter sea
bays at my back door, the wind
has ice on its breath,
that day's warmth, I have it still,
I've gathered it.

Christine Evans

WELSH INN PARLOUR

Keep that old gramophone going.
For heaven's sake don't let's just sit and think.
Talk? Why, whatever should we talk about?
We know what everybody's been doing.
Let's have a good time. Let's have a drink.
Let's hear the band play, hear the boys shout.
Let's have some noise to kick the blue devils out.
Keep the old gramophone going.

And half a mile away
There's silence on the hills and the stars' slow dance.
It's cold out there. But one might sit and think
With a great-coat on. One might even kneel and pray.
At any rate one could give one's soul a chance,
And the world wouldn't have to shrink
To a blur of noise and drink
This way.

There, the world's firm shape,
It's true and lasting shape not to be denied,
Background of all the ages that make man's day,
Stands to the dark as a cape
To sea, juts chinlike into the cosmic tide.
There, you could see the universe wheel and obey
Laws that your children learn at their schools. And you play
The gramophone, to escape.

Will you not escape from escaping? See, the moon
Comes and the stars draw back. For such as me
Your Welsh hills and your bright skies are spread out.
Break those scratched records, smash that bastard croon.
The world's whole past and all futurity
Are waiting on the mountainside. The rout
Of heaven do homage to you. Their soundless shout
Drowns out the loud empty tune.

Geoffrey Faber

CADER IDRIS

I

The mountain was warmer then
as I shinned its green slopes
to the polished peak,
to where God had sat on the seventh day
to bless the Mawddach estuary.

In the towering sêt-fawr
I recited the names of Quaker farms
quivering below in the hot fields
from Gelli-lwyd to Bryncrug.

And with the sun,
a red coracle on the sea,
down to tŷ Nain for cold meat and pickle,
scuttling into bed from the ghosts
groaning in the tall dark wardrobes.

II

Today,
my head heavy with the night's beer,
the slopes were steeper,
the rocks sharper.

Above Lyn Cau
clouds heaved with rain,

and those with faith
strong enough to move mountains
crawled like ladybirds on the distant ridge.

Below, twisting in the rain,
the path to the warm cwm.

Huw Jones

INNOCENT DYING

Grey is Nant Iago, grey
With slate planes and break-offs
From the darker roughs
Shot dead in the mines on Cedris. They

Lie flat now, assembled, flat
As the lives of old miners.
Calms immerse
Them, hold them in a cold mercy, set

Grey in their faces, grey
Run weedless, the surface
Clean. It is
Only a skate now to confluence, shy

Death in Dysynni, death
By confusion. Close by at
This gorsy spit
You can see the swathe of green weed beneath

The wave of Dysynni, wave
Going humped with the fields' knap
That's higher up.
A step farther shows you Iago, grave

And resistless, hand
His cap in, simple
With years. The full
River swills undyed from his token end.

Roland Mathias

THE WELSH HILL COUNTRY

Too far for you to see
The fluke and the foot-rot and the fat maggot
Gnawing the skin from the small bones,
The sheep are grazing at Bwlch-y-Fedwen,
Arranged romantically in the usual manner
On a bleak background of bald stone.

Too far for you to see
The moss and the mould on the cold chimneys,
The nettles growing through the cracked doors,
The houses stand empty at Nant-yr-Eira.
There are holes in the roofs that are thatched with sunlight,
And the fields are reverting to the bare moor.

Too far, too far to see
The set of his eyes and the slow phthisis
Wasting his frame under the ripped coat,
There's a man still farming at Ty'n-y-Fawnog,
Contributing grimly to the accepted pattern,
The embryo music dead in his throat.

R S Thomas

ABOVE TREGARON

This is a way to come in winter. This is a way
Of steep gradients, bad corners for cars,
It is metalled now, but this is a way
Trodden out by cattle, paced yet by the ghosts
Of drovers. The valleys ring with echoes,
When the car-horn sounds, of wise horsemen
Calling across the streams, the slow black herds
Steaming and jostling, the corgi's yelp.
The sweet breath of cows still hangs in the air
Between rock, bracken and milk-foamed water.
Away from the road stand the farmhouses,
The loneliest it is said, even in this land
Of lonely places, and on the high ground
Between Irfon and Camddwr you are as far away
As you will ever be from the world's madness.

The drivers you pass wave and nod a greeting,
Recreating you as a person from a statistic.
Look on it for the last time; in a few years
The pinetrees will have hidden it in their darkness.
Even now perhaps it is not quite right
To take this road when there are easier routes.
Flying from madness, maybe we bring it with us,
Patronising romantics, envying the last survivors
Of an old way of life, projecting our dreams
On this conveniently empty scenery, deserted
By its sons for the hard bright streets we come from.
We pass them perhaps on the road, our journey
An interlude, theirs a beginning, an end.
Pause on the watershed, look round, pass on,
Leave it behind. Anyway its all dead, you'll tell me,
Like everything else traditional in Wales
And not before time too. That is why I say
This is a way to come in winter.

Harri Webb

NANT-Y-CERDIN

In high morning I am haunted
                by long-ago mornings —
and even those were ghost-ridden
                by a more distant morning
never quite remembered
                but never dying at noon.
Today when wheatears
                flash from sunny rocks
and new loose-limbed lambs
stagger appalled through the stony stream
                after stolid ewes;
when daffodils blow in the nettle-garden
                of a farm with broken windows,
and in a remote brown valley
the clammy standing stone
                grows warm to touch —
even today ghosts come
                whispering of a ghost.

94

Could there ever be a morning unhaunted,
a spring shining
             with no sunlight but its own?
Only the first, perhaps,
             the lost ideal morning,
the one that must be found,
must be lived or haunt me always,
the lost morning on forgotten hills.

                           Ruth Bidgood

PLYNLIMON FAWR

I am a wide surf of sound.
Grey herons float in my valleys,
long-winged and silent.
A white circle of stones
is my beacon, my church.
My blood is the earth's blood.
I offer no easy shelter.
My rocks will not stretch
above man's head
like the dark trees of Hyddgen.
I father wild buzzards
while brown larks haunt my clouds.
I share in the high wind's loud
struggle of living belief.
I am a rocky shelf, wound
into a hymn-source of sound.

                           David Goddard

ON PEN Y FAN

I will not lift up my eyes to mountains.
To walk on hills is to parade your arrogance.
Is to look down on people.
Yet all peaks are relative;
It depends on your viewpoint.

Aircraft look down and sneer at mountain tops,
Their pilots wink at the altimeter's dark eye.
But aircraft crash before landing,
Or shortly after take off.
Put not your trust in turbines.

At Newport generators jerk current
Down miles of cables, coils, and wire capillaries.
Bold electricians switch and cut.
But circuits short and stutter.
Routine maintenance sets in.

At Merthyr assembly lines are tamer —
Newmachines make tools to tool yetunmade machines.
Parallel men serve them in rows,
With some sacrifices and
Mechanical obedience.

Even Breconshire hills are mechanised,
Triangulated, probed, trudged over and contoured.
What for? Tourists kill time climbing
Or walking. Soft substitute.
A mountain is a machine.

Brian Morris

BEYOND TREFIL

Hawthorn bushes, witches' hair.

Crows buoyed on up-currents
at the head of a valley —
black ink, quill
scraping air.

Inscrutable sheep staring
into a space
in your skull
the wind inhabits.

I have dreamt
of those farms down there
among cuckoo-clock trees
you blow for the season,

not strung together
in a net of wires
to catch the outside world —
no aerials jetting pictures.

I hold a lamb:
it kicks inside the womb
of the mountains,
the spring of its muscles
not meek and mild.

Pen-y-Fan, snow-wrinkled forehead
critical of my offering,
frowning on the farms
which float like rafts
on a lake of grass.

Mike Jenkins

THE MOUNTAIN OVER ABERDARE

From this high quarried ledge I see
The place for which the Quakers once
Collected clothes, my fathers' home,
Our stubborn bankrupt village sprawled
In jaded dusk beneath its nameless hills;
The drab streets strung across the cwm,
Derelict workings, tips of slag
The gospellers and gamblers use
And children scrutting for the coal
That winter dole cannot purvey;
Allotments where the collier digs
While engines hack the coal within his brain;
Grey Hebron in a rigid cramp,
White cheap-jack cinema, the church
Stretched like a sow beside the stream;
And mourners in their Sunday best

Holding a tiny funeral, singing hymns
That drift insidious as the rain
Which rises from the steaming fields
And swathes about the skyline crags
Till all the upland gorse is drenched
And all the creaking mountain gates
Drip brittle tears of crystal peace;
And in a curtained parlour women hug
Huge grief, and anger against God.
But now the dusk, more charitable than Quakers,
Veils the cracked cottages with drifting may
And rubs the hard day off the slate.
The colliers squatting on the ashtip
Listen to one who holds them still with tales,
While that white frock that floats down the dark alley
Looks just like Christ; and in the lane
The clink of coins among the gamblers
Suggests the thirty pieces of silver.

I watch the clouded years
Rune the rough foreheads of these moody hills,
This wet evening, in a lost age.

Alun Lewis

HILLS

Down under the gloom on the cold floor
Of the forking Valley, among the villages,
Each a little mound of glow-worm lights,
The men that passed me by lie buried
Under this load of darkness deepening.

I have stood aside when they flooded down
The slope from two pits, the sound of their boots
Like chattering of tipped hail over roofs;
I can remember like applause the sound
Of their speech and laughter, the smell of their
    pit-clothes.

On the hill-top, ambushed by rising stars,
Beneath a pine-tree giving up its scent
Into the night like some monstrous blossom,
A man stands suffering, with tears salt
And cold upon his mouth for very pity.

Glyn Jones

PEACE IN THE WELSH HILLS

Calm is the landscape when the storm has passed,
Brighter the fields, and fresh with fallen rain.
Where gales beat out new colour from the hills
Rivers fly faster, and upon their banks
Birds preen their wings, and irises revive.
Not so the cities burnt alive with fire
Of man's destruction: when their smoke is spent,
No phoenix rises from the ruined walls.

I ponder now the grief of many rooms.
Was it a dream, that age, when fingers found
A satisfaction sleeping in dumb stone,
When walls were built responding to the touch
In whose high gables, in the lengthening days,
Martins would nest? Though crops, though lives, would fail,
Though friends dispersed, unchanged the walls would stay,
And still those wings return to build in Spring.

Here, where the earth is green, where heaven is true
Opening the windows, touched with earliest dawn,
In the first frost of cool September days,
Chrysanthemum weather, presaging great birth,
Who in his heart could murmur or complain:
'The light we look for is not in this land'?
That light is present, and that distant time
Is always here, continually redeemed.

There is a city we must build with joy
Exactly where the fallen city sleeps.
There is one road through village, town and field,
On whose robust foundation Chaucer dreamed

A ride could wed the opposites in man.
There proud walls may endure, and low walls feed
The imagination if they have a vine
Or shadowy barn made rich with gathered corn.

Great mansions fear from their surrounding trees
The invasion of a wintry desolation
Filling their rooms with leaves. And cottages
Bring the sky down as flickering candles do,
Leaning on their own shadows. I have seen
Vases and polished brass reflect black windows
And draw the ceiling down to their vibrations,
Thick, deep, and white-washed, like a bank of snow.

To live entwined in pastoral loveliness
May rest the eyes, throw pictures on the mind,
But most we need a metaphor of stone
Such as those painters had whose mountain-cities
Cast long, low shadows on the Umbrian hills.
There, in some courtyard on the cobbled stone,
A fountain plays, and through a cherub's mouth
Ages are linked by water in the sunlight.

All of good faith that fountain may recall,
Woman, musician, boy, or else a scholar
Reading a Latin book. They seem distinct,
And yet are one, because tranquillity
Affirms the Judgement. So, in these Welsh hills,
I marvel, waking from a dream of stone,
That such a peace surrounds me, while the city
For which all long has never yet been built.

Vernon Watkins

SNOW ON THE MOUNTAIN

There was a girl riding a white pony
Which seemed an elemental part
Of the snow. A crow cut a clean line
Across the hill, which we grasped as a rope
To pull us up the pale diagonal.

100

The point was to be first at the top
Of the mountain. Our laughter bounced far
Below us like five fists full of pebbles. About us
Lay the snow, deep in the hollows,
Very clean and dry, untouched.

I arrived breathless, my head breaking
The surface of the glittering light, thinking
No place could claim more beauty, white
Slag tips like cones of sugar spun
By the pit wheels under Machen mountains.

I sat on a rock in the sun, watching
My snowboys play. Pit villages shine
Like anthracite. Completed, the pale rider
Rode away. I turned to him, and saw
His joy fall like the laughter down a dark
Crack. The black crow shadowed him.

Gillian Clarke

THE RHONDDA HILLS ARE TALL AND LEAN

The Rhondda hills are tall and lean
Like greyhounds stripped-down for speed,
But the townships running close at their feet
Are going all out to take the lead.

The long-legged hills and the puffing towns
Are neck to neck in this hard race:
The towns lack style but are full of tricks
And the hills are tough in spite of their grace.

Clifford Dyment

WHEN WE WALKED TO MERTHYR TYDFIL

When we walked to Merthyr Tydfil, in the moonlight
   long ago,
When the mountain tracks were frozen and the crests were
   capped with snow,
We had tales and songs between us, and souls too young
   to fret,
And we had hopes and visions which the heart remembers
   yet.

The winds from the farthest mountains blew about us as
   we strode,
But we were warm and merry on the crooked freezing road,
And there were lamp-lit homesteads to south and east and
   west,
And we watched the round moon smiling on those little
   lights of rest.

The moon is still as radiant and the homely hills remain,
But the magic of those evenings we shall not meet again.
For we were boyish dreamers in a world we did not know
When we walked to Merthyr Tydfil in the moonlight
   long ago.

Idris Davies

from MERTHYR

Lord, when they kill me, let the job be thorough
And carried out behind that county borough
Known as Merthyr, in Glamorganshire.
It would be best if it could happen, Sir,
Upon some great green roof, some Beacon slope
Those monstrous clouds of childhood slid their soap
Snouts over, into the valley. The season,
Sir, for shooting, summer; and love the reason.
On that hill, varnished in the glazing tide
Of evening, stand me, with the petrified
Plantations, the long blue spoonful of the lake,
The gold stook-tufted acres without break
Below me, and the distant corduroy

Glass of the river — which, a mitching boy,
I fished — flowing as though to quench
The smouldering coalfield in its open trench
Of steamy valley, fifteen miles away.
Here, Sir, are more arrangements for that day:-
Lay me, lead-loaded, below the mourning satin
Of some burnt-out oak; the skylark's chirpy Latin
Be my '*Daeth yr awr*'; gather the black
Flocks for bleaters — sweet grass their ham — upon the back
Of lonely Fan Gihirych; let night's branchy tree
Glow with silver-coated planets over me.

Glyn Jones

from IN HOSPITAL: POONA

Last night I did not fight for sleep
But lay awake from midnight while the world
Turned its slow features to the moving deep
Of darkness, till I knew that you were furled,

Beloved, in the same dark watch as I.
And sixty degrees of longitude beside
Vanished as though a swan in ecstasy
Had spanned the distance from your sleeping side.

And like to swan or moon the whole of Wales
Glided within the parish of my care:
I saw the green tide leap on Cardigan,
Your red yacht riding like a legend there,

And the great mountains, Dafydd and Llewelyn,
Plynlimmon, Cader Idris and Eryri
Threshing the darkness back from head and fin,
And also the small nameless mining valley

Whose slopes are scratched with streets and sprawling graves
Dark in the lap of firwoods and great boulders
Where you lay waiting, listening to the waves —
My hot hands touched your white despondent shoulders

— And then ten thousand miles of daylight grew
Between us, and I heard the wild daws crake
In India's starving throat; whereat I knew
That Time upon the heart can break
But love survives the venom of the snake.

Alun Lewis

THE SMALL WINDOW

In Wales there are jewels
To gather, but with the eye
Only. A hill lights up
Suddenly; a field trembles
With colour and goes out
In its turn; in one day
You can witness the extent
Of the spectrum and grow rich

With looking. Have a care;
This wealth is for the few
And chosen. Those who crowd
A small window dirty it
With their breathing, though sublime
And inexhaustible the view.

R S Thomas

The Human Animal on the Hill

OVER THE DROP

He clings to the bulge of the cloud,
Feeling its glossy whale-bulk urge against his chest.
The air's spinning cascade
Hollows down the entire drop
Between zenith and globe and he knows that falling
This time will lose him the world.
He remembers Sadak
'Searching for the waters of oblivion',
The giant with the hairless skull
Down in the sordid basement of the mountains,
Dwarfed by the hairy ogre-torsos of the tree-ferns,
The nude limbs of succulents, his twisted
Hawser muscles crucified around the brute boulder.
And he remembers Fawcett
Leading the top pitch of Nagasaki Grooves
High on Great End in Borrowdale,
His brown arm sprouting from the blue singlet
With an ivy's clasp, with a gibbon's flair,
With a human's instant calculation
Of the dizzy chances.   His own toes touch
The cloud's iced underside, the vapour tendrils twine
Into a cat's cradle, and like the gulfing pressure
Under the buzzard's wing the air buoys him upwards,
His fingers sculpt snow-holds, he hauls himself home.

David Craig

THE ONES THAT GET AWAY

They're out early, human ravens,
combing the rocks, feeling in the cracks,
peering out under the overhangs
as if they're about to be attacked
or have lost something important.

Or found it,
here, at the moor's jaw,
bright pallete of anoraks and voices
— Yorkshire, Devon, Oxbridge —

on red, green yellow and iris
   ropes
   rising
with their lives in their hands.

Moving slowly over the brown diamonds,
coming to grips
with grief
on that slab, frantically fingerprinting
the severe British faces,
anglers of bones and loneliness, their hands

- fish
  deep
    in that
      crack!

        Edwin Drummond

CRAGSMAN

His heels, slow
and poised, swing out
like wings.

In the amphitheatre
sky has dimension
as though through a camera.

Creased by dusk perspective
a disappearance of angle
simply aggravates
the shock of its texture.

A scythe's exposure follows.
It is of the dualism:
keeping one eye on the horizon;

the other turned inward
is maintained by abstraction:
one climber,
one valley,

severed by an ocean,
with one human mind
latched to a Langdale wall,
fixed like a lighthouse.

Chat is restricted to resting,
a few words spun over granite
like powder-snow.

An edge where stove-light shows
concavity,
slipped depth muffles rockfall.

The sparks trail
surreal arms
scribing parabolas in flight,

geometry of a man's fall
between two stabilities.

When sunlight works
in refraction
sérac dews the earth
in ivory.

Ice-axe and screw
stab and pull
like starlings on snow.

Winter brings these steel birds,
the solid-feeders,
visored
to their eyries.

David J Morley

CLIMBERS

fodder
for agape enthusiasms   all the
cruder
lethargies   they lie and bask
on some raw slab and do not ask
other
than that the holds be not too close
together

G J F Dutton

LIKE AN ANIMAL

My son is like an animal.
Before he moves on the rock
His brown eyes jump from hold to hold
Nervous and sure and quick
As a rat on a high timber
Or a field-mouse poised on a straw.
His hands and arms are limber
As a gibbon looping from tree
To lower tree to bush
In a headlong balanced rush.
Peter steadies himself,
Gathers himself for the move,
The tips of his feet frictioning
As a lizard clings to a slab.
His fingers reach for the groove,
The hold is not enough,
His toes are edging off,
His gravity-centre goes
In a long rising lunge,
His fingers hook with a sloth's grip
Onto the next ledge,
And the move, the charge, the momentum
Carry him on and up.

David Craig

THE CRAGSMAN

In this short span
between my finger-tips on the smooth edge
and these tense feet cramped to the crystal ledge
I hold the life of man.
Consciously I embrace
arched from the mountain rock on which I stand
to the firm limit of my lifted hand
the front of time and space:-
    For what is there in all the world for me
        but what I know and see?
    And what remains of all I see and know,
        if I let go?

With this full breath
bracing my sinews as I upward move
boldly reliant to the rift above
I measure life from death.
With each strong thrust
I feel all motion and all vital force
borne on my strength and hazarding their course
in my self-trust:-
    There is no movement of what kind it be
        but has its source in me;
    and should these muscles falter to release
        motion itself must cease.

In these two eyes
that search the splendour of the earth, and seek
the sombre mysteries on plain and peak,
all vision wakes and dies.
With these my ears
that listen for the sound of lakes asleep
and love the larger rumour from the deep,
the eternal hears:-
    For all of beauty that this life can give
        lives only while I live;
    and with the light my hurried vision lends
        all beauty ends.

Geoffrey Winthrop Young

SNAKES AND LADDERS

alone that spring day on the cliff below the summit
face pressed to stone face & fingers sticky
swollen in the dusty slits

climbing swift as a lucky counter, until chance
made incautious, & spreadeagled limbs
began to tremble in their torsion
stiff & powerless

before fear the body fell back into space dropped
face upwards to nothing but clear sky
thought & image flash as meteors
burning unknown out

& then the bracken broke the fall. lay staring
as if listening to a great shout, as if
the rope of mind had snapped. death
crouched

disguised as a boulder an inch beyond his skull.

Dave Calder

THE LIVING ROCK

The grey, gregarious rock swarms
With gaily clad human insects,
Fragile and gaudy as butterflies
In scarlet, orange, yellow, blue.
Their climber paraphenalia
Emphasising every move.

Some clumsy, awkward over the crags,
Others poised delicately,
In tense expectancy,
Before making a move, as
Controlled and graceful
As any ballet dancer.

Problems of every day life
Forgotten in the anguish,
Passion, elation of the moment,
Granite-faced they contemplate,
Every nerve strained
In intense concentration.

Then that superb moment
When, supremacy established,
The conqueror conquered,
Self esteem satisfied,
They allow themselves
Their secret insect smile.

Startled, the passer-by is spellbound
By the welcoming, beckoning rock
Bedecked and bestrewn,
Alive and alert
With artistry, agility,
Movement and colour, and life.

Until night falls.
The rock,
Deserted, dark,
Hard and uncompromising,
Lies gaunt, and grey,
. . . . and dead.

Thelma James

THE CLIFF

He broke through trees, cursing the brambles
that tore in his clothes, his ankles cricking
in rock holes hidden by the underbrush:
at last four yards of sunlight, and the cliff.
His deductions, his route-finding, were all true.
Now his eyes stroked it in love, noting
the unswept ledges, the moss, the blocks poised
to fall at a touch and the tasks to climb,
a network of possession in chimney and slab.

113

The rock was rough rust, warm. He turned
and blundered back to the world for a companion.
Why did he never return? The foiled purpose
lies unseen on the crag and will never be found
by the groping eyes of others. Winter and summer
the cliff glooms rawly. It is not waiting for anyone.

Geoffrey Byrne-Sutton

ICE LEADER

Upward daunting
double jointing
front pointing.
Mate taunting,
'Let me have a go'.

Axe slipping.
Knuckles ripping.
Blood dripping.
Mind tripping,
colours on the snow.

Ice flaking.
Crampons scraping.
Hold making.
Weight taking.
Watch it down below.

Quite dramatic.
Acrobatic.
Photographic.
Instamatic.
Hold it half a mo.

Core freezing.
Body seizing.
Angle easing.
Top teasing.
Only a stone's throw.

Dave Bathgate

AN EMBARRASSMENT

It's nothing to laugh at, let me tell you now.
Here I stand on slender green suede feet
Balanced on nothing much. Head back, hands low;
Responsive but relaxed; cool; giving
It plenty of daylight; sensing the warm dry rock,
The sun on my back; properly helmeted.
The speckled rope, the best that money can buy,
Runs further perhaps than I could honestly wish
To a staunch observant second well belayed.
The move protected by a threaded tape
Inserted neatly where nothing else would fit.
Ready to go . . . not dreaming I have clipped
The runner's crab in the bight of my Tarbuck knot.

George Watkins

THE CLIMB

It was pure entropy, one long continuoushering
of one another up one fantasticky overhangled
grimpetigoed gabbroken drippinging
slabyrinth after another, danglingerining
for hoarse hours on that nylonely rope
on pitch after pitchblack above some crack-acking
verticaliginous chasm till, our ascending ended,
we emerged at last into the Whitsunset, often
not even at the summit and then at once descended
since the end of those forays was never, I now know,
the ending. It was the climb itself that was climax.

Eddie Flintoff

INTO ROCK

He stretched to fit the rock
He crouched and eeled to fit the rock
Thinned and flexed to fit the rock
Spreadeagled on its burnished sheets
Feeling his fingers hone to claws

He chimneyed up the gigantic split
Sitting in air like an ejecting pilot
While the sky out there
Blazed at him and the granite ground his spine
Then surfaced from the fissure like a mole

Bearing the chimney's pressure in his hunch
Its rising in his springing tendons
Its darkness in the gleam behind his eyes

Bearing the face's crystals in his fingerprints
Its cracking torsions in his wrists
Its drop in the air beneath his arches

It moulded him. He was its casting.
His clay was kneaded to its bas-relief.
His brain infolded, mimicking its strata.
And when he called, and the echo heard his note,
It parodied his language.

David Craig

THE CRUX

A protuberance of granite,
A finger-hold is all,
Yet the catalyst between being
Or non-being.
Metaphor and hyperbole end here,
The rest is action — plain, unvarnished.
A convulsion of mind and muscle
Bringing
A triumphant awareness of self.
A clamour of furious blood
Pumps and scours.

Fingers throb to the rasp of rock.
Eyes absorb the perfection of
Embedded crystals.
Ears capture the querulous lamb-call
Drifting up a thousand feet of thin, blue air.
Heat.
Sweat.
Salt bristle under the claggy tongue.

A brief scramble up a few feet
Of steep, bare rock
On a summer's day;
And the world sings,
To its golden edges.

Tom Bowker

THE ROCK IS

The rock is
smooth and cool
to the touch, it
is just there
and will not
change though I
step up and
pull on it, jam
my hands and
feet into its
cracks, rest on
small ledges, say
I have conquered
it or at least
come to terms.

I feel my
body move in
unlikely ways over
improbable places,
hang and stretch
on the edge of
balancing, but I

do not even
conquer myself or
come to terms with
my fear. Is it
the act or
the intention, the
climbing or
the conception, that
moves up steep
walls on small
holds?

Joe R Fitschen

THE CLIMB

Cramped on the rain-greaved steep of rock,
shouldering its grey weight, inching round
outcrop and nudge till light is black
and brailling fingers, flake and crack
and footscrape, taut to mock and trick,
sometimes there is no way down.

The lift of sky seduced us here
to make the pathless sheer a feat
significant in hope and fear,
but, pinned upon the need of near,
we hear the whisper at the ear.
Sometimes there is no retreat.

The straddled chimney, the shifting stone,
the slip and scatter of chuckled shock
into its echo, and the grown
demands of hands are ours alone
to tease us with the strength we own,
and always there is no way back.

Robin Skelton

THE WOUND

Thirlmere
soft as meadow,
larch, or alcohol.
Castle Rock of Triermain
hard as Harlot's Face
steep as Overhanging
Bastion, the scar across
the clean north face
that, once seen,
sears the mind.

Pulling past the holly
carefully, contained,
I seek to seal the wound
of panic on this crag
ten years ago.

The wall's small sharp holds
seduce the fingers,
a seeping corner draws
the rhythm and the confidence
of comfortably bridged feet
to a ledge above the larches
green fingering the spring air.

What follows is simple therapy
a relaxing rehearsal
of the crux above
from tempting ramp
to testing step
blind round a block
to land on the platform
of dreams, pinnacle anchored.

A step from the pinnacle point
closes with essences:
finger pocket, foot friction,
trusting to rock and moving
on its subtle surfaces.

Four human points stitch
up the scar until, together
man and rock cast out
on air. Undercut feet step
down, fingers find flake
after flake, reaching, panting,
fired above space
pull up to face
a Chinese lantern
of a yew stem, shiny
from sweaty grabs and
hollowed by sighs.

Beyond this tree
the world is whole,
each detail newly made,
from last rough rock
to soft grass mound
into the sunlight
healed, annealed.

Terry Gifford

AWAY . . . . .
BREATH
YOUR
TAKES
THAT
G
N
A
H
R
E
V
O
5b
A
OF
R
E
H
C
R
O
C
S
A
HAS
THE SECOND
T
U
B
IT
COMMEND
TO
LITTLE
HAS
PITCH
FIRST
THE

NEW ROUTE: E2. 4c. 5b.

Des Hannigan

THEY WHO STAND AND WAIT DO NOT NECESSARILY DO MUCH SERVING

Is this really where I belong?
With rusty sardine cans, beer bottles
And shit inadequately hidden under stones?
Their rucksacks propped against a cairn
And Heino's track shoes moored to a rock
With prussik loops all reassure me they'll return.
I know about real fear now; not the sort
Where you put on a show and scream and shout;
But *there* I knew, in that crevice, my feet slipping
Slowly towards the sea seething hundreds of feet below
As I pressed them, bridging up against the roof,
Hearing unknowing voices chaffing on a lobster boat
Moored under the lee of the teflon cliffs,
And *their* voices, 'Climbing!' 'Take in!' 'Below!'
Their voices, Davey and Rob, familiar, safe,
Yet far and far away. Not knowing here I was
Stuck in this silly posture, remembering
Not to squash the yellow flower
That was safe on this ledge until I came.
Fear is having no-one to share it with —
Would I have been afraid if Rob had reappeared?
— Scoffed 'Good heavens, mum, how the hell did you
    get there?'
But there was only me to inch fearfully across
Remembering Davey's 'good holds will appear,'
And usually they did, and then the top,
And the gathering thunderclouds, and sitting here
Hearing their voices, safe again, waiting,
Brushing away the bluebottles, moving my peeling face
To dodge the sun. Best for the moment to wait here,
Not risk adventure on my own.
Later perhaps.

Anne Spillard

122

THE HARD MEN

Some men write poems upon stone
And I don't mean sculptors.
They gaze upon a fall of crag
And sense its secrets.
Then, according to their temper,
Patiently or headlong,
They write an epic upon it.
Muscle metaphors across overhangs,
Traverse a delicate line of verbs
Over emptiness.
Clichés are truths here,
'Brave as a lion'
'Cool as a cucumber'
But no one states it and few see it
Save those linked to the same frail
Umbilical.
Though those that follow later may
Grasp the gist of it.
But should you say 'This was a feat
Of incredible cool courage without
Regard of cost.'
You would be more than likely told
'Get lost'.

Tom Bowker

ROCK

No I wouldn't say he was a dangerous climber
but he'd lose control of himself, get all worked up
with the rock, almost personal, as if he reckoned
that if trusted, it might let him down;
he'd uncoil the rope at the cliff's foot and
banging his hammer on the crack shout 'brainless bitch
you're as proud as eternity, you've helped
twenty of my friends drop to their deaths,
yet you can't move around like we can and you can't
    climb up'
— then, scrabbling and grunting, he would make a jump
and land at the top so fast there just wasn't time

for the rock to act; for his logic was simple,
if he could fall off a cliff he could also climb it.
Not like another I knew, who'd coax black rock
for hours, as a royal lover
will stroke a girl's hair half the night (and only then
dare make what in most men's repertoires
are the opening moves). He'd fondle the crack
with the palms of his hands, lowering each wrist in turn
to feed the fingers with blood; finally, when the rock lay
most relaxed, glide slowly up it like a dancer.
A queer thing, but the rock was almost like a woman,
forgiving this one his seduction (he died
not by striking but in a snowstorm, peacefully)
— and punishing that one's rape by breaking him.

R J Wathen

THE ROCK CLIMBER

Upon the genial rock,
rising in grey facades to the untouched sky,
I lay my frail hand
and strive to venture upward.

My unchained eye
goes where my feet may not.

I stand upon a little ledge,
neither of earth nor sky,
detached from harsh reality
upon peaks of imagination.

And there,
in the breadth of rock and air,
I am a human spider,
spinning a single gleaming thread
up the bastions of the battlemented crag.

Dave Gingell

GIANT

A thousand metres sheer,
Diamond buttressed, mammoth shouldered,
Dagger at the stars,
He shrugs presumptuous shoulders off in avalanche
As stallions switch flies from their flanks,
And endures perenially battering blizzards.
Epochs ago when mountains were holy —
Not playgrounds but temples —
They named him,
Those dawn-men who danced in his shadow,
'Sentinel', 'Shepherd' and 'Giant.'
They knew he was old then,
Even as he was old when Megalithic Man
Set stones on the moor,
Aligned to him,
When sighting setting suns;
An eternal solstice recorder,
Recorder of Time itself.

Eternal?
His body is built of sea-snail shells.
He is a tower of ancient bones
Folded and piled when continents collided,
Churning Everests out of abysses.

And he rots at the edges!
Dissolves by drips from leprous ledges,
Crumbles like cheese from frost-shattering ridges.

A stone falls from the face,
Clatters and claps down the screes
To the well-heads of rivers
That grind rock on rock
And roll all their grist to the sea.

. . . Till the snails grope again where the giant stood,
Under yellow water, feeling flat, blue mud.

A J Hastie

HE WAS A GREAT CLIMBER

He was a great climber. He said
' — Climb, but I don't know why.
     Had a dream.
Was drifting up a precipice, there were no holds,
     Nought beneath,
But I, caught, straining, dark.
Then the cliff was not, and I cleared.
     But my footsteps trudged on high
High, and alone.
And then a thing, swaying, swinging light
     In the air above.
A young man. A form. And I looked up, smiled,
I rose, looked down, and the sun shone white
On snow.'
He said, ' — and another dream.
For they watched as I went, and my hand grew great
That I trod the cliff far up.
     And they watched.
And my hand grew greater, huge, behind:
     But I must, I must
See down for a hold, a crack, and my eyes
Stared, cramped, by my knees, and a crevice, but filled
With the little green fronds of moss that were green and straight.
And they watched, watched, from forests in the head.
And the hand grew more,
I feared,
     My eyes went small. And I died.
It was no grist, but I pondered.'

And the Wise Man said
     'I have plucked it deep,
Have thought from many masters.
     Crush of emotion
How it effervesces, breaks, how it talks in the night.
But I too pondered.
     I fell into a sleep and I dreamt,
And it had been a dream,
I know not what dream.'

'Yes,' said the Climber, 'Yes, and mine?
You can say?'

126

But the Wise Man had gone,
And there, a little further, he met a man,
With a rope and a rucksack, walking.
And he asked, 'You, too, are a climber?'
'No,' he said, 'for I climb, as you see,
But not now I am a climber.'
And the Wise Man said, 'If I might come and speak — '
But he — he stopped, he sat down by the roadside,
Put a hand to his eyes. For he wept.
So the Wise Man turned,
                    stepped back,
For indeed, there came
                    the great climber.
And they, too, stayed,
                    pointed thoughts at
Many subjects.
                    For the dew stood wet
Among the stones of the wall,
And it seemed well to wait
                    a little.

And I said, 'But what was the meaning
Of the story, story of the three men?'
But he said, 'No,
                    A tale of one man
And of three armies.'

Menlove Edwards

THE DON BROWN ROUTE

Over your head the climbing blue
Sky observes your lonely foot.
Through the lens of language I
Focus on the Don Brown Route.

From where I am, even if I shout,
You will not hear. You climb in slow
Motion on silence on the face
Full of happy, full of woe.

Today is very nothing like
Any other day that once soared
In this place. My lens suddenly
Is crossed with the black of a near bird.

Today is almost without winds
And I can see your fingers brush
Your next hold clean and the sand drift
Fine like the smoke of your own ash.

Through the lens of language each
Act hangs for a long time.
Floated out in the iodine air
Your motion comes to me like home

Ing birds meaning to say something
I should be able to read. Reach
For the hold three feet above your pressing
Cheek bright at the edge of your stretch.

Set your Northern toe-cap in
To where your own weather has set
A ledge of spar like an offered journey
Across the cobbles of your street.

At least I am not putting you off
Through the dumb lens I see you through.
I can't nudge your climbing foot
Or shout out to you what to do.

Yet do not lean too far in
To the father face or it will
Astonish you with a granite kiss
And send you packing over the sill.

If you fall, remember no one will see
You tumbling lonely down. Only
I through this bad focus will see.
Why do you imagine Gravity lonely?

And over your head the climbing blue
Sky observes your lonely foot.
Stopped in the lens of language you
Slowly establish the Don Brown Route.

W S Graham

HEIGHTS

Let not the hunters who through chimneys stalk
swift clouds, or like eagles from buttress and rocknose
chase the elusive light, look down on those
who merely wander and worship as they walk:

A pilgrim in the valley may in his soul
see the glory of a mountain and see it whole.

Gregory Blunt

LANDSCAPE AS WEREWOLF

Near here, the last grey wolf
In England was clubbed down. Still,
After two hundred years, the same pinched wind
Rakes through his cairn of bones

As he squats quiet, watching daylight seep
Away from the scarred granite, and its going drain
The hills' bare faces. Far below,
A tiny bus twists on its stringy path
And scuttles home around a darkening bend.

The fells contract, regroup in starker forms;
Dusk tightens on them, as the wind gets up
And stretches hungrily: tensed at the nape,
The coarse heath bristles like a living pelt.

The sheep are all penned in. Down at the pub
They sing, and shuttle darts: the hostellers
Dubbin their heavy boots. Above the crags
The first stars prick their eyes and bide their time.

William Dunlop

THE RUNE AND THE ECHO

THE CLIMBERS:

'Now and tomorrow
O hill-gods grant us
the breadth of your vision,
the calm of your vapours —
granite's stability,
heather's tenacity,
cataract's purity,
poise of your pinnacles
reaching to heaven.'

THE ECHO:

'Now and forever
our ways be unto you
challenge and conquest
stern and sufficing —
white peace of our snows,
grey grief of our rains,
flame of our sunsets,
freedom of eagles —
a dream in our dust.'

Brenda G Macrow

A HILL

Only a hill: earth set a little higher
    above the face of earth: a larger view
of little fields and roads: a little nigher
    to clouds and silence: what is that to you?
Only a hill; but all of life to me,
up there, between the sunset and the sea.

Lift but a hand: the beating of the heart
    answers with hope and thrill of conscious force.
Look upward: thought, unhindered, soars apart
    in still pursuit upon a loftier course.
Climb but a little hill: you too may find
the clouds ebb surely from your clearer mind.

Action and soul are one: the leaping blood
    drives hope into the heart; a purer air
sweetens the breath of thought; the doubting mood
    is shallow vapour on the face of care.
Life's sorrows rise no higher than our hedges;
the distant view has heaven about its edges.

Look from a height: the city and the plain
    and the near clouds are but as one in seeming;
all earth is but a link in the dim chain
    that binds our little seeing to our dreaming;
life, with its limits merged in larger truth,
looks as it once looked from our heights of youth.

Only a hill: yes, looked at from below:
    facing the usual sea, the frequent west.
Tighten the muscle, feel the strong blood flow,
    and set your foot upon the utmost crest!
There, where the realms of thought and effort cease,
wakes on your heart a world of dreams, and peace.

Geoffrey Winthrop Young

CROSSING THE MOOR

Always observing us unseen
eyes the shape of blades of grass
follow our progress, let us pass
through the nervous green.

Munching maggoty sheep on the hill
hustle away as we come too near,
larks and grouse fly out, and fear
holds the moor still.

Should we turn, we would not see
ears as still as straight stone
attuned to us and us alone
tracking silently.

Should we turn, we would not hear
the snuffle of noses near the ground
quivering over a scent they found
as we passed here.

Nor would we see the vigilant sky,
nor feel the open moorland track
growing over itself behind our back
as we blundered by.

Cal Clothier

THE HIKER

An occasional cloud smokes from
The sun, hills fade in haze.
And like tangled insignias trees bunch
Decoratively along the horizon
To which fields fold in road-cracked
Sheets. A silver mark denotes a lake
Lying in some glacially-thumbed hollow,
While points of sound stab everywhere
As intermittent bird calls break in air.

The hiker leans a sweat-clammed
Back to age-old rock, his mind
Induced to stillness surveying distance:
The stress of the scramble
Up stone-encrusted unyielding paths
Has forced a glut of blood to veins
And now the palpitating slow view
Quiets weariness and a soft languor
Loosens all his limbs —
Till imagined further freedoms
Of topography draw him on again
And rested, liberated, he climbs.

William Oxley

CLIMBING THE MOUNTAIN

The ridge my eye holds to
Sharp in the sky
Twenty yards ahead
Is never the summit.
It is always further.
So I heave myself on
With boosted will —
Forward to the summit.
The level step
There! The buzzard maybe,
And the scarce primula!
Then the completer view:
Walls I could not see beyond
Walking below
Shall be a net of shadows
A prisoner may walk across.
The main street, haughty,
With honours glittering,
When seen from the peak
Shall be reduced to the ranks
Of highways working
In the unfolding plan
Of pasture, ploughland, rivers, hills.
Ah, the view from the peak —
But the ridge my eye holds to
Sharp in the sky
Twenty yards ahead
Is never the summit.
It is always further.
So I go on
With boosted will —
Forward to the summit,
For it is the way of a man
Half blinded by land
To be healed by horizons.

Clifford Dyment

SIX OF US CLIMBED THE HILL

Six of us climbed the hill energetically.
It was evening, the sky in front was streaked red
as a tulip field. Bunched importantly we
walked unseeing absorbed in our exchange, heads
down — talking. But our words weren't taken up.
It seemed almost as if they weren't wanted
for the stern hills let each rebuked sound drop
to the ground. Our breath, disinherited, died.
One by one we grew silent, our arrogance
catching and tearing on burnt heather,
our voices we'd thought of such significance
cancelled. Then we were seven together
not six as before and listening to the peewit
our words, resurrected, touched the summit.

Caroline Gourlay

TO WALK ON HILLS

To walk on hills is to employ legs
As porters of the head and heart
Jointly adventuring towards
Perhaps true equanimity.

To walk on hills is to see sights
And hear sounds unfamiliar.
When in wind the pine-tree roars,
When crags with bleatings echo,
When water foams below the fall,
Heart records that journey
As memorable indeed;
Head reserves opinion,
Confused by the wind.

A view of three shires and the sea!
Seldom so much at once appears
Of the coloured world, says heart.
Head is glum, says nothing.
Legs become weary, halting

To sprawl in a rock's shelter,
While the sun drowsily blinks
On head at last brought low —
This giddied passenger of legs
That has no word to utter.

Heart does double duty,
As heart, and as head,
With portentous trifling.
A castle on its crag perched
Across the miles between is viewed
With awe as across years.
Now a daisy pleases,
Pleases and astounds, even,
That on a garden lawn could blow
All summer long with no esteem.
And the buzzard's horrid poise,
And the plover's misery,
And the important beetle's
Blue-green-shiny back . . .

To walk on hills is to employ legs
To march away and lose the day.
Confess, have you known shepherds?
And are they not a witless race
Prone to quaint visions?
Not thus from solitude
(Solitude sobers only)
But from long hilltop striding.

Robert Graves

THE LAST MILE

                                    . . . Dies irae, dies illa . . .
Dark, dark the clouds approaching and still'd the skylark's song;
A cold, sharp wind blowing
And sunless above.   *. . . Dies irae, dies illa . . .*

The distant, threatening thunder rolls o'er black and sullen hills:
It nears
And I am alone.   *. . . solvet saeclum in favilla . . .*

The long miles stretch behind me, the countless
Pain-racked footsteps not yet a memory —
And more to come — ahead
The path leads on, on, ever upward, seemingly
Unending.   ... *quantus tremor est futurus* ...

Closer the thunder. Suddenly
Great lightning leaps across the tortured heavens:
I am afraid.
The storm breaks.   ... *tuba mirum spargens sonum* ...

Blindly I stagger through the wall of lashing water
As beneath my feet the gullies turn to rushing
    torrents: ... *per sepulchra regionum* ...

So far, and yet it seems so far to go —
The darkness is around me and
There is no refuge.   ... *mors stupebit et natura* ...
Again the lightning flashes.   ... *cum resurget creatura* ...

And thunder crashes like a thousand drums
And I am afraid.   ... *gere curam mei finis* ...

But
Yonder a slender pencil 'gainst the skyline stands
Briefly revealed and quickly gone. A few steps more —
Drag, exhausted on. Fight through the
Clutching rain;
Bend into the
Screaming wind: a few steps more
And it is over.
I am not afraid.   ... *sanctus, sanctus, sanctus* ...

I am not alone —   ... *sanctus, sanctus, sanctus* ...
My journey is completed, and
I am home, for
Before me stands the radio mast at
    Ravenscar.   ... *Hosanna in excelsis* ...

Eric F Engler

136

A BATHE IN THE ESK POOLS

Strip off those worn routines
    You use like clothes.
Step naked as you will be dead
    Into the running vice
Of this cold pool.

Let water round you wind
    Its burning sheet
Till you feel solid enough to slip
    Out of yourself and leave
A veritable mould,

A mortal hollow to be filled
    With a water body,
That over boulder and fall will keep
    Its momentary shape
But flow for ever.

Patric Dickinson

LISTENING

Aria in a couloir,
atonic doloroso:
a shifting atmosphere
precludes silence.

Over many hours,
the sea being
twenty miles distant
beyond hills,

sound seems vestigial
like a brilliant
inactive
dendri-nerve.

Traditional
to chant
and then
be silent.

This I envy:
what a mountain starts with
has taken
eight thousand years
to emulate.

David J Morley

CAIRN

Stairs leading nowhere, roof
To no accommodation, monument
To itself, half-scattered.

An old badge of belonging
To the available heights,
A shrug and a smile, as though

Having climbed two thousand feet
You could climb a few feet more
And the view might be different.

John Fuller

OUTWARD BOUND

Two campers (King Lear and his clown?)
Smile to see the skies come down.
The shaken mind finds metaphors
In winds that shake the great outdoors.
As roofs and fences fall in storms
The tranquil mind's protective forms
Collapse when passion, grief and fear
Stir. We will spend a fortnight here.

138

To this small wilderness we bring
Ourselves to play at suffering,
To swim in lonely bays, immerse
In the destructive elements, nurse
Our bare forked bodies by wood fires
Where ox-tail soup in mugs inspires
The tender flesh. By rocks we cough
And shiver in the wind, throw off
What history has lent, and lie
Naked, alone, under the sky.

Of course, not one of us prefers
The cold; we are sun-worshippers,
Wilderness-and storm-defiers,
Neither masochists nor liars.
Cheeks whipped by freezing rain go numb.
The baffled blood is stirred, will come
Again, glowing like my mind when Lear
Speaks in the words of Shakespeare.
Under duress trying to sing
In tune, foretasting suffering
That we will swallow whole, the storm
Endured, we hope to come to harm
At home, with better dignity
Or style or courage. Anyway
I like to camp and read King Lear.
We had a lovely fortnight here.

James Simmons

PATHS

I am the dotted lines on the map:
footpaths exist only when they are walked on.
I am gravel tracks through woodland; I am
field paths, the muddy ledge by the stream,
the stepping-stones. I am the grassy lane
open between waist-high bracken where sheep
fidget. I am the track to the top
skirting and scaling rocks. I am the cairn.

Here on the brow of the world I stop,
set my stone face to the wind, and turn
to each wide quarter. I am that I am.

Fleur Adcock

WALKING ON THE CLIFF

But for a sleepy gull that yawned
   And spread its wings and dropping disappeared
This evening would have dawned
   To the eternity my flesh has feared.

For too intent on a blackcap
   Perched like a miser on the yellow furze
High over Birling Gap,
   That sang 'Gold is a blessing not a curse,'

How near I was to stepping over
   The brink where the gull dropped to soar beneath.
While now safe as a lover
   I walk the cliff-edge arm in arm with Death.

Andrew Young

from ELEGY VIII

You are the climber who became aware
suddenly of the mute hostility
of mountains; as the wind plucked at your hair,
balanced between the known and the unknown
        you turned, and found yourself to be
frozen and weary and alone, alone.

Now that the mountains and the quiet lake
threaten no longer, you have found no peace,
only this most uneasy armistice,
even at night, when you will lie awake
watching the darkness, listening to the silence,
or fight to keep your balance
upon the polished buttress of a dream.
        You hug the stone
but that most void composure is unbroken
        even at night when you awaken
sober and thirsty and alone, alone.

William Bell

HARBOROUGH ROCKS

A man in breeches, gear a bright skirt, picked out,
bridges, rope held by a thread, the flowering rain:
where we left off, and when, and which of us, pick up again

and where, low crags blocked off at the foot as well by bad light,
white: that we each were there then as thin spun as the thread,
anchor, if I had got the job, or not met you now dead

begin to run, like ants, uncovering, I put the stone back
to resurrect what pattern in black I presume, do not presume,
not I on this date, bridging this little particular gloom:

brightness contained by grey, wet, a red apple lying in a drab
tangle, for picking up, for how long, where we left off, ropes
    coiled,
secured, to carry off: when I stood life on this rock it held.

Libby Houston

141

PAUSE

Pause, stand on the scree edge and look back,
You who too hastily — Watch carefully again,
There is the cliff; its Eastern incline steep
With furrows there and there: How well I
Know them. When we were climbing there,
Do you remember, how from that tiny earthwork,
You remember, stretching; then upon the slab:
How powerful the fingers . . .
And then that other day, rocks wet, wet everything,
How on that bare wall on the right,
Where from the stance a craftsman riskily . . .

And there again, still on that Eastern slope,
Day after day repeats, day after day
The clouds pass over, or the wind occurs,
Or snow. Sparse growth on it, on this
Dull cliff, dead or asleep or living.
But the thoughts return.

Or am I mourning for the dead?
And is it you? You, where
That stream of sunlight shows
The texture. You. Watch
Carefully again: there it is
Steep and solid there, broken more
Here over on the left. Yes
It is you, you only.
And on your form the dusts will come,
Thy walls do lichen grow.

On with your coat: walk jauntily
And turn your back: be gone
Over the springy turf: so
Should we celebrate departure.

Menlove Edwards

RAINING OUTSIDE

the sea the forest
and the city.
all
rooted on rock.

only man and only
a few men
spend weekends
tempting themselves
maybe to fall off it
maybe to stay on.

and you complain
                    at the window
my verse is not sufficiently explicit
does not reflect
                    the human situation.

G J F Dutton

THE FALL

Fear was the worst part,
Mind-blowing, gut-wrenching fear,
It was that alright.
Smashing bulkheads inside my skull
Rending at my vitals
Was the awful inevitability that my
Strength had gone.
My eyes recorded my flaccid fingers
Uncurling from the rock.
There was *nothing* I could do,
I fell.
At once the fear fled,
I went 'bionic'.
An aborted steve austin tumbling
Slowly and endlessly through space.
Mind and eyes recording,
With extra-sensory clarity,
The glint of sun on the lake,

Scafell's gleaming snow-cap,
A dusting of crystals on the cragface,
My friends' white, gawping faces
As I wheeled past.
'Is this how it all ends?'
Then I was gaffed, brutally, by the nylon.
The rock hammered at my skull
And clawed at my skin,
As the world painfully righted itself,
And the fear came spewing back.
Minutes later it was all over.
My friends, sick-faced, sat on the grass
Monica nursing scorched hands and
Sobbing quietly,
Whilst I tended my scrapes and bruises.
I climbed again.
But fear had blown a fuse,
Tripped, burnt-out, calcified,
A circuit in my brain
And it was never the same.

Tom Bowker

ON LOCATION

This was on Skye — the black-haired spaniel first in the corrie,
and then my mother with her shepherd's old boots, you
dropped, shed, forging ahead to climb
the Inaccessible Pinnacle, of all things, with a roadmap,
telling her to wait, cold, lately-wed, at the foot there, where
the mountain-cloud received you out of her sight.

I led the Great Tor's east ridge on the Gower last summer
and at the top, in the sun, among flowers, looking down
on a black-backed bird flying high below me
and the clear deep-water covered sand, I suddenly saw
you, with your arms wide, reckless, glorious
on pinnacles above the sea or clouds
in the pre-war photographs, or one — one in particular
looking down on you at the top, so small, not up —
as if I'd been expecting unawares
you, whom I don't remember, to be there
to welcome me with a voice I'd like to recognize.

144

It was when your feet no longer touched
rock, or indeed the earth — when you were far far higher,
telling her, reckless in keeping, only to wait,
that presumed dead you vanished quite.
I suppose you too fell like Icarus, made to swallow
all your presumption in the seconds of spinning
down for deep water with a trail of black and fire —
the dazzling figure in that photograph
might equally well have been gathered like Elijah
into a fiery chariot, to mount still higher,
doffing the body at last the quicker to rise.

Flat snaps, my father, and black and white at that,
giving me my leads, I follow, older
than you were, ever — measuring my reach
to make a guess at yours, at least.
Bruises and blood show up in close-up and colour.
Cold wind, a cold scent; waiting around gets colder.

Libby Houston

N. F.

Four months ago
You died. Though I accept the fact
I can't believe in it; it's natural
Still to include you in plans, to think next Easter
We'll come here with you, as we should have come
Last. That chance went by, and now
You'll not climb here again.
Something's missing for good now
From our life, something
To grow old with happily
As the years passed, and hours
Grew calmer, less needing to be snatched at.
To say *I miss you* is meaningless;
But I've come through the storm
And where each ridge and gully was your friend
I stand imagining the good design
For ever incomplete.

Up there you fell —
No use to ask what happened; no use to wonder
If you felt sudden anger, or surprise,
Or even a shock of fear, or only knew
A jerk, a fainting exhilaration of speed.
A painless blow, and light.
You fell; you've gone somehow, leaving us
The broken ruin of your body (that
Which we knew supple, hard, reliable)
And some possessions — books, maps,
Climbing gear — which we use thankfully,
Remembering you, and how you stood
One day, and what you said
While tea was making, and that you were
Always as sure and true as the hills' selves.

I shall go back
To that different life into which
You sometimes came; but for a long time yet
I shall expect to meet you on the dark
Road by Mirehouse, or see you knitting
Vigorously in the cold dining room
At Dungeon Ghyll, or fill your cup
When you arrive from Carlisle hot and tired,
And talk with you of good far places
Where in some happier season we may go.
And always, I believe,
When — on whatever errand — I approach
The sixth milestone towards Windermere,
Or the tall birch past Rosthwaite, or
The gap behind the Arrowhead,
I shall be seized with a certain numb surprise
That if I turn my head I cannot see you.

There wasn't much
That I could ever give you — only love
For your friend, and for the hills you loved
And rocks — and I suppose
This winter-offering of words
Would only half-amuse you, if you lived,
And, if now somehow you're aware of it,
Will not come very near you.
But, while I stand here
Below the snow-streaked crag on which you died,

I send you thanks
For all the days I knew you, for your friendly
Acceptance of me, your encouragement,
For your steady, calm example, for
Your presence, strong and homely as an oak tree.
Goodbye. You were good to know.

Anon.

NO SOUND COULD BE HEARD

No sound could be heard on the mountain side.
No sign could be seen that a man had died.
We brought him down from the rocky slope
and retrieved his gear and the tangled rope.
And above, on the crags from which he fell,
we could find no clues that would ever tell
that here he came to his journey's end
and that we who remain have lost a friend.

Dave Gingell

ON A DYING BOY

Oh leave his body broken on the rocks
where fainting sense may drown beneath the sound

of the complaining surf. His spirit mocks
our ignorant attempts to hem it round:
as eagerly as body sought the ground
into its native ocean must it flow.
Oh let his body lie where it was found,
there's nothing we can do to help him now.

And hide his face under his tattered coat
until the women come to where he lies,
they come to bind the silence in his throat
and shut the eternal darkness in his eyes,

to wash the cold sweat of his agonies
and wash the blood that's clotted on his brow.
Cover his face from the unfriendly skies,
there's nothing we can do to help him now.

And watch even his enemies forget him,
and skies forget his sobs, the rocks his blood;
and think how neither rock nor sky dared let him
grow old enough for evil or for good;
and then forget him too. Even if we could
bring back the flower that's fallen from the bough,
bring back the flower that never left the bud,
there's nothing we can do to help him now.

William Bell

A MOUNTAIN RESCUE

Safe, from the farmhouse window
we watched in the gathering dusk
the helicopter, jewelled with navigation lights
more splendidly than any gaudy insect,
circle the black cone of Tryfan,
endlessly manoeuvring to gain or lose
a few feet of height, some balance of thrusts.

It was curiously beautiful, yet the beauty
we could not have seen but for the terrible fall
of a climber missing his handhold in
the blustering wind.

Having been glad to see the aerial
dance of the machine, so much more beautiful
by dusk than by day, we were glad
to hear of the rescue and to know
that this strange and jewelled machine
carried a precise and practical compassion,
as, safe, from the farmhouse window
we watched in the gathering dusk
its gaudy insect rite that rendered mercy.

Frederic Vanson

148

HE TELLS OF HIS ASCENT

Lord Grace, I am so weary of this climb!
Almost it seems as if a light-flung stone
Would hit the cairn, but yet I cannot reach it.
So near, and yet so far! Slipping, I turn.

Below me lesser heights assault my gaze
And mock the prayer I lift to unanswering heaven;
For there they triumph, there their banners wave,
There they exult — the climbers who chose ease
And took the lower mountains in their grasp,
Flaunting simulacrum of strength and power;
Whilst I, who mastered rock and grim ascent,
And passed them, am requited by fatigue
And the grey clutch of vulture-eyed despair.
Harsh prize, strange recompense! What have I done?
Why did I leave the forest slopes for this? —
That now I wish the peak would rive and fall
And roll its crags upon my drumming ears,
For that would end me, that would bring me ease!
I slip, I turn, I wish the unwished-for doom
O foe of God, death-glad Perversity! —
For well I know that Bliss is hedged with Pain,
And every citadel projects its wall,
And Paradise is talon'd with the grave.
Plain as yon slope the cairn will be attained.

Herbert E Palmer

RAISON D'ETRE

Those who accept the challenge of the hills
In wind and rain, to feel the bitter lash
And revel in morass and water splash;
Who do not mind the soakings and the chills
To hear floodwater thunder in the gills;
Who walk in darkness by the lightning flash
And watch the cragtorn boulders downward crash,
Knowing the odds the mountain maims and kills,
What do they ask of Life but living so,
Of Death the sublimation of their day?
Rejecting not the ones that Fate laid low;
An impulse strong as theirs spurred on the frail:
Life has no course to finish or to fail;
Failure is all to end in blind decay.

Kenneth Milburn

BELAY POINTS

1   'Being there' is enough
We climb,
Tracing a route
out of time.

2   It's those people
most alive
live most
for their secret prize.

3   Climbers know that life's a bright flower
that grows an inch from death.
You don't have to pick blooms
to enjoy their scent.

Hamish Brown

TITLE

This is no Peak
Aloft among the snow;
No friendly folk will wait with bated breath
For my return;
'Tis my concern —
A hundred feet or so
Is all the hazard that I have with Death
And all I seek.

Yet here I stand;
No matter who has title to the land,
Nor who may follow in the marks I make,
No man can take
From me this moment when, in Time and Space,
I own this place.

John C Lyth

TWO PEAKS

Loneliness is a cold lack:
Solitude, fullness of want.
Climb that first peak —
No one is there, you're giddy,
Cannot get going down,
Shudder, are frozen.

Climb Solitude, and look
At the shiny teeming valley —
The sweet smoke of hearts and bodies
Rising as day darkens.
Coming down is going on:
You feel, you are, chosen.

Patric Dickinson

HOME FROM THE HILL

Coming home from the hill: do you remember
    The cold, the bitterness, the despair,
The sodden snowflakes of a wet December?
    Do you remember? You were there.

Do you remember how we had redoubled
    Effort on effort, and all of it in vain?
Clouds parted, but because our hearts were troubled
    We missed the rainbow — only saw the rain.

Coming home from the hill that bleak December
    Do you remember how the world seemed lost?
These heights were not worth winning — you'll remember —
    Without his company who loved them most.

Archie Mitchell

RACHEL
(On Dow Crag)

The silence of snowfall,
The laughter of young becks,
The joy of lark song,
And the peace of the tarn
Flow through the seasons of your face
As you stand beside me.

High on the fell
The wind dances with your hair,
And the sighs of the clouds
Are for you, you alone.
As Nature courts
A fellow spirit.

Alone, you touch me with morning,
And the burning cold of your sunset
Laps me round with a misty, mourning promise.
You are Nature's child
Compounded from pure elements,
And my bastard spirit is subdued.

Robert G Griffiths

A STARE FROM THE MOUNTAIN

As the sun slants, the best of it over,
Into the trug of Usk from the summary
West, masking the struts, the wicker rents
With plush, with a stuff of shaded
Greens gentling the upper, thistly fields,
The thicker bush of forest, ploughland
Cuts of red already stiff in their winter
Folds, tricking the human aberration
Into the same still life, a whole
Kindred lit with the right intensity,
Painted safe to a fortunate choice
Of colours, I stand on Yscir mountain,
Head above wind level, putting the frozen
Questions that the poles demand. Fieldfares
Break from the half-leaved oak as I
Walk a few tentative feet. The fetlock
Hairs, the mane, the portly glassblown
Outline of a pony natured white
Shine between me and the sun, the animal
Marked with redemption from a hidden
Source. I look involuntarily, all
Of a sudden in need of a gleam
Lining my shadow. But nothing there
Satisfies, nothing anywhere in the sparse
Clip of the mountain, only that down
In the valley bottom is a reed-
Plume of smoke fining the rubbish-tip,
The town, taken by sun and arked,
Burning its pages from the Domesday Book.

Roland Mathias

153

UNDER THE MOUNTAIN

Seen from above
The foam in the curving bay is a goose-quill
That feathers ... unfeathers ... itself.

Seen from above
The field is a flap and the haycocks buttons
To keep it flush with the earth.

Seen from above
The house is a silent gadget whose purpose
Was long since obsolete.

But when you get down
The breakers are cold scum and the wrack
Sizzles with stinking life.

When you get down
The field is a failed or a worth-while crop, the source
Of back-ache if not heartache.

And when you get down
The house is a maelstrom of loves and hates where you —
Having got down — belong.

Louis MacNeice

The Green Rim of Ireland

HAMISH BROWN

PRELUDE

Still south I went and west and south again,
Through Wicklow from the morning till the night,
And far from cities, and the sites of men,
Lived with the sunshine and the moon's delight.

I knew the stars, the flowers, and the birds,
The grey and wintry sides of many glens,
And did but half remember human words,
In converse with the mountains, moors, and fens.

J M Synge

DISTANCES

I remember mysterious stirrings
As a child when the sun caught the grey roof
Of a house, tree-hidden, on a distant
Hill, flash of white gable, the gun-grey slate.
That particular small hill in drumlin
Country, those particular never-touched
Conifers lost in distance, that magic
Twenty-thousand years from distant Dublin.

Here, now, the Wicklow foothills blaze luminous
Sapphire embossed on silver, a bird turns,
Disappears, then a sudden crow erupts
From the field where calcimine sheeps' heads burn
Into my cagey stanza. Write it down.
The heart mightn't make it to the next town.

Maurice Scully

MORNING FROM KNOCKAULIN

remember the dew how white it was?
the flashes of plastic at Allen in the bluish distance?
remember the smokefibres slowly untangling
over the midlands little cattle
lying down the fields and the fox
treading startled turning
into the gorse at the royal fort

overlooking Kilcullen?
                     down there you had
housewives with the radio on, children
crouching to their lessons, men
busy as the sand lorry — a Dinky toy plying the road

remember?

Desmond Egan

THE HILL OF FIRE

I saw five counties of Munster
From the top of Scrolm hill,
And later the grey blankets of rain
Swaddling the far fields until

They seemed to disappear in greyness.
Minutes later, the rain was gone,
And the salmon-heavy Cashen
Like a river of silver shone.

The hob-nailed hours trudge slowly
Through that country; the brown
Mountain, bald-headed, lords it
Over the peaceful pastures down

Along the hillside. A name for every field —
Boland's meadow, marvellously green,
And the humped, crooked shoulder
Of grassy Garnagoyteen.

A touch of cold coming in the air,
I threw one last look around
At my mysterious province, and turned my back
On the cold purity of high ground.

From low ground, I saw the sun
Change the entire
World; that towering bulk became
A hill of fire.

Brendan Kennelly

BALLYDAVID, BY GALTYMORE

Ballydavid, by Galtymore,
That is a place to rest you now!

Under the historian's oak —
A colour burst among the pines
That ambush the long descent
From the turf-edged, booleying heights
Of O'Loughman's Keep.

There's a high spring on Galtymore
And I've heard young laughter from its slopes
Tripping from green and golden fields
That mile to Tipperary town
Beyond the Vale of Aherlow.

Such crimson years that oak has known
To give to us such benison.
Sure, all life is a mountainy road!
Peace then, for this corner of it —
And the big view.

Ballydavid, by Galtymore,
That is a place to rest you now!

Hamish Brown

ON GALTYMORE

A shake in time of
the mind's kaleidoscope
and scraps of marbled light
fall to their place where

we plod the mountain sideways
heads bent to the wet
pilgrims slowly spiralling
intent on silence

from the opposite face
crooked regiments of sheep
following a straggled vision
send us faint bleated messages

leaning on sticks
we turn and stare across
waiting for breath and faith

Joan Keefe

COMERAGHS

The curlew whistles for the coming rain,
The cloud curls down the corries till the lake's
Steel mirror's misted over: on the plain
Below, its sudden shadow drops and makes
A shroud of darkness. Here, upon the heights,
The wind sings to himself as he makes stride
Across the emptiness and the torn light
Chequers and patches all the mountainside.

A solitary world and desolate
That humbles arrogance and mocks man's will.
Here is no mercy to compassionate
The weak or help the strong. Here on the hill
Only the indifferent wind may dare to play
Only the curlew make abiding stay.

Patrick Warner

ADVENT

The mists at Cūl Rūa
Seep the mountain
And heatherfields for miles.

But there are signs of sunlight
Soon to come breaking over
Our bodies, setting us on fire

With explosion of colour
And so tender colour everywhere
Scarcely possible.

Padraig Daly

THE PAPS OF DANA

The mountains stand, and stare around,
They are far too proud to speak!

Altho' they are rooted in the ground,
Up they go — peak after peak,

Beyond the tallest house; and still
Climbing over tree and hill,

Until you'd think they'd never stop
Going up, top over top,

Into the clouds — Still I mark
That a linnet, thrush or lark,

Flying just as high, can sing
As if he'd not done anything!

I think that mountains ought to be
Taught a little modesty!

James Stephens

161

MACGILLYCUDDY'S REEKS

With a name like that you are apt to think
Some joker set his hand on the mountain game.
(Perhaps its the chancy rhyme of Reeks with breeks?)
It's a committee-creation name, or the sort of name
Bandied about in the slapstick of O'Pantomime.
Mind, when you go flying on the lubricated grass
Of Cnoc an Toinne it may have some justification
You think. But you'd be wrong. The Reeks are great
Mountains and before greatness names are forgotten
And metaphorical hats raised in white recognition.
These are peaks fit for the legendary heroes. The din
Of battle is often enough crashing on their crags
But it is clean fighting, and with spectators welcome.
The names are built, tower on tower, battlement-
Linked, moated, buttressed, defended by storm
(a western gale can fire rain hard as arrowheads):
Knocknapeasta, Cummeennapeasta, Cruach Mhor,
Caher and Beenkeragh, Carrauntoohil, Curraghmore . . .
You need good lungs for that lot, and powerful legs,
And no fear of heights. Choose your weapons all the same;
The Reeks, though great, climb down to our little game.

James Macmillan

WIND ON THE REEKS

The clouds pass endlessly — like waves curling
Over the Reek's reefs, spraying bravely, bravely
On the climbing sailor on the shrouds of time.
I saw childhood glitter in the clouds,
Shadows on the old man's Cruach cairn
But the salt lips licking were mine, were mine.
My scrambling feet scraped waves, fossilised, yet I
Walked unsubstantial as the oval clouds
That hinted winds no eye can spy,
A cold essence of things, raw from the sea,
To emphasize our temporality.

James Macmillan

KENMARE BAY

Caha to the south, MacGillycuddy to the north,
This bay lies, a giant bowl
Of blue water, held reverently
Between enormous palms.

Villages in valleys
Semaphore their presence
With a glitter of windows
From a far tilled coast,

Where fields clamber the mountains
Laboriously as persons,
To falter into granite,
Underbelly of cloud.

A frieze of pines
Provides green peace for a black crow
To holler at the sea
And at the motor-boat

Which noses between
Seaweeded islands, rhinestone inlets,
Scattering the sea-pies
Whose red beaks flash

Above visitors' hats
Like scalping knives.

John Montague

OLD ROADS

Missing from the map, the abandoned roads
Reach across the mountain, threading into
Clefts and valleys, shuffle between thick
Hedges of flowery thorn.
The grass flows into tracks of wheels,
Mowed evenly by the careful sheep;
Drenched, it guards the gaps of silence
Only trampled on the pattern day.

And if, an odd time, late
At night, a cart passes
Splashing in a burst stream, crunching bones,
The wavering candle hung by the shaft
Slaps light against a single gable
Catches a flat tombstone
Shaking a nervous beam in a white face

Their arthritic fingers
Their stiffening grasp cannot
Hold long on the hillside —
Slowly the old roads lose their grip.

Eiléan ni Chuilleanáin

CRO NA CAILLIGHE, BEARNA NA GAOITHE

On a cold bare hill stand
stone cabins of the two hags
where the wind throws its force
with the shape of the ridge:
the mountain does not yield
even to hold them in a hollow
but pins them to exposed wastes,
consigned by a myth born
in upland fields once fertile.
I walk beside their shadows
to find what lies in the legend
of death at the vast jaw of cliff,
wonder at names given to stones
when stories shortened winter nights.

Steve MacDonogh

ENTAIL

On the stone anvil of Brandon
sledge-hammer of the sea
pounds soul between power and patience
to an infinity.

164

Eastward come combers rolling,
westward headlands face;
under grey sky, under mountain
all time, small space.

In the worn realism
of that Atlantic shield
is no speciousness
romance could yield

even to the memory of exile;
yet still my impoverished ghosts
tramp through my brain, calling
to that ultimate coast.

Geoffrey Byrne-Sutton

BRANDON BAY

The wild white seabirds of Brandon
   from the fall of the cliffs to the caves
      stoop on the watch
      as they cry their wish
      with a swoop for the catch
      of the shoaling fish
   from the sullen plunge of the waves.
On the brow of Brandon is mist, and rest
      from the racing sky: --
the rollers break upon Brandon,
         Brandon the blessed,
      and the seagulls cry.

The peat-brown children of Brandon
   in the gusts of the wet grey sand
      with still eyes glance
      under rain-roughed hair
      and their brown bodies dance
      wind-tattered and bare
   where the spray drives bleak on the land.

At the base of Brandon is hollow, and nest
    under rainy sky: —
and the children scatter on Brandon,
        Brandon the blessed,
    with a shrill sea cry.

The broad-browed fishers of Brandon,
    torn sails dipped to the foam,
      bid life bold
      for a crust hard won;
      till they spy red gold
      in the Western sun,
and hunger waits them at home.
The brood of Brandon flits to the west
    as the seabirds fly: —
and there's only old men in Brandon,
      only children on Brandon,
        Brandon the blessed,
    as the years go by.

Geoffrey Winthrop Young

BRANDON

Do you remember Brandon,
Our mountain in the west:
Brandon that looks on oceans,
Brandon of the blessed?

Do you remember Brandon
In hoary frost one day
With Smerwick heather burning
And curraghs in the Bay?

Do you remember Brandon
And marching pilgrim feet
And blowing mists around us
Where saints and sinners meet?

Do you remember Brandon
With staff in youthful fist,
The turf reek in our nostrils,
Hair silvered by the mist?

Do you remember Brandon
When still too young to talk
And do you mind the conquest
When first we made the walk?

Do you remember Brandon
(The *aire-cnoc gear* a jibe)
When we could climb all mountains
And love a girl beside?

Do you remember Brandon,
Our swim in Nalacken,
And the first pint in Dingle
When we returned as men?

Do you remember Brandon
When penitence was real
And hearts knew true devotion
To follow that ideal?

Do you remember Brandon,
Brandon of the blessed,
Brandon that looks on oceans —
A tideway to the west?

Do you remember Brandon,
A lifetime now away,
The oath we took on leaving
To lie by Brandon Bay?

Do you remember Brandon?
It's there I think to fly
While yet there is tomorrow —
For Brandon, and goodbye.

Hamish Brown

MEMORIES ACROSS DEAD GROUND

We travelled the shore road and none went on before —
Three yards from the salt weed where the long water came
Lapping at the quiet land as a deer might come
And white in sunlight stood the bony hills of Clare.
We went past the white farm and the haymaking,
Their white horse from Connemara and the helpers,
Aproned Mother, Nun on leave, the Son, the Father
And bonnetted children busy at their raking.
No sound (and all here's tumult) save a dripping oar
Mirrored on crystal air and one voice over water.
Grass here bends from the wind of bombs and the thrown
    flame
And white in sunlight stand the bony hills of Clare.

Teresa L Gray

ON MWEELREA

1
I was lowering my body on to yours
When I put my ear to the mountain's side
And eavesdropped on water washing itself
In the locked bath-house of the underground.

When I dipped my hand among hidden sounds
It was the water's pulse at wrist and groin,
It was the water that reminded me
To leave all of my jugs and cups behind.

2
The slopes of the mountain were commonage
For me clambering over the low walls
To look for the rings of autumn mushrooms
That ripple out across the centuries.

I had made myself the worried shepherd
Of snipe twisting the grass into curls
And tiny thatches where they hid away,
Of the sheep that grazed your maidenhair.

168

3

September grew to shadows on Mweelrea
Once the lambs had descended from the ridge
With their fleeces dyed, tinges of sunset,
Rowan berries, and the bracken rusting.

Behind my eyelids I could just make out
In a wash of blood and light and water
Your body colouring the mountainside
Like uncut poppies in the stubbly fields.

Michael Longley

THE MEADOWSWEET THE HOLY MOUNTAIN

Beyond the meadowsweet, the holy mountain,
Holy Croagh Patrick rises, transcending legend,
Veiled in a far sunset, the flame from the skies.

Mile on vagrant mile, the meadowsweet wanders,
The long quiet of pool and sky to inherit.
Likewise the pilgrims journey through the evening land.

Stone and silvery water, the earth and air
Dissolve in sweetness, lulling the darkening curlew
On the lonely bog consumed in a dying fire.

Pilgrim, is this your forestaste of Paradise:
The flowering waters sweet in the summer wild?
The traveller remarks agreeably the fine

Spirea ulmaria of the bogland parts.
Blown down time to shadow an alien sun
It is the anguish numbs and for ever the heart.

Under the holy mountain all are one.

Diana McLoghlen

PILGRIMS ON CROAGH PATRICK

Here they go clambering for soul's arrears
As if dog-weariness could blot their tears
Against the thundering doom that weights the skies
And threatens every hope to pulverise.

Meanwhile, in mockery of what they seek
In prick of thorn and bruise of rock and reek
Of cloud, a drifting music ghosts the air
From faery caverns lighted by the hair
Of unforgotten women wise to know
That laughter is the only seed to sow
For flowers that can blossom out of snow.

George Brandon Saul

WAKING IN ACHILL

Some small birds tease the silence at night's end
With little scraping voices that chirp and cheep,
Backcombing the rain-washed air
Until the sleeper has abandoned sleep
To lie not stirring, between a dream and waking.
What lies beyond the window's dawn-pale square?
Gossiping birds, yes: and a star hangs there.

Open the window to the morning star;
The birds, folded in feathers, are suddenly still;
The silence gathers itself together. Lean on the sill
And listen. From an unseen farm a cockerel crows,
A dog barks, once; far off the sea is breaking
On an invisible bleached strand, below the hill
Patterned with ghostly sheep.
This is the tangible silence of world's end.

Then a lark launches his song, unlatches the morning,
Climbs where the first light grows:
Golden, like a young girl shaking out her hair.

Margaret Rhodes

SLIGO

The terrace has made way
for the shifting scree;

the scorched hill absorbs
whatever little springs
from the remote stones;

the coarse grass
and saltsmitten weeds
hide the luminous land.

I have stood with you here
listening to the harsh briars
and the loss of this wilderness,

barren, soundless
like the pause in some elegy.

Hugh Maxton

GLENCOLMCILLE 1972

then we were standing on the top
its boggy surface yielding underfoot

there was cold from a salmon sea   and mist
over the valley we were passing through

our breaths hung too whisped above it
making it somehow ours i thought

but it was hard to talk
hard to be consoled

better to find the track, scramble down
before it got too dark

we still had to pitch a tent
somewhere
under the silent mountain

Desmond Egan

MAP LICHEN ON SLIEVETOOEY

Up on this bare summit
where fierce weathers pare
heather and peat down
to its skeletal bone
until the cairns groan
like gods in labour
I check my route and
watch a hare white in
its winter coat sit
back in a gap of light
scanning a stone whose
lichen maps
worlds
unknown to me and
cartography.

Francis Harvey

DONEGAL

Here on the dim horizon the humped hills,
Blurred with rain, turn their backs to the wind
And huddle together. The fretted gray Atlantic
Boils at their feet. And then the cloud is gone
And silver light spills from the sky again.

This is my magic ground. Oh may no bitter fate
Prevent my returning.
And let there be this light on the water for me
At the end of all journeys.

Evangeline Paterson

IN THE LIGHT ON THE STONES IN THE RAIN

Mostly, in West Donegal,
it is rock and light, and water, but rock above all,
and rain, to-day it is rain, rain falling softly in veils
on foxglove and fuchsia and furze;
and, plaintively calling all day by the sea,
in the mist and the spray,
back and forth in the rain wheel the birds,
plover and curlew and teal.
And then there are men,
in the light on the stones in the rain,
sometimes men, but not often,
for mostly in West Donegal
it is rock and light, and water, not men,
and to-day, to-day it is rain, rain falling softly in veils
on foxglove and fuchsia and furze,
and on birds.

Francis Harvey

THE STARLING LAKE

My sorrow that I am not by the little dún
By the lake of the starlings at Rosses under the hill,
And the larks there, singing over the fields of dew,
Or evening there and the sedges still,
For plain I see now the length of the yellow sand.
And Lissadell far off and its leafy ways,
And the holy mountain whose mighty heart
Gathers into it all the coloured days.
My sorrow that I am not by the little dún
By the lake of the starlings at evening when all is still,
And still in whispering sedges the herons stand.
'Tis there I would nestle at rest till the quivering moon
Uprose in the golden quiet over the hill.

Seumas O'Sullivan

MIST ON ERRIGAL

I struck off where I thought the road would lie.
   The turf road dwindled to a stony track.
Wet, lumpy moorland changed to slopes of dry
   Close-growing heath, streams babbled at my back.

On and up till Errigal I found
   Raising its shrine of quartzite to the sky;
Close, clinging mist came up and down and round
   Enveloping the puny thing called I.

In the mist-hidden heights a something moved
   Dislodging rocks which clattered down the scree,
Click, clack, click-clacking down the grooved
   And weathered shute of stones a yard from me

And stopping with a thud in something soft.
   The cloud cleared and I saw the mountain lake
Shine like a sickle in a harvest loft
   Through the dim dust which thirsty threshers make.

For one brief moment smothered things appeared —
   A cottage glimmered by the corn field edge
And blunt and pointed summits round me reared
   Their rocky heads to heaven, ledge on ledge.

Then rain came and the mist grew thicker still,
   Rock pipits twittered flying down the wind,
Sheep moaned from some high hidden window-sill,
   And huge hill midges at my ear-drums whined.

Patric Stevenson

RADHARC AN EARGAIL

From the distance, it was almost edible —
the cake of ceremony.
The appearance of virtue's dress.
The clouds veiled its fierceness.

In the desolation of Donegal,
the valleys and passes
were trenches warning hills
from the face of Errigal.

Lakes, standing without direction,
tried to gape a reflection
in their refracting lenses.

Peat spread out like lava,
painting the bracken and grasses
a murky amber, infecting the boot
and, in strange mutations
coughing up silvered tree-stumps.

Below Errigal, only sheep scrounged
a living from moongrown grass,
only the snaking streams
signposted a destination.

Alone, Errigal stood, glowering down.
Clouds smoked upwards
like volcanic eruptions,
the locust-rain swept in
on a man who carried his gate
on the crux of his back, alone,
heedless of the mountain
which stood, a lesson in stone.

Mike Jenkins

ON MOUNT MUCKISH

This hill could stage the end-play of a move
Of tribes their lifelong by the sagas haunted,
The peak-led lightning dramatise the roof,
The cairn sum up whole tent-sleep peoples depending
Like us on stones to record the hard-won norm
Through which our race its vagrant passion manned,
Put out of pet now, grooved in cyclic harm,
The close of death is grave, we will not rant.

Faint in the hulabulloo the ghostly tribes
Shake in our fathers' handsome act of death.
Temple, town-hall fall with silent pipes.
All the love-legends of the abandoned earth,
When the intestate loins have spent their race,
Would come to mind with tears and forfeit voice.

Denis Devlin

RETURN

Now, on this golden autumn day,
    While yet the wine of heather spills
Over the moors, I take my way
    To my heart's haven in the hills.

Where I shall see the blue smoke rise
    From cottage fires of fragrant turf
And listen to the curlews' cries
    And hear the beating of the surf.

And see, once more, in my heart's home
    The arc of gleaming golden sand
Fringed with a flounce of lacy foam
    Broider'd with shells, where sea birds stand.

And red and gold the rowan trees
    Shine on the shore of Loch na Doon
And I shall see on silvered seas
    The splendour of the Hunters' moon.

Soon I shall see, tho' sunlight die
    The sight beloved over all
Serene against the evening sky
    The dear blue hills of Donegal.

K G Sullivan

SLEMISH

Slemish rises from the green
a scaled reptile of prehistory,
its gravestone face you clamber and climb
for mystery, the paths wind
respect for rooted rock
which mocks as rain rolls away:
there are no valleys where shelter
can be had, or water gathered.

But the green surrounding
(rather, so many greens
each one deserves a colour)
sentenced off in stone quadrilaterals
which, in moistness of Springtime
are nets, the cows bobbing
like gulls, on tides of grass.

At the base of Slemish fences stop,
farms stand their distance, wary,
tracks circle and then, regard
the strange lizard thrust up, a mound
of buried schemes and circumstances.
As if, to drag yourself up
clawing at thistle and pawing for foothold
were enough to awaken the mountain.

At the top you may sit with St. Patrick
doubting you exist beyond the wheel and helmet;
you may see the planters arrive with guns
primed with ambition and ploughs behind.
All of this, pointing back to the ice
scratching at the surface of time,
moving ridges and valleys as if they were dunes
yet leaving Slemish to resist any question.

Mike Jenkins

THE GAP

Fencing a rough place on the mountain
where the stirk was killed
he took a chill and came home shivering,
refused the doctor, enduring the wide bed
a few hours longer than usual;
for a week now he has sat
on a chair to the right of the hearth,
spitting against the turf and lighting his pipe,
reading the children's schoolbooks, and hearing reports
of how they are managing to save the hay without him,
as one day
they shall have to manage everything.

John Hewitt

LETTER FROM THE MOURNES

From the cupped peace of these aloof
Uncertain hills, a quiet hint
Of a corner-lurking past, the leaf
Murmuring on the wary tree,
I pen with glib erratic point
Irrelevant lines to the squat city
Dour in its suit of dust, the blunt
Thunder of traffic lulling your room,
Booming a grotesque lullaby.
(Here the wheels are out of time,
Like a drift of smoke loose on the sea.)
Here, in the mountains, where a crazy folk
Coax the sullen soil to yield,
Whose prayers are that the weather walk
Softly, sitting on a stone
In the centre of a lean, mean field
Where a rabbit goggles and is gone,
The silver sheep silent and cold:

Watching the soft sweet swoop of the hills,
I nurse a vague nostalgic prayer,
Shy as the stammer of lame stone walls,
For a golden harvesting this year:
Pray that a miracle may flower,
Though the seeds are wrong, and the soil is sour.

Roy McFadden

MOURNE GRANITE

Mourne granite cradled me. The clay
Of mid-Down carried
The imprint of my growing foot.
I swung my satchel
In the shadow of the clanging yards.
— And wouldn't have it otherwise. The rock
Ran milk for me. The fields
Were a green playground. Gunmen
Were none to stalk the city
Like a bad conscience.
                    Disaster
When it came chose my middle age.
My eyes have seen
Eden subverted, but needed glasses for it.

Victor Price

LINES BY SLIEVE DONARD

The men who made these walls,
Rimming the higher ground with younger stone,
Aproned with mist or shoulder-high in sun,
Their hands absorbed and yet contemplative,
Pausing, did they lift their hands to hear
The hunted echo scurrying through the whin,
Peer for the shadow driving the stuttering sheep
Askew in flight, and the cattle lumbering
In the swollen valleys glittering with fear?

— And speculate,
Above the parishes and baronies,
Picking out spires like pins and the roads' threads,
On some disaster climbing the rockface
To where their obstinate regiment of stone,
Boulder to boulder, guards the empty peak.

Roy McFadden

THE GOAT OF SLIEVE DONARD

I saw an old white goat on the slope of Slieve Donard,
Nibbling daintily at the herb leaves that grow in the
    crevasses,
And I thought of James Stephens —
He wrote of an old white goat within my remembering,
Seven years ago I read —
Now it comes back
Full of the dreaming black beautiful crags.
I shall drink of the white goat's milk,
The old white goat of Slieve Donard,
Slieve Donard where the herbs of wisdom grow,
The herbs of the Secret of Life that the old white goat
    has nibbled,
And I shall live longer than Methuselah,
Brother to no man.

Patrick Kavanagh

FEBRUARY CALM

So calm it was that near my feet
Slieve Foy, inverted, lay complete,
And crags two-thousand feet in air
Swayed gently in the ripples there
(No breath was felt to stir a hair).

I thought, the summer tourist will
But seldom see the mirrored hill
Repeat with symmetry so true
Each rocky knoll and every hue —
The sky-blue and the mountain-blue.

Then to complete idyllic calm
And banish things disposed to harm,
Bells from Rostrevor and Omeath
Rang o'er the water; 'I believe
In God the Father . . . ' And I leave

The Lough with its bright mirrored rim
And go to church to worship Him,
The Primal Artist, who is found
In everything spread forth around,
Which man has left without a wound.

Patric Stevenson

ON SLIEVE GULLION

On Slieve Gullion men and mountain meet,
O'Hanlon's territory, the rapparee,
Home of gods, backdrop for a cattle raid,
The Lake of Cailliagh Bearra at the top
That slaked the severed head of Conaire Mor:

To the south the Border and Ravensdale
Where, a week ago, the torturers left
Not even an eyelash under the leaves
Or a tooth for MacCecht the cupbearer
To rinse, then wonder where the water went.

Today through a gap in the hedge I spy
A blackened face, the disembodied head
Of a mummer who has lost his bearings
Or, from the garrison at Dromintee,
A paratrooper on reconnaissance.

He draws a helicopter after him,
His beret far below, a wine-red spot
Swallowed by heathery patches and ling
As he sweats up the slopes of Slieve Gullion
With forty pounds of history on his back.

Both strangers here, we pass in silence
For he and I have dried the lakes and streams
And Conaire said too long ago: 'Noble
And valiant is MacCecht the cupbearer
Who brings water that a king may drink.'

Michael Longley

BALLYKINLAR: MAY 1940

One standing on the empty beach
beyond the sandhills, threw wide his arms
with an oratorical gesture to beseech
the blue and unresponsive hills:

    let now Cuchulain or some of the old gods
    descend from the mountains, with chariot wheels
    scything the hordes of evil, wielding again
    the battle-axe for justice, before all else fails.

And yet, the Red Branch withered at the last
now only a shadow in the mind of man
the victors and the victims — they are all lost
and the shed blood forgotten.
      Not out of the hills
must come the conquering host, but from the deep
recesses of the heart before the darkness falls.

Patrick Maybin

SHANCODUFF

My black hills have never seen the sun rising,
Eternally they look north towards Armagh.
Lot's wife would not be salt if she had been
Incurious as my black hills that are happy
When dawn whitens Glassdrumond chapel.

My hills hoard the bright shillings of March
While the sun searches in every pocket.
They are my Alps and I have climbed the Matterhorn
With a sheaf of hay for three perishing calves
In the field under the Big Fort of Rocksavage.

The sleety winds fondle the rushy beards of Shancoduff
While the cattle drovers sheltering in Featherna Bush
Look up and say: 'Who owns them hungry hills
That the water-hen and snipe must have forsaken?
A poet? Then by heavens he must be poor'.
I hear and is my heart not badly shaken?

Patrick Kavanagh

MONAGHAN HILLS

Monaghan hills,
You have made me the sort of man I am
A fellow who can never care a damn
For Everestic thrills.

The country of my mind
Has a hundred little heads
On none of which foot-room for genius.

Because of you I am a half-faithed ploughman
Shallow furrows at my heels.
Because of you I am a beggar of song
And a coward in thunder.

If I had been born among the Mournes
Even in Forkhill,
I might have echo-corners in my soul
Repeating the dawn laughter.

I might have climbed to know the glory
Of toppling from the roof of seeing —
O Monaghan hills when is writ your story
A carbon copy will unfold my being.

Patrick Kavanagh

HOME

The faraway hills are green but these
are greener. My brother roamed the world
and seemed to know everything. He boasted it
until I burst, 'Well you don't know John Joe Farrell,'

the butcher's son, my friend. I balanced all beside
a field in County Meath, its crooked acres falling
south. We called a hill *Sliabh na Cailli*, the hag's mountain,
but that's the way it is for lowlanders will call

a small incline a mountain and mountain-men mention
a hill and point to Everest. Things were themselves.
We bore them as the Cuckoo Clarke bore his origin,
humbled, naturally. We were masters of reserve.

'Why?' 'That's the why,' 'Ah why?' 'Because . . . '
When all fruit fails we welcome haws.

Peter Fallon

184

THE INNER HILLS

I cannot paint the loveliness of things,
    Pouring clear colour into gracious form,
Yet in my soul beat the caged skylark's wings,
    And the huge mountains tower above the storm.

Gleaming they stand, cloud-haunted, near the sky,
    Oh, shall I do the Divine Hills a wrong?
Hardly I dare, in wildest ecstasy,
    Drag their great glory into my small song.

Eva Gore-Booth

Habitation and Habitat

JANET AND COLIN BORD

A DURABLE MUSIC

Most walls now are prose
defining private places —
our insubstantial theories
of domesticity, work
or loneliness held in place
by the rational argument of bricks,
chunky with imperatives.
Mortar may overcivilise
the sensible heart.
Most walls now are prose.

But some are an old poet's work,
undulant and epic forms
tongued and hearted to perfection
in slate or stone's own rhythm,
not a cadence out of shape.
Some master of the long dry line
has measured his craft against the fells,
a true hyperborean makar.
I see his grey muse striding
through the north's bold weather,
inspired curlews rhyming
with the wind.

Rodney Pybus

PURPLE INK

I've left behind the card that, day by day
For long months past, time-clocked in purple ink,
Has counted every minute of my stay
Amidst the din and clatter, oily stink
And complicated industry of this
Rush-hurried modern world. I have instead
A smaller folded yellow card, that is
My passport key to freedom ...
                                    ... and a bed
In this high lonely hostel on the bounds
Of human habitation, where the steep
Lane ends; and curlews' cry, and distant sounds

189

Of wind-blown rushes, streams, and bleating sheep
Are heard, until the shadows of the hills
Grow deeper, and the downward drifting tide
Of cloud obliterates the peaks, and fills
The hollows in between, and slowly, wide
Gray wreaths of mist creep down the mountain slopes
And urge us to ... the Common Room. Where snaps
Are shown, & 'experts' talk of nylon ropes,
And cycle gears, and blisters, and of home.
Then someone asks 'the 'eight o' that round 'ill
At back 'o th'ostel, 'ere', while others roam
The continent with oft-told tales that will
Be told a hundred times again. We speak
Of Firbank's book, and Coxhead's, that we've read;
Of songs of Wales, and legends of the bleak
High cliffs, and fairy tales. And then ...

                                             ... to bed;
Some drowsy cross-talk, and the last bare feet
Pad over to switch off the light, and peace
Comes quietly, like the mist-born dew. And peat
And pines bring scented dreams ...

                                    ... that cease
And are forgotten when the Morning brings
All colours slowly back to earth, and fills
The brave new day with light, and swiftly flings
The mist far up into the singing hills.
Another lively day of freedom lies
Ahead, in which to ramble, see, & think ...
BRYN HALL LLANLLECHID was my gateway to the skies,
Stamped on my yellow card, in purple ink.

Anon

190

from THE RAIN AND THE TENT

Meanwhile
the rain falls,
little bombs
on our green walls.

We are sitting, John and I, with last week's butter
the crossword and Anna Karenina
while the candle gutters
on the biscuit tin
and the rain tightens the guys

and the moth reels
against the wind-blown tent
and the cigarette smoke
swings tick-tock like a funny bloke
edging round a lamp-post in his cups

and the moth wheels
into the candle
and dies.

R J Wathen

THE BOTHY

The flame of the pine-logs
Leapt high against the timbered walls.
We sat
Huddled in overcoats, toasting our toes
And eating bacon, like savages,
Out of the frying-pan!
Then we lay down, still in our coats and mufflers,
On sacks of straw to sleep.
And the cold crept in;
And the wind crept in;
And the fire died;
And the floor-boards prodded our bodies through the sacks.

And I thought
Of a comfortable hotel in Aberdeen

With hot and cold running water, and beds like thistledown —
(But dared not, of course, mention it!)

Yet, it was worth it —
Everything was worth it —
To be alone again among the mountains —
To know that they were gathered all about us —
That we had only to go outside to see them standing
In all their naked beauty in the moonlight
With their white heads pillowed on the sky
And the dark
Forests folded, like blankets, round their feet.
And we knew
That we would have endured much more than this
Just to feel that they were near us
Watching
While we tried to sleep.

Brenda G Macrow

OCTOBER AT STAOINEAG BOTHY

Was it worth it,
that draughty train, and
the growing strain of
bulging packs as we
laboured along these unending tracks?

Was it worth it,
that fitful sleep, the
creeping frost and the
creak of boards as tired
bodies twitched and tossed
seeking rest?

Yes, it was worth it
for that golden glen, the
yellow birches and tawny
ferns, the glorious solitude
of corrie and ben, replenishing
our hearts again.

Yes, it was worth it
for one view alone,
a glittering-blue sky and overnight
snow, all gilded by the pale-gold
glow of morning sun.
Until, jewel-like, all shone as one,
exquisite and dazzling.
And as we marvelled, it dimmed and
was gone.

Yes, it was worth it,
that physical grind,
to find
such peace of mind.

Rennie McOwan

PEANMEANACH

Soft the stones so near the sands
that squeak a welcome if you go
a step beyond our world's end.
Crackle on the tangle. Feel the guard stones
   of the bay.
Lurk your fingers in the cracks
between the rocks of houses ruined now
and clasp the hands of years away
that made the slabs to kiss so gentle
where soft the sea kneels to the land.
Turfed and whole, they must have seemed
a new piece of the shore.
Grand, to build up from the ground
your own place (scooped but not removed
from local earth and stone)
a haven at the heart of things.
Made, but not your own.

Leen Volwerk

HUT

it is almost too simple
here under the mountain,
snow flying
lightning
and roaring water.

the unwashed plates.
and the weather too obviously bad
to go out.
six men
in a bare room

walking from window
to fire and back again.
each one
identical
but for the others.

simple as
condoning the galaxies,
given the time
what infinite
can help it. white

sheeting the window,
thunder over the flood,
six men
laughing
keeping the fire bright

and if it had happened,
we should have described the avalanche.
boot. splinter
of chair.
somebody else's photograph.

G J F Dutton

DEEPDALE CAMP

between the drumlins' soft breasts
we lay back
replete as the resting turf
and let night come
to the rattle of beck boulders
and conversation
stilled by flares of shooting stars
entranced by arches of orbit
silent moments of firey extinction.

silent next morning
the sheep suffered the crow
at its empty eye-sockets
stirring a leg only
as we passed.

Terry Gifford

UNDER MY FEET THE YEARS BIDE TIME

I have come briefly
to be something other
than a stranger in this
bleak, unpeopled place
where once, grain bare
cleft wood was fitted
handily length to length
and peat cover opened
for the apples of the earth.
Here, on this furrowed face
long left
lazy bed
I will lay
me down
and watch
a million masts
running with the wind
smoke across the earth.

David Boyd

WHERE ONCE WAS HOME

Silent and lonely to-day are the hillsides,
    Sheep at their grazing and grouse on the wing;
Vanished the tartan that rallied at bidding,
    To follow a chieftain or fight for a king.

Heather is crowning the path of the drovers,
    Laughter is stilled where the lonely deer roam;
Bracken is crowding its way to the lintels,
    Nettles are growing where once was a home.

D C Cuthbertson

GLEN GLASS, AUTUMN

The glen is grey now,
Grey for the want of men
To make bright fields
Of women in the doorways
And children crowding from school.
The roofs are fallen
And the thin wind scours
Bare hearth-stones.
There is no harvest now,
No long-learnt understanding
Of the ways of herded beasts.
There are none to share
This bane, that blessing.
No one stands in the pass,
Eyes narrowed,
To look for another coming.

Yet there are echoes of anger
In the stags' roar.
The stare and soar
Of eagles
Flings a dare.
Fish leap
The torrent,
Wild swans ride the long
Grey waters of the loch

And the hare
Has his unhindered kingdom
On the hill.
Only a man's sadness,
Rising sharp in word or song,
Is stilled now.
Grief is buried deep.

Katharine Stewart

DEPOPULATION OF THE HILLS

Leave it, leave it — the hole under the door
Was a mouth through which the rough wind spoke
Ever more sharply; the dank hand
Of age was busy on the walls
Scrawling in blurred characters
Messages of hate and fear.

Leave it, leave it — the cold rain began
At summer end — there is no road
Over the bog, and winter comes
With mud above the axletree.

Leave it, leave it — the rain dripped
Day and night from the patched roof
Sagging beneath its load of sky.

Did the earth help them, time befriend
These last survivors? Did the spring grass
Heal winter's ravages? The grass
Wrecked them in its draughty tides,
Grew from the chimney-stack like smoke,
Burned its way through the weak timbers.
That was nature's jest, the sides
Of the old hulk cracked, but not with mirth.

R S Thomas

PENNINE RUIN

Watching through empty stone
Where once perhaps a face
Pressed, on ancient glass.

Gone now, only air and wind
To blow in vacancy.

The walls stand straight and strong
Only crumbling in corners;
And green fern grows in crevices
Where pictures hung or some
Memento of a life that passed.

Only the wind makes music now
In winter. Swallows, the only living
Souls to call it home, have flown away,
Leaving the eternal silence of its
Emptiness. Stone slates slide
A few more in every gale
Uncovering rafters to hang
And fall like broken bones.
And the barn, once warm and
Cattle-smelling, is cold, wet stone.

Stone. On stairway, each step hollowed
By tired feet of generations gone.
And stone grown green
Where water drips.

What spirits linger here?
Souls of a life long gone.
Children born and dying;
Bitterness, the long fight
With wind and sour land;
The twisting, frantic wind
That tears at fortitude.
Heartaches and defeat,
Bright hopes reduced to dust.

Given up, stone back to stone,
The house alone,
Abandoned, till the moor
Takes back its own.

Chriss Brandon

from NA PRÁTAÍ DUBHA

Dungarvan was a long and winding street
Of low whitewashed houses:
The Square was still a potato field
Full of the blackened fruit;
The hake was scarce, the fever ran everywhere.

In the countryside, bailiffs were emptying
The small houses;
They met little resistance.
The mountains would never be peopled again.
Whole hamlets were abandoned now forever.

Stones among nettles, a fuchsia hedge.
Mounds of fallen mud
Tell of the dead storying.
Some tried to grow crops on the reaghs
And fell by their unfinished ridges.

Mothers followed their children
In mock funerals:
There were processions at dawn
To the top of the road;
The burial place, America at the farthest turn.

Padraig Daly

CONDY

He lives alone in the shadow of
mountains; his tilted stony acres
fray the clouds; he takes
eight years out of a dog and knows
his ewes better than the sons
he never had. The horizon is
his fence, his sheep range free
and yet his mind is
penned, his spirit tethered. He climbs
through darkness into
the light on summits but hears

no voices from a cloud. He fears
death — the rickle of bleached
bones in lonely places — and in drink
weeps for himself and his brothers
and for all the others
on whom the shadow of mountains
fell.

Francis Harvey

MOOR SIGNS

Onto the moor of minding
I will go — my roving acres
one dog's life ago.
There's little linking, many ways
are covered that have been.
Much of the moor is ditched
and organised; the curlew
keening.

And still the dyke lines lie,
foundations of a system that gave way.
Below the forestry, the scars of farms.
Below the will of man, the earth.

I look for moor signs to identify
inside their houses, families,
my people, self;
a land informed with us,
our bones in time.

Between the Solway
and the threatened hills around our edges
moor and machar of our making.

Robin Munro

STONE

Arcadia was never here.
Ice-needles tortured the thin soil,
spring snow lay long by the north wall,
yet the peat-fire had a summer heart.
Waves of life receding left
jetsam of stone — grey megaliths
half-sunk in tussocky grass now
but still processional on the ridge above,
leading into a mystery:
in a cranny of the valley, a ring of stones
that sheltered a hearth once: a roofless hut
of later years, perched high upstream
under the shadow of cairned hills.
The rushes cut each autumn
to mend the thatch, one year
were cut no more; over the centuries
the path was lost. Only stone lasts here.
Stone proclaims life, affirms a future
by virtue of so many pasts,
yet baffles questioning. As I touch walls
warm in the sun today, and feel
so many summers gentle to my hand
and yet withheld, I would crush stone
in my fist, if I could, till truth's milk ran.

Ruth Bidgood

ANCIENT CAIRN

Who built this cairn on this wild hill;
who shaped this pile, rough stone on stone?
Who, toiling here, sought to fulfil
a dream, a promise? Who — alone,
perhaps, and lonely — thought in this way
to leave a mark in this wild place?

And for whom — or what? Is a day,
a month, a year, some form of grace
commemorated here — a love,
a hope — or is this pile of stones
a silent, supplicatory dove
wooing peace for old, dead bones?

Gordon Allen North

FARMER'S BOY

It is a naked country without trees;
Scourged by winds from the seas;
Bald and bare;
Harsh with sounds that drive like stones through
the air ...
They do say
There were forests here once on a day;
But the great wars stole them away.

And when I walk at noon upon the bare,
The beaten ridge, where
The grass grows,
Where once, they say, the pines climbed in rows,
I do hear
A singing like to harps in my ear,
And like a ship at sea the wind goes.

Rose Macaulay

A FIRE OF TURF

In summer time I foot the turf
And lay the sods to dry,
South wind and lark's song, and the sun far up in
the sky.
I pile them on the turf stack
Against the time of snow,
Black frost, a gale from the north, who minds what
winds will blow?

Now winter's here, make up the fire,
And let you bolt the door.
A wind across the mountains, a draught across the
    floor,
I'll not be heeding cold or rain,
Or moaning of the wind,
With the turf fire, the hearth stone, the notions in
    my mind.

Winifred M Letts

BIRTH

On the hottest, stillest day of the summer
A calf was born in a field
At Pant-y-Cetris; two buzzards
Measured the volume of the sky;
The hills brimmed with incoming
Night. In the long grass we could see
The cow, her sides heaving, a focus
Of restlessness in the complete calm,
Her calling at odds with silence.

The light flowed out leaving stars
And clarity. Hot and slippery, the scalding
Baby came, and the cow stood up, her cool
Flanks like white flowers in the dark.
We waited while the calf struggled
To stand, moved as though this
Were the first time. I could feel the soft sucking
Of the new-born, the tugging pleasure
Of bruised reordering, the signal
Of milk's incoming tide, and satisfaction
Fall like a clean sheet around us.

Gillian Clarke

HILL FARM

The farm rides the swell
of the moor like
a raft,
square sail fixed
to the sky.

Fields break
into outcrops of foam,
the farmer gentles
his cargo,
chickens and cows;
watches his
ballast of corn.

It is the edge of
a storm,
lightning-flashes of gorse,
the heather
engorged with purple;
his wife
adjusts the canvas,
tightens rope.

Isobel Thrilling

OLD AARON

Slow moving now;
Too frail to face the gale.
Near ninety years this farm has been his home.
The mountain Pass
May beckon to the the dale
But now he cannot climb where Herdwicks roam.

Worn out and done?
His grandson won't agree,
For now the blizzard sweeps across the fell,
And warm in bed
He thanks the Lord that he
Brought down those sheep to shelter — safe and well

'Old Aaron knew,'
He murmured once again,
With grief and loss avoided by a hair;
Forewarned, forearmed
As when foretold 'the rain
Will flood the pasture, and the bridge won't bear.'

He'd read the sky
And talked with mountain mist,
He'd listened, each nuance for Nature's cue
And so tonight
A treasured child was kissed
Goodbye — goodbye. Oh yes, old Aaron knew.

Edna M Cass

from THE ANIMALS

This is no place for the sentimental
Anthropomorphic view of the animal creation.
These sheep are creatures who tread among boglands,
Shave the meadows as close as a razor,
Assume the shape and coloration of a boulder
On the strewn hillside,
Who unceremoniously cuff their white lambs
With a teaching hoof,
And feed the thin soil with their heedless droppings.

Frederick Vanson

THE EWE

She was so proud
there on the turf, blue boundless above
and great hills lolling in sunshine, stretched
this once serene, Snowdon with all his sons.
There she had lain,
there on a swell of turf, her labour come

this April morning, and all creation sang
with the birds to her courage, as if that day, alone,
she the world's darling bore the loveliest thing
the world had seen.

It was her first.
It hurt her, a pain accepted, pulse of pain
joining with hills around, with cliff, with stream,
witness the act of love; then it was done.
She licked him clean,
a trembling thing, her world's one child, her tongue
loosing from bond of slime, wall of her womb,
to see the sun, to see the sky, to be
her lamb, to taste milk that to none before
tasted so good.

So she got up
unsteady, so proud, and then edging away
he followed calling, her child, but never looked
at the crumpled grass, his birthplace, at the blood,
at the cord;
and this her gut, token of end or birth,
sign of creation, relic of parted love,
a white gull, fugitive from storm today,
pecked at and gnawed and gobbled, emptily
screamed and cried.

Wilfrid Noyce

RAMS

Their horns are pure baroque,
as thick at the root as a man's wrist.
They have golden eyes and Roman noses.
All the ewes love them.

They are well-equipped to love back.
In their prime they balance;
the sex at one end of their bodies
equalling the right to use it at the other.

When two of them come face to face
in the mating season
a spark jumps the gap.
Their heads drive forward like cannon balls.
Solid granite hills splinter into echoes.

They never wrestle, as stags and bulls do.
They slug it out. The hardest puncher wins.
Sometimes they back up so far for a blow
they lose sight of one another
and just start grazing.

They are infinitely and indefatigably stupid.
You can rescue the same one
from the same bramble bush
fifty times.
Such a massive casing to guard such a tiny brain
— as if Fort Knox were built to house a single penny!

But year by year those horns add growth.
The sex is outstripped in the end;
the balance tilts in the direction of the head.

I found a dead ram once.
It was trapped by the forefeet
in the dark waters of a peatbog,
drowned before help could arrive
by the sheer weight of its skull.
Maiden ewes were grazing near it,
immune to its clangorous lust.
It knelt on the bank, hunched over its own image,
its great head buried in the great head facing it.
Its horns, going forward in the old way,
had battered through at last to the other side.

Alasdair Maclean

THE SHEEP

Then we looked
and saw on every side
the empty moorland
stretching far away
from where she struggled
on encumbered back
swollen with young
legs crook'd and feebly stirring.

We knew enough
though none was country bred
to leap the tussocks
of that peaty marsh
intent to grasp
tangled oily fleece
and curving horns
to lift and ease her turning.

Now we looked
and saw still watching her
the carrion crows
abruptly urged to flight
craving to finish
the foul thing begun
whilst she — eyeless —
stood in darkness, unaware.

Jean Grant

BEHOLD THE LAMB

You were first.
The ewe licked clean ochre and lake
But you would not move.
Weighted with stones yet
Dead your dead head floats,
Better dead than sheep,

The thin worm slurred in your gut,
The rot in your feet,
The red dog creeping at dawn.
Better than dipped in the hard white water,
Your stomach furred,
Your head hardboiled.

Better dead than dyed
In a bowl of pale whin petals.
Better than rolling down the hill,
Pale skull flaking.
First to break.
First for the scream of the clean bite.

Better dead with your delph head floating.

Paul Muldoon

LINES

Sheep paths are useful lines
on the face of hills.
Braes with many
are good to go on.

A thrawn sheep track
lines up with the rock, missing
the marsh. Sweir to
cross the burn, it will cross,
in time, in the best way,
the old way.

They bring mire on themselves
who take a swaggering walk
or move like motorways
on hills. Shepherds know (and poets should)
the sense in sheep path lines.

Robin Munro

DRYSTONE WALLS

A sudden withdrawal of light — grey
thickens to the dull glisten of slanting rain,
moorland's dusty brown brightens and the air
is filled with a new chill, stinging flesh of face,
stiffening fingers.

        Line of black wall
that divides the fell, hints at shelter.
I crush in the lee, hunched in my warmth,
knees pressed from the worst of the weather.
Wind plays the wall like shattered pipes,
something between sigh and whistle, air on stone,
forced through crevices left by shrewd makers
to split the wind's push.

        And I hear, too,
the rush of gale over moor beyond,
the very grass soughing in the blast, flattened
under naked pressure.

        No compromise here
— a fragile beat of conscious life held
against vast emptiness of space, time;
dead wall makers could not tame the wild,
nor contain the cold threat the rain brings.
But a place to breathe from, from which to assert
even hopes or human truths.

        Walls have gates.

Colin Speakman

THE WALLERS

Astride a granite fell the wallers meet
and iron clogs on rocks clatter
as men ascend a sullen scree.
Slow-limbed, in hodden grey they pace the land
and subdued voices down the mountain slope
resound until at last a bargain is agreed —
a Contract by Wilson, his mark,
and Thompson, his cross,
a wall before the old year end,
a wall before the frost.

In canvas shack the dykers bivouac below the ridge
and hands at a touch reach to set a crag of slate to rest.

Through yards of scattered stone quiet minds pick,
through bracken and scree
and length by length a course appears,
a shadow below the fell.

It falls to place, the wall, unhurriedly.
It advances over cleft and beck until,
long weeks breached and gone,
hard against a barren slope it humps.

At this the dykers seem to slow.
Through mist they move,
and days of rain
as stone on stone is lodged.
Thus grey November booms and fades
and only then the mountain slope
is crossed.

Two months done from first unpromising
cast of rock to a new dyke running harsh
with standing stone.
A wall before the old year end;
a wall complete and built to last.

It seemed, indeed, the only way to build a wall.

Irvine Hunt

211

WALL

The wall walks the fell —
Grey millipede on slow
Stone hooves;
Its slack back hollowed
At gulleys and grooves,
Or shouldering over
Old boulders
Too big to be rolled away.
Fallen fragments
Of the high crags
Crawl in the walk of the wall.

A dry-stone wall
Is a wall and a wall.
Leaning together
(Cumberland-and-Westmorland
Champion wrestlers),
Greening and weathering,
Flank by flank,
With filling of rubble
Between the two —
A double-rank
Stone dyke:
Flags and through-
stones jutting out sideways,
Like the steps of a stile.

A wall walks slowly.
At each give of the ground,
Each creak of the rock's ribs,
It puts its foot gingerly,
Arches its hog-holes,
Lets cobble and knee-joint
Settle and grip.
As the slipping fellside
Erodes and drifts,
The wall shifts with it,
Is always on the move.

They built a wall slowly,
A day a week;
Built it to stand,
But not stand still.
They built a wall to walk.

Norman Nicholson

QUARRYMEN

By echoes in long barrows of the tribal mind,
I know our wildthorn roots were heeled by those who,
At the barnacled and fallow edge of the world, turned
And stood with beaker, axe and horn to pledge, with
Embyro tongues of our chiselled vernacular, that here
Was oak and mistletoe; strewn oracular bones; and
Miracle scarp of days and moons for the Cymry, that
We stay — wedged, and sharp, in this place of stones.

Rock-bound, ancestral wraiths sigh like gossamer tunes
On ossicles of the secret ear, when the rude cliffs
Were hewn and runed crags cleft with crude tools.

Know us by the slate — dragged caesarean from flanks
Of man-hung cwm; the silicotic lung in rumbled storms.
Lilies of the mountains weep for my brothers from your
    corms,
For they became bunched umbels, pale gathered in clouds
And stalked for hunchedback, grey-lagged tombs.

Yet, — these strata are floral and stacked for me —
Where the huge, salt wind scrolls the screes,
The prayer-mat grass and hassock thrift;
Where the tides trade shells for wild gulled cries
And waders fife the drift of dusk in the wake
Of the days that sound in our orison sea.

And the zion of galleries that soars through our life
Brails me to these shores and storied grail of ground.

T Ll Williams

213

THE MOUNTAIN CHAPEL

Chapel and gravestones, old and few,
Are shrouded by a mountain fold
From sound and view
Of life. The loss of the brook's voice
Falls like a shadow. All they hear is
The eternal noise
Of wind whistling in grass more shrill
Than aught as human as a sword,
And saying still:

"Tis but a moment since man's birth,
And in another moment more
Man lies in earth
For ever; but I am the same
Now, and shall be, even as I was
Before he came:
Till there is nothing I shall be.'

Yet there the sun shines after noon
So cheerfully
The place almost seems peopled, nor
Lacks cottage chimney, cottage hearth:
It is not more
In size than is a cottage, less
Than any other empty home
In homeliness.
It has a garden of wild flowers
And finest grass and gravestones warm
In sunshine hours
The year through. Men behind the glass
Stand once a week, singing, and drown
The whistling grass
Their ponies munch. And yet somewhere
Near or far off there's some man could
Live happy here,
Or one of the gods perhaps, were they
Not of inhuman statue dire

As poets say
Who have not seen them clearly, if
At sound of any wind of the world
In grass-blades stiff
They would not startle and shudder cold
Under the sun. When Gods were young
This wind was old.

Edward Thomas

BEN GRIAM BEG HILL FORT, SUTHERLAND

Those straggling heaps of reddish stone
Stand cold amid the wind and snow,
Telling tales of time long gone.
When wolf and lynx were hunters here
And man had other men to fear.

— Such fear it must have been
To cause the bitter raising of those walls
Away up here where the air is keen ...
A chilly haven in the battle
To save their lives and keep their cattle.

Straining bent against the gale,
I hear the wrenching grasps of men
Joined with the wind in universal wail.
— Hard harmony of toil piled the stones,
A battered token of aching bones.

Did this wall save sheep and cattle beast
To crop upon the Sutherland plain?
Or did the corbies make a feast?
Ghosts or wind raise a haunting moan —
I flee the hill, reminded I'm alone.

Leen Volwerk

WADE'S ROADS

Troop colours marked their highroad's run
    When Wade's men drove the ways.
Pennants of Ker and Harrison
    Had all the moor ablaze.
But when you and I went wandering
    Along the broken foss,
        Azaleas were the flags we met,
        With saxifrage and violet;
        And Alpine lady's mantle set
    Her colours in the moss.

A centinel of Montague's
    With curses filled the day
When a wagon wheel had broken loose
    On a traverse north of Spey.
But when you and I went wandering
    A whaup was calling clear;
        The ptarmigan were lazing round;
        A cock-grouse crest was blazing round,
        And a yell hind stood a-gazing round --
    The sentry of the deer.

So up the glen and o'er the ridge
    Wade's soldiers sweat and strain,
With here a traverse, there a bridge
    To build in sleet and rain.
But when you and I went wandering
    We dandered down the way,
        And the broken bridge was a resting-place,
        And the water mirrored your happy face,
        While the trout went jink in their old-time race,
    And life was holiday.

J B Salmond

THE PYLONS

The secret of these hills was stone, and cottages
Of that stone made,
And crumbling roads
That turned on sudden hidden villages.

Now over these small hills, they have built the concrete
That trails black wire;
Pylons, those pillars
Bare like nude giant girls that have no secret.

The valley with its gilt and evening look
And the green chestnut
Of customary root,
Are mocked dry like the parched bed of a brook.

But far above and far as sight endures
Like whips of anger
With lightning's danger
There runs the quick perspective of the future.

This dwarfs our emerald country by its trek
So tall with prophecy:
Dreaming of cities
Where often clouds shall lean their swan-white neck.

Stephen Spender

WINDSCALE

The toadstool towers infest the shore:
Stink-horns that propagate and spore
    Wherever the wind blows.
Scafell looks down from the bracken band,
And sees hell in a grain of sand,
    And feels the canker itch between his toes.

This is a land where dirt is clean,
And poison pasture, quick and green,
    And storm sky, bright and bare;
Where sewers flow with milk, and meat
Is carved up for the fire to eat,
    And children suffocate in God's fresh air.

Norman Nicholson

DEATH OF A GIANT

Strange creature
can you not hear me

I have lain here undisturbed
long before your kind first walked
upon this earth
I have suffered ice ages
great floods
and burning heat

I have seen you evolve
grow
and multiply
I have also felt your wars

Yet
I have survived all of these
until now
must you end my time
by breaking me into a thousand pieces

strange creature
can you not hear me.

John Walsh

SUNSETS

When the sunset burned the snow
It stoked a wrath of memory.
I looked, not over a splendid world,
One man on his million-acre peace,
Not at my freedom eagled in the sky,
Not at love soft as spindrift silk ...
I saw blood in the red, and sweat,
And tears, for wars still to be waged
Before man can walk the heights clear
Of sharp, cramponing conscience.

It is so easy to admire sunsets on Ben More.
Would I rise to such admiration in Soweto say?
I doubt it. That sort of superiority isn't mine.
To admire sunsets under those circumstances
Is to have scaled heaped Everests of fire.

Hamish Brown

THOUGHTS IN AN AREA OF OUTSTANDING NATURAL BEAUTY

You haven't lived, they said to me,
Until you've seen our hills, our sea,
Our mountains strong from age to age,
Our fortress and our heritage.
So, dutifully here I stand
To view the splendours of our land,
The castled crag, the fabled shore,
So now I've lived, and I'd say more:
Until you've known this shame, this stress,
This beauty that is meaningless,
That's bought and sold on every side,
You haven't lived — you haven't died.

Harri Webb

THE MOUNTAIN

Back yard for the nation,
space plotted and pathed
for the frittering fret of humanity.
Have they a right to be here,
who miss the sign of the sky
and the rock face?

The mountain gave them directions enough
and they erected posts with arrows,
laid paths with processed granite.
The mountain should have given them hope,
and all they found was soggy newsprint.
The mountain should have given them awe,
and they prepared a display on granite batholiths.
The mountain should have tested their strength and faith,
but, graded and routed at base, they clutched plastic maps
or followed the people in front.
The mountain should have given them God,
and they swore in their gym-shoes,
at the Almighty who made the stones so sharp.

Turnstiled mountain,
worn by the shrieking and cursing,
tattered by picnics,
torn by the crowd;
Why will they take,
who cannot see what it gives?

R A Hector

HOLOCAUST

A month's drought:

eastwinds bleed the land.
Earth cracks, anguished . . .

A straggle of Sunday hikers
threads the moor. The peat-scab
breaks: its dust spews from bootsoles
like distended tongues.

Laughter of disregard:
a black fan opens
from a tidalwave of flame . . .

The moor inverts its image
in the sky: a desert sunset
shocked into midday dusk.

Beneath it men lose eyebrows,
hair and shirts. A fire engine,
caught in a tortured curve of flame,
shatters like a landmine.

Sheep, hares, foxes panic upwind,
stampeding to clear air. They burst
from the blaze like brands —
streaks of terror, incandescent.

Haze thickens. The sky is a sandstorm,
battle-brown. Heath peels faster
than a man can run. Peat burns inward —
fire gulps it twelve feet down.

The forestry erupts. Bulldozers
smash tracks through spruce. Peat
burns under them: trunks flare again.
The digger crews move in . . .

The conflagration is contained. The peat
is a roasting quicksand. It smoulders
like a lavaspread — the outer crust of hell.

Grouse, curlew, plover dip
above their offsprings' crematorium:
a five mile tract of carcasses.

Farmers sell off the remnants
of their flocks: the commons an ashpit,
dead for fifteen years.

Surveillance is maintained. Danger
could break again before the rain ...

Roads are closed: car jams
and cameras turned back.

The watchers wait for cloud.

Ian Taylor

Hills to the North

WALKING IN MIST

At first the River Noe
Like a snake's belly gleamed below
And then in a mist was lost;
The hill too vanished like a ghost
And all the day was gone
Except the damp grey light that round me shone.

From Lose Hill to Mam Tor,
Darkness held me and before,
I gave the track its head;
But as I followed where it led,
That light went all the way
As though I made and carried my own day.

Andrew Young

PENNINES

Much older than Rome,
blue-black backbone
— Bleaklow, Kinder, Mam Tor —
England's lungs.

They have rolled themselves well,
hurled hills
of peat, gritstone and cold-blooded rain,
world's emeralds.

A sea in suspense
over Manchester, Sheffield, Leeds,
the wild roof of the North,
smelting stars
on a dark night.

Every year, several people
disappear up there,
elusive as the blackberries.

Edwin Drummond

PENNINE COUNTRY

In the beginning
God stuck his thumb-print
on these hills,
in peat, sour grass,
the ritual scourging by wind,
and then forgot.

Until the time
our fathers came,
dug-in on slaty scree,
performed their bloody-minded miracle,
conjuring drab towns out of mist,
and still survive in us.

Surely, some day
this doggedness will earn
a blessing,
the peat ooze fat,
the cold streams run wine,
and corn spring from the bare rock.

If not, no matter.
We shall stick it out.
You can't just sling your hook
when the wrong half
belongs to you
by squatter's right.

John Ward

PENNINE

The northern uplands, England's backbone,
Are lonely. Their grasses are cracked
Down the centre, ribs scarred by roads.
Grey sheep bleat
Pitifully. Silence is ignored.

Ineffectual lapwings moan
Helplessly. Like a dismayed girl undressed
Briefly surprised, the hills clutch rags of reeds
Close, and drag wind-dried bracken
Over bare gipsy breasts.

Carole Robertson

KINDER SCOUT

Hares, on this sodden mountain.
White, surprised by the thaw,
Appear like moments of vision
Then silently melt away
Between a communion of boulders
That shape a rain washed sky.
Now water repeats to silence
The name of a running stream
And, falling, creates a presence
That lives while the stream flows on
But would die like a man from the absence
Of water, and turn to stone.

I climb to the source of the water
And watch it break from the turf —
So a child comes out of its mother
To traffic with death and life —
And know that the stream is neither
This cup where it murmurs one small
Word to the lichen and gravel,
Or its leap from that sudden fall
To a salt and tidal river,
Since just as my life exceeds
Its day of birth and dying,
This headlong water evades
The definition of boulders
That give it shape for one breath
And has a purpose such details
Are not familiar with.

Darkness covers the mountain:
Why must we travel this way
Over hags of peat and boulders?
That I shall never know,
But hares, like moments of vision,
Run white and then melt away.

Thomas Blackburn

KINDER DOWNFALL

On the sprung arch of a new night
stars waver and blink.
Eyes
slink up a silence of ice
on the eelwet wall
as though of feet ascending on holds
now preserved in Winter amber.

I intrude on your once accustomed stance,
witness to the white thrust of the cosmos
rising from these stunned stones.
No thunder breaks from the fury of this flood
you stayed behind to watch so many times,
tight locked in silence
it and I
wait your not expected presence.

On a last drift of light
melting drops
dance and bleed
through the red bar of a done sun,
and your shade fades to silence
under the wind's broad keel.
Along the moorland rims
the wine-mouthed valley tocsin
peals a soft-tongued greeting.
Somewhere,
water falls
unseen.

John Storer

MANOEUVRES ON KINDER SCOUT

Reaching Kinder's river-bed
after a morning's trek
and the game is on.
Sheep silhouetted against the grey sky
become Apache look-outs
the boys dodge. They
follow the twisting river,
keeping low to the sandy bottom
as it drains the Kinder plateau,
running to spill at the Downfall's sheer drop.
We head South with the water
oozing between high peat walls
that block all landscape,
all escape under the blanket sky.
The boys run small risks,
soakings as they leap boulders
over the gathering force of the water.
Arrow-noises zing and zip
from their mouths into the spongy banks.

I let them whoop ahead and occupy
myself in walking. Then
turning a bend come across them
in a hushed huddle. The eldest boy, Routledge
cups a ball of fluff in his hands.
Feet away, a hen grouse waddles back
and forth for our attention —
'I'm bigger, take me, I'm bigger.'
A nursery-book sacrifice.
Routledge smiles, makes a fist to hold
her chick, helpless, brushed with beginnings
of colour. Then, like some pageant hero,
he lowers that blind ball of feathers
to the heather roots.
He turns and leads us on.
One asks, 'Why ... ?'
'There's some things you didn't oughta ... '
Hen and chick melt back into the scrub
before our boot-marks can fill
and fade in water.

We unpack lunch
sitting on the edge of the world.
At Kinder Downfall the peat-trickles bunch
into a tumbling rush of water
the windy uplift turned to mist
that bathes us. Light spumes off the plovers
that catch and ride the air's power.
The talking dies — we are breathless at the show.
All morning we've crossed the plateau,
so, watered and fed now, we turn for home.
Mission complete, the schoolboy platoon
races on beyond my ken to Grindsbrook Clough.
Climbing the parapet of one more peat-gulley
I find myself alone,
the wind scouring my ears like shells,
my eyes loaded by the span of humped peat.
The world is weighed under loss.
Now, pinned to this map's one contour,
I see, stark and simple, the reality
of an absolute:

          this levelled
table-top world spread above its two poles
— Manchester, Sheffield —
and those cities laid waste
in a terror of nuclear heat,
brick and flesh charred peat-black
in a sear of thick light.

          Strange snows
will cover this mountain.
That history is held sure,
deep in the darkness of the peat,
deep below the jagged hulk
of a Dornier, its pilot's fist
clenched for thirty years.
That bomber, overshooting factories,
the web of searchlights, slides down
year by year to its real target.

Tony Curtis

BLEAKLOW

In conjuring mist's dissolving grey
    bleating sheep vanish and reappear,
Drizzle-bedraggled stand like mutton, staring
    with effrontery and eyelash affectation.
Baaing to refute their proverbial foolishness
    and absurd woolliness, their mandibles
Circle distractedly, and absent-mindedly
    they stoop to crop the rough grass.

The moors were always outside the door,
    waves of landscape waiting to wash over us,
Undulating horizons crowding and listening
    with an anxious silence swallowing voices.
At night their massive shadows lay
    like dragons asleep against the stars
And sodium lamps of distant roads
    were luminous footprints over their backs.

Sheltering behind walls from a sheering gale,
    snowdrift sheep
Were iced in their cells all winterlong
    emerging lifeless to lie in the stream,
Leaving grey wool entangled
               in the barb-wire wind,
And the vacant orbits of their weathered skulls.

Gnat-plagued in shimmering summertime,
    I laboured up the stony path
To the wind-marauding top
    and scrambled gulleys of eroded peat
On Bleaklow's moorland wilderness,
    over dark brown fibrous moor
To the cottongrass where the windvoice drones
    and the curlew cries on Featherbed Moss.

Writhing round boulders of millstone grit
    glistening in the wet
A torrent of glassy serpents
    slides down the mat-grass hillside,
Chirruping and twistling over quartz pebbles
    and falls into ferny hollows in the rocks,
Frond wells where humic smells rise
    from cushioned mosses in a green mosaic.

231

The rough stone walls are algal green
    in that damp season
And I clambered one
        to glimpse a fleeting hare,
Drank the cold springwater ceremonially
        and kicked an autumn puffball
For its smokey cloud of spores.

Now between house-ends
    moors rise like funeral mounds
And I ascend these childhood landmarks
    to view the smoke-corroded city.
Immune to urban metamorphoses
        they form a promontory
To watch the glaciers pass.

R J Wood

ON MIDDLETON EDGE

If this life-saving rock should fail
Yielding too much to my embrace
And rock and I to death should race,
The rock would stay there in the dale
While I, breaking my fall,
Would still go on
Farther than any wandering star has gone.

Andrew Young

from REMEMBRANCE
(Walking above Glossop)

Last night I watched the red tide fall,
Forgotten souls each poppy head.
The old men nod, return through time,
But for our young, a list — of dead.

232

The ones who fought, that we might live,
Who still remain, though life is done.
Today each year I seek the hills,
To pay a tribute for my son.

How many? — of the men who died,
Forsaking all — and their life-blood,
If given the choice, would gladly change,
To Bleaklow peat — from Flanders mud.

Geoff Milburn

BLACK HILL

The blackness intensified by rain-sodden peat
Black oozing mud and squelching feet,
'Go back! Go back! Go back!'
The startled grouse will cry,
But here there is no turning.

Grim shapeless mounds,
Vague outlines in a misty scene
And shadowy figures
Are all that might be seen.
The startled grouse flies up:
'Go back! Go back! Go back!'
But take no heed.

Amorphous dome of wasting peat
Scoured and blackened by an atmosphere
Polluted by the sooty rain;
Product of a ring of towns
Weeping from the skies
And shared
By Blackface Sheep,
Black-bottomed sheep,
The black sheep of Black Hill.

Kenneth Oldham

ANGLEZARKE

Campion has something
obvious to say,

as you follow on,
writing toeholds
in a golden tower,
one spine of grit
since morning.

Creeping Jenny clings
like noon,

as you stretch skywards,
like a cave-painting
with simple lines,
swapping faces with men
of stone.

Speedwell's life
approaches my own,

as you rappel,
slinging echoes
of sense in space,
uprooting pullies
in green sky.

Vervain extinguishes its flowers
one by one,

as you arch sideways,
like hyphal frost
across simple lines,
to an altered vision
of living rock.

Campion has something
obvious to say.

Alison, Orpine, Avens
watch.

David J Morley

SCOTCHMAN'S STUMP

Fifteen hundred feet above the sea
Glinting in cloud-gaps thirty miles away
Beyond the Mersey Bar,
The pillar stands where he died.
A short stump of iron, holding
To his memory an inscribed plate:

William Henderson, traveller,
A native of Annan, Dumfriesshire,
Barbarously murdered
On Rivington Moor
At noonday in November
in eighteen hundred and thirty-eight.

On this ground where the clubs
Thudded down, and his head
Broke under crushed defending fingers,
He dropped to the tussocked grass.
Near him, pools of dark peat-water
Grew slow spirals of red.

This is where his life's track and the ambush
Locked, after whatever wheeling incomputable
Configurations clicked into place
And doomed him, wandering from Annan
Over this clouded hump. It is a suitable
Haunt for the violent. For storms, for men.

Now from the television mast,
From a thousand feet, the staywires
Drop, thick as thighs, and plunge
Into the ground, anchored,
Slabbed with concrete, deep
Under the embedded heather.

The mast drags eyes up its white leap
To the sky, away from his eight-foot
Iron pillar, black, dark as the landscape,
Jutting like a crude thorn. The rage
Of his killing is rooted yet,
In the earth's bulk and indifference.

He died, the inscription states,
In the twentieth year of his age.

John Cassidy

HEPTONSTALL

— old man
Of the hills, propped out for air
On his wet bench —
Lets his memories leak.

He no longer calls the time of day
Across to Stoodley, soured on that opposite ridge.
And Stoodley has turned his back
On the Museum silence.

He ignores Blackstone Edge —
A huddle of wet stones and damp smokes
Decrepit under sunsets.

He no longer asks
Whether Pecket under East Wind
Is still living.

He raises no hand
Towards Hathershelf. He knows
The day has passed
For reunion with ancestors.

He knows
Midgley will never return.

The mantel clock ticks in the lonely parlour
On the heights road, where the face
Blue with arthritic stasis
And heart good for nothing now
Lies deep in the chair-back, angled
From the window-skylines,
Letting time moan its amnesia
Through the telegraph wires.

As the fragments
Of the broken circle of the hills
Drift apart.

Ted Hughes

THE MOORS AT NIGHT

November moors are wonderful when day is dusky-eyed,
And winds are clean and eager as a strong man for his bride,
When there's fine sweet rain a-blowing down a gallant path
    we know —
A still path, a hill-path — the path to Ringinglow.
And we two took the moor-ways as the gloaming-lights
    crept out,
The moonless ways of Autumn with the hill-mist all about,
We strode through olden glamour to the Land of Heart's
    Desire,
The tragic land, the magic land — the land of Derbyshire.
There were miles of windy going, with your hair blown back
    like flame;
There were drifts of raptured music when the hill wind
    breathed your name,
Oh, the ancient dreams we startled on the ancient path
    we took,
The old way, the cold way — the way to Burbage Brook.
The little frightened stars crept out in leagues of lonely sky;
The naked trees and shadowy poles like ghosts went striding by;
The moaning wires were with us, and the great hills loomed
    ahead,
The blind hills, the kind hills — we followed where they led.
The shapeless stumbling walls lurched past, and crooked
    thorns wind-bent;
The young desires came crowding back in strange bewilderment;
All splendid dreams that ever were — Love set their flames
    astart;
The olden dreams, the golden dreams came running to my
    heart.
November moors were wonderful with star-dusk all around,
And mimic selves beneath our feet: star-shadows on the ground;
But the old days sang me forward with their lilting bells
    a-swing,
The long days, the strong days, the greening-days of Spring.
Spring broke across the autumn-moors, though with me as I
    strode
Were sleet and wind and starlight on the gallant open road.
My soul was faint with throstle songs and leagues of foaming
    may,
They thrilled the world, they filled the world — the Springs
    of Yesterday.

My autumn-moors were lit with youth. I dreamed we knew
    again
The grass-grown sides of Cavedale and the stream in Quiet
    Lane,
The Roman Road to Stanage and the cliffs of Monsal Dale,
The singing burns and springing ferns in lonely Cordwell Vale.
Oh! Autumn-moors are magical when day is dusky-eyed,
When misty hills are beckoning, and you are at my side.
But soon the celandines will dance, and all the birds will sing,
And Love will wake, and hearts will break when Winter flames
    to Spring!

E A Renshaw

ON HAWORTH MOOR

Coupled in silent mist and married habit.
we share the morning moor with sheep and grounded twite,
become a part of their seclusion, until a waking breeze
turns back the coverlet of cloud, and searching sun
dissolves the myth of solitude.

At Brontë Bridge we sit and watch a snake
of haversacks and walking boots go by; warmth livens
the mood of the moor and middle-aged men in running-strip
pant, like greyhounds, up a painful track,
chasing the fleet-foot hare of their youth.

Sheep and twite are startled by the sight of youths
with shouldered cycles, sprinting a snort of hill
to Within's Height; and now another snake, townsfolk smiling,
repeating a weekend's parole. There are more helloes
in the still of this moor than in a week of city streets.

Maurice Rutherford

NOTHING CHANGES

Nothing changes on this moor,
nothing.
Time remains forever, lost
like sheep wool,
suspended on the wire fences.
The wind moans today,
as always,
for the demise of yesterday,
then dies too,
leaving only the rustle
of a crinoline
to disturb the awesome silence.
Across a stream,
a flat stone, broken,
but not by Brontë feet.
A presence here,
glimpsed fleetingly,
a face of tears,
gazing parsonagewards,
seeing an old man in abject loneliness
preparing a sermon,
and crucifying himself over and over again
in pious exultation of a new life,
whilst the old,
like dust caught in a ray of sun,
drifts slowly down the steep
canyon of cobblestones
into immortality.

C L Riley

BARDEN FELL

Time took
all autumn and winter
coming up to April, to burnish this landscape.

You hear
only the blood in your veins
and a sigh from a long way away that goes further.

Many streams
sandal the foothills,
lace a light lodging for the day and the night.

Now shadows
peel off under
blue thumbs, spreading hands of sky.

I am purged
by the draining of floods,
and return my horizon gently to the necessary frame.

Jane Wilson

PENNINES IN APRIL

If this country were a sea (that is solid rock
Deeper than any sea) these hills heaving
Out of the east, mass behind mass, at this height
Hoisting heather and stones to the sky
Must burst upwards and topple into Lancashire.

Perhaps, as the earth turns, such ground-stresses
Do come rolling westward through the locked land.
Now, measuring the miles of silence
Your eye takes the strain: through

Landscapes gliding blue as water
Those barrellings of strength are heaving slowly and heave
To your feet and surf upwards
In a still, fiery air, hauling the imagination,
Carrying the larks upward.

Ted Hughes

WINTER, YORKSHIRE

Lime screes scar the slope,
The exoskeleton of the mountainside.
A north-east wind blows from the coal counties.

Come wind, channel the lead hills.
Come snow, whiten the mole-heaps,
Come grey goose, lunge over the villages,
Take the numb air in your long throat.
Come ice, rim the boulders,
Grip the ghyll by its one pulsing vein.
Come lichen, hoar the fences.

Cold water-veins, bowed mountain-shoulders,
Broken stone-heaps, give yourselves to the winter.

David Craig

LIMESTONE DAYS

take any facet of a day
add green immense mammalian hills
to mould an average archetype
of hackneyed landscape boulder strewn
to avatar of limestone lawns

then paint in vivid white a roll
of unrepeating clouds where in
the labyrinths of mind a sound
of silent skies in turquoise light
comes billowing in the grassy wind

take sun and stone and sound and sight
a smell of northern alps and streams
that generate a solitude
of caves a lacy underground
to conduit abrasive rain

see time expand exquisitely
when nothing urgent matters time
as moving shapes of stones and clouds
reflect the razored hay bleached fields
dissolving in the tenuous air

take clean carved rock a soft
and living marble dazed with heat
caressing rounded spiky grass
in praise to lords of loving air
for limestone's partnership with sky

Roy Brown

ON FAIRSNAPE, BLEASDALE
(Ascension Day)

Here on the hill together we are become
Suddenly more than men.
Clouds claim us and the bodiless wind
Blowing through holes in the wall;
Nothing is above us; over all
We stand like gods upon a storm-grey cairn.
Behind our backs dark woods and fells unfold
Through muted distances; a distant peak
Dwarfs all the rest, yet we remain as giants
Among the slow stone lumber of our summit.

But facing west, away and away the plain
Carries us down, across vague miles of grey
To where the last land slides into the sea.
Only the church below has anchorage —
A ship of stone riding the centuries
On a changing tide of leaves.

Phoebe Hesketh

ABOVE THE SNOWLINE, RIBBLESDALE

Rain on the quilted valley turns to sleet
a contour-line or two up from this cosy,
still green and undulating land, dealt out

as fields by man to man. I walk here, easy,
towards the mazy beck's tree-guarded source
in moss-upholstered grotto. This is lazy.

Above the valley a grey mountain rears
its desert, indistinct, half-lost in sky,
only defined by dotted lines, the layers

of jutting crags, spaced intermittently
in courses that break through the snow and prove
the peak still present as, imperiously,

it summons me from softness. I must leave
familiar sheltered crannies for the bleak
moor where lost sheep fend for themselves or starve.

The ineffectual sleet, to beat me back,
pecks at my face as, through the bristling sedge
and scurfy grass, I trudge along the track

to where the sleet turns gentle. At moor's edge
snow-flurries cease and wind abates. The peak
looms white as holy ghost or ermined judge.

Ravens command dead silence. I forsook
my waterloud oasis for this old
eroding stack of stones, to hear it speak:

silence is all I'm told.

Anna Adams

243

THREE PEAKS

I Ingleborough

Island in a sea of space. Some old God of time and air
clawed out the land, left this gigantic core, chiselled
grit steps out of the ripped edge which defy tides
of light that smash against the high, wild shore.

Hill fortress. The last Brigantes hung to that flat, bare waste —
the losers, the betrayed. Boulders were walls, huts to hold out
gales crueller than Roman sword, whilst they must wait, watch
and siege-long starve away. There was no other place.

It has endured. The far plains shiver with life
— this an austere, inescapable thought towering high
above all swirling, sullied drifts of comforting words.
Warriors, your cries still rise to that bleak and bitter sky.

II Pen y Ghent

Hill of the border, where the bare fells end
and surge up to this massy sphinx of black grit
that lies along the valley's horizon: head raised
to gaze, had it eyes, across the flattened land.

In mist an enigma; a cold force that will emerge,
loom like a shadow above streamlets' leak
or murk of thorn; the droplets coalesce, darkness,
a whisper, a shape that expands like a spreading bruise.

The face is raw, wet rock that frosts have shattered
and shaled. In cracks saxifrage push delicate flowers
above touch leaves, tiny, purple in bright April light
— tatters of royal, priestly gown that sparkle like blood.

III Whernside

A vast, upturned ark of rocks. Querns,
stones for mills were hewed here, bumped, rolling down
long slopes, crushing fingers, toes, grazing thighs
to lie in yards or revolve by slow streams.

Whaleback, tapering to a high narrow fin.
The blunt head has shallow tarns, pools in peat,
upstaring stagnant eyes. Cairns spike the nose
and walls criss cross the huge corpse like chains

Turned fossil. Yet green with moss and sparse grass.
The muscles have turned their vigour to grit;
thick hide is metamorphosed to pasture;
landlocked, it blends away in ageing rain.

Colin Speakman

GARSDALE AFTER DROUGHT

Purple cloud and double rainbows
Telescope the dale
Scatter the cars
Like metal petals.
Why do they want to go?
Is beauty only in a sunny view?
The fell's face feels the balmy freshness
Of the first rain for weeks.
Baked in the stifling valley,
Waiting for this storm
Where does it find the patience?
The farmer's learnt to wait
To take what nature brings.
He knows if you wait long enough
There will be a change.

Richard H French

WILD BOAR FELL

A curlew by the roadside makes me pause
And curiously I wait to watch it fly;
Four white fell-ponies nod up, swing away,
In crooked file they trek on up the moor,

Till horseless, birdless, I am left to see
How wall-decked Mallerstang lies deep in haze
With field and farmhouse backed by ash and elms
Burnt-brown as rushes in this April heat

Below; there once the Eden rose to moat
Round wrecked Pendragon, soon to be restored,
Though little less must be this valley since

de Morville restless one full Easter night
Sought out the rising blackness of Wild Boar
Found Becket's profile there and fled for France.

Michael Ffinch

WENSLEYDALE

Today all things compose
A magical incantation:
From change or death immune
The leopard in the hedge
Is dappled with the rose,
And just beyond Sight, Imagination
An eagle from the sun
Stoops from his golden ledge.

Bird, fish, animal,
The witness of the hills
Whose testament is mute,
The lissom river's length —
All the enchanting dale
Within the heart and mind distils
Its creatures form and fruit,
Its superhuman strength.

246

You can spread out a map
And say the Dale is spread;
The hill's a contour-line
And the river is a word:
As from the subtlest trap
You get at most the living dead,
A cold and empty skin
Or a stuffed singing bird.

Men to each other are
Maps read in curtained rooms,
And human intercourse
By conventional sign and scale
Can only go so far —
Until the sudden traveller comes
Who folds the map and goes
Into the magic dale.

There is the land that plays
Chameleon to the weather,
There curlew upon the scree
Or trout sleek in the pool
By natural synthesis
Fulfil the body and soul together
And life in every key
Is right and beautiful.

Compass and Map are gone
For Love must needs destroy
All things vicarious:
He has the measure of
The soul and the skeleton,
Yet his immeasurable joy
By flesh and blood is ours,
Is ours, is now, my love.

Patric Dickinson

ARKENGARTHDALE

The clouds have withered, lost their icy bloom;
Each frost-sharp fleece has slackened, spread and merged
Into a grudging grey. The inert world,
Its strength sapped, feels no silent stir of growth.
A few bewildered snowflakes drift about,
Scrapings from the sky. Yet down the Dales
A warmer time will come. The road from Reeth
Will summon up its strength and turn its back
Upon the huddling houses, thick with stone,
And make its way upwards into the moors
And into summer. Twisting first one way,
Then bending back upon its tracks again,
It hauls itself slowly up Galva's flank,
Where adders hide among the heather-tufts.
The road is stubborn like the moors themselves.
It curves, climbs, dips, then climbs again — one last
Heave, and it stops for breath. While down below
The whole dale, fresh with sunlight, lies spread out.

I've often made this journey, always felt
A growing wonder at the view. Sometime
No doubt, when summer hangs and sways above
The moors, I'll see it all again; and life,
Now muffled with the body's cares, will flow
Gurgling and rippling through my veins, just like
The winding beck that makes the whole dale fresh.

Rayne Mackinnon

DALES IN PARADISE

There must be dales in Paradise,
Where Wharfe and Aire and Swale
Fulfil their several destinies
And tell their various tale:
Flinging themselves just when they choose
Into the honest arms of Ouse!

There must be dales in Paradise
Which you and I will find
And walk together dalesmen-wise
And smile (since God is kind)
At all the foreign people there
Enchanted by our blessed air!

There must be dales in Paradise
With noble tops atween:
Swart fells uprearing to the skies
And stretching to the green —
And ower t'tops we two shall go,
Knee-deep in ling or broom or snow!

There must be dales in Paradise
Where nappy ale is sold,
And beef and pickles — even Pies
Such as we've known of old!
And we will find a parlour there
And call for pints for all to share!

A J Brown

A SALTING OF SNOW

The farmer said,
Just a salting of snow —
an odd way of putting it
for salt and snow we usually see
in the mess of busy streets.

But it was aptly right
with the fawn haunches of the Howgills
spread with the salt-snow
and nicely grilling in a winter sun
set at a low number.

We raised the dust of it
as we tramped white fells
the short day through.
Just a salting of snow,
but enough to flavour
the day so the ordinary
turned into a feast.

Hamish Brown

THE SNOW HORSE

The Easter traffic veered round to the fells
    and I hemmed-in behind a Highlands Tour
    expected soon to glimpse the Lune, but saw,
as if scarred out in chalk on Southern hills,

a giant horse with tail and winded mane
    turned by the melting snow. The flank and legs
    were drift-filled runnels sheer down from the crags,
for there the sculptor cut his surest line;

the sleek white head, I knew, was lightly held,
    to the hovering sun an easy prey.
Yet in that fleeting poise there seemed to rest

in charactery a peace that England lost;
    till passed, I sought attesting words to hold
what few more hours of sun must melt away.

Michael Ffinch

250

WALKING DOWNHILL, HIGH CUP NICK

After the breathless climb
    and all that exertion of will
to contract the aching muscles, time after time,
    and carry ourselves uphill,

the body goes on its own
    on the downward path. Sure feet
find out their way over rocky ground, unshown
    by any conscious thought.

The skeleton's stack of bones
    adjusts its effortless balance
to variations of incline, and sliding stones.
    Gravity leads this dance

down from the windswept top
    where waterfall spray flew up
in the blast of air from the hillside's hollow cup
    that serves as a wind-trap,

so streams performed handsprings
    on the limestone sill's high edge;
stood on their heads, did acrobatic things
    on each succeeding ledge.

Drenched through, we could not stand
    for long to see blue hills
and, far below, the ravelled tinsel strand
    of levelled waterfalls,

but recklessly, down the track,
    bear height's exhilaration
and knowledge that it's hard work to climb back
    to that exalted station.

Anna Adams

CROSS FELL

This enhancing view:
The ever changing atmosphere of cloud and storm,
Of shafts of sun on distant peaks,
Or glimmering on some strip of shore;
The golden lake and radiant strand;
All these, and more,
Are offered at your door,
Should tents be pitched the night on Cross Fell's summit.
And if the wind restrains from veering to a Helm,
You *might* observe the dawn!

Kenneth Oldham

I DREAMT LAST NIGHT

I dreamt last night of England and the rain,
grey clouds across the Yorkshire hills, and mist
haunting the moors, curled low in every grain;
close huddled sheep keeping bedraggled tryst

behind a broken wall; smell of wet heather;
music of rushing streams; beat of the wind;
one solitary shepherd ... 'Mucky weather!' ...
'Aye, dampish, ... an' ah've three young lambs ti find.'

Bill Cowley

THIXENDALE

I went alone there once and in rare moments recalled
how five lanes, some single-tracked with passing-places
(like Scottish roads), reached it by creating calm
between chalk screes grass speckled green on white.
Empty fields edged quarries where nothing needed to
    happen.

I could not revisit a quietness too near
for shared adventure. We dared to crave cragged peaks,

lakes, gorges, rapacious torrents, to struggle through passes
and glimpse
beyond cols blue southern seas, or to sweat across plains
peopled grey with cities, purpled with arteries
directing traffic over involved intersections
to streak red, white, day, night towards convoluted junctions.

Now I have been there again I shall remember
always the truth of tranquillity's colour.

Rainwater sinking through chalk makes unexpected springs,
dry valleys, elsewhere suddenly full streams,
ponds that surprise with their identity.

Through my mind this memory percolates.

A place I can never dwell in, no house is mine,
no rooted association demands. I know
merely what I remember and what that does
to me who live on windblown alluvium, journey
over impermeable rock, archaean,
volcanic or hard conglomerate.

Brian Merrikin Hill

LOCKWOOD GILL

Pearl-blue water below, bright between winter pines;
stream pouring suddenly over black rocks — wild jumble
of great stones tossed down by eroding centuries
that lumber past slowly like the heron
there over the bracken howes where the gill narrows.

Above, the sea-roke sweeps across smooth swithened ling
obliterating far horizons of time; on the high moor
a Bronze Age stone stands brooding
carved into runic channels
by the knife of the North-east wind.

Bill Cowley

STORM LONGING

Come, friends of my heart, to the hills we'll fly,
  Where the high winds never rest,
But storm and cry on the Riggs that lie
  To the eastward crest on crest;
Where rain and sleet in tempest beat
  Round many an ancient Cross,
From Crookstaff Hill to Wheeldale Gill,
  From Bloworth to Yarlsey Moss.
When the sea-roke spread on Botton Head
  Rolls down to the dale beneath,
And our way we thread with careful tread
  Through the gloom of the trackless heath;
When the sea-wind snarls from Stony Marls
  And the sky's a leaden cloud
That hides the brow of Shunner Howe
  Like a Norseman's funeral shroud.
But what reck we of roke or storm
  Or the furies overhead?
A song we'll sing as on we swing
  With sure and steady tread.
Though boggets growl and ratchets howl
  As we tramp on side by side,
Through the night that's black with storm and wrack
  Our steps the gods shall guide.

Bill Cowley

THE SCOTCH ROAD

Sheep, wiser than the Romans —
Not straight between two points
Follow the slope round and across —
Contour to the col.

Drovers too would use this track
Humping sacks of wool,
Or cursing cattle up the fell
And over into Scotland.

Soon Windscarth Wyke and White Fell Head
Are blown around by snow
And Arant Haw and Bruntscar Syke
Dance under white cloaks too.

But in the hills, the story's there
(No history book can tell so well)
By Standing Stone and track and gill
By names on maps they tell the tale.

Yet we have left the hills
To follow easy roads.
Will man come back
To walk the tracks of long ago?

Richard H French

TO MY MOUNTAIN

Since I must love your north
of darkness, cold, and pain,
the snow, the lonely glen,
let me love true worth,

the strength of the hard rock,
the deafening stream of wind
that carries sense away
swifter than flowing blood.

Heather is harsh to tears
and the rough moors
give the buried face no peace
but make me rise,

and oh, the sweet scent, and purple skies!

Kathleen Raine

OCTOBER IN EDEN, NORTHUMBERLAND

Above Eden I stood
transfixed
as summer nudged from sleep
encroaching autumn's lease
with one, brief, laughing day

that ran careless
of the winter-waiting hills.

The constricted trace
of human racing stilled
cushioned, soft, on bracken;
and my heart was a small
bird singing
high in the bordering blue

unafraid that a single
feather's tip could touch eternity.

Free, fast-falling space
tumbled through light and air
past crag and heath
to spread in a gesture of green
across the valley; but a sense
of ghosts troubled the earth

and there were tears
tasting of apples on my tongue.

Innocent was the flower crushed
underfoot as at last the day
turned to look at the hills
waiting — a grim night and
a burning moon — beyond Eden.

Brenda Whincup

A WALK ALONG THE WALL

A rattle of snow; an iron lane;
Looking for shelter from the wind,
I thought the spinney would just do.
Its thick-laced branches were of yew
Rooted upon a tump or mound
Like a mole that grows on skin.
And when I climbed that little hill
I found no spinney, but a pool,
A weedy circle of blank water
Where a fish, a somersaulter,
Leapt once, to make silence still.

A rustic boathouse flaked a stale
Reflection; the ragged yews
Stood on their caked bed of shed leaves
To deaden the forgotten pond
And encroach, a dark surround,
What a secure abundance made
Its one-time pleasance, with cold shade.

To this new trophy of decline
I preferred the colder wind,
So turned away, to mount the chine
That runs across Northumberland;
Picked up, while snow and sunlight fell,
The stretched arm of the Roman wall,
Where like steel bobbins, shiningly,
Vehicular metal shuttles by,
Sealed, encapsulated from
That moorland and skylit loom.

Where the wall was, is the road;
Still you may see on either side
Ditch and vallum, each a wound
Living on the living ground.
There the vallum, wide and hollow,
Is windbreak for lamb and ewe;
Which by farmstead, wood, and field,
I followed to Heavenfield.

Here a votive altar is
A half-forgotten saint's cross-base,
Whose pilgrim chapel, on the scarp,
Looks across the ruined north
From a long obliterate
Celt and English battle-place
Where, come a millenium, Wade
Drove through his military road.

But a coeval's left his mark
In the bus-stop by Brunton park;
A freestone box, which yet like a
Vallum, cross, or votive altar
Is memorial to long bygone.
The Victorian fishpond
Came to memory as I read
The *In Memoriam* overhead.
Rank, a name, regiment, then
      1940
   France Belgium
    1941-43
  Egypt Libya Italy
   ... Killed Nijmegen.

David Wright

THE ROMAN WALL

Though moss and lichen crawl
   These square-set stones still keep their serried ranks
Guarding the ancient wall,
   That whitlow-grass with lively silver pranks.

Time they could not keep back
   More than the wind that from the snow-streaked north
Taking the air for track
   Flows lightly over to the south shires forth.

Each stone might be a cist
   Where memory sleeps in dust and nothing tells
More than the silent mist
   That smokes along the heather-blackened fells.

Twitching its ears as pink
  As blushing scallops loved by Romans once
A lamb leaps to its drink
  And, as the quavering cry breaks on the stones,

Time like a leaf down-drops
  And pacing by the stars and thorn-trees' sough
A Roman sentry stops
  And hears the water lapping on Crag Lough.

Andrew Young

THE JOURNEY

As I went over fossil hill
I gathered up small jointed stones,
And I remembered the archaic sea
Where once these pebbles were my bones.

As I walked on the Roman wall
The wind blew southward from the pole.
Oh I have been that violence hurled
Against the ramparts of the world.

At nightfall in an empty kirk
I felt the fear of all my deaths:
Shapes I had seen with animal eyes
Crowded the dark with mysteries.

I stood beside a tumbling beck
Where thistles grew upon a mound
That many a day had been my home,
Where now my heart rots in the ground.

I was the trout that haunts the pool,
The shadowy presence of the stream.
Of many many lives I leave
The scattered bone and broken wing.

I was the dying animal
Whose cold eye closes on a jagged thorn,
Whose carcass soon is choked with moss,
Whose skull is hidden by the fern.

My footprints sink in shifting sand
And barley-fields have drunk my blood,
My wisdom traced the spiral of a shell,
My labour raised a cairn upon a fell.

Far I have come and far must go,
In many a grave my sorrow lies,
But always from dead fingers grow
Flowers that I bless with living eyes.

Kathleen Raine

KIELDER

North of the Wall is a countryside of clean, bare hills,
Gleaned smooth by ice sheets of another age;
Over Kimmins Cross and on through Willow Bog,
And onto Sadbury Hill,
And here a cloudscape
Reminding you that the clouds and the weather
Are as much a part of the Pennine Way
As the hills, themselves.

Behind us now, the loughs and Wall,
In front is the ever changing scene:
The clean sweeping hills are here replaced
By the verdant cloak of heavy green.
Expanding forests of the spruce
Have overwhelmed this smooth landscape
With towering spires, a living screen,
With broad, straight gaps, the firebreaks, in between.

Thus we pass through the span of forests
And out again to the windswept moor
With fawns and browns of wiry grasses
Replacing the forest's needled floor.
Behind us now lie the whole of the Pennines,
Though a few reared heads mark Lakeland still,
But the north sweeping landscape now acclaims
The burnished flame of the Cheviot Hill.

Kenneth Oldham

SILENT CHEVIOT

I did not know that what I sought
   Was silence, quality elusive,
So that a sheepdog barking brought
   No sound that might have seemed intrusive.

In Bizzel Burn that winter's day,
   A quiet, not a silent place
Up which I made my breathy way,
   There were a score of sounds to trace:

The distant barking far below
   In Dunsdale's fold still struck the air
To counterpoint the rattling flow
   Of Bizzel down its rocky stair.

The soaring breeze came whispering
   Across the crags, it stroked the grass,
Among the blades went scurrying
   And through the heather made its pass.

Across the peaty cloughs I strode
   Where mist no distance would allow,
Where bog creaked softly under load
   — A frozen Marne on Cheviot's brow.

An eastward path from summit holding,
   Arm in arm I walked the breeze,
The mist around us both enfolding
   In a dreamy sort of peace.

Then what I sought at last was found,
   This wilderness no hostile plain,
Where for a moment all around
   Was silence in its perfect reign.

Tom Rix

HELL-GATE MOOR: AN ODE

Beyond the flowering valley and the green
Of tossing lawns, high-couching 'neath the sheen
Of infinite blue heavens, sleeps Hell's moor,

Like some Prometheus form, whose lineaments
The Northern goddess throned in Asgard bore,
But dreamed her spirit's fairness reared in stone,
And hurled her from the storm-surged battlements.

Above her the winds wrestle, and the roar
Of hurricanes rolls planetwards; but ever
She, dreaming, broods, -- shunning Earth's radiant vales.

Hers is a sullen splendour; it doth sever
Her from those green still places where there fails
No grain of plenty heaped for harvesting,
Where life moves lightly as the Ages fly.

Above her soars the music of the sky;
But under her — all meaner things that sing
Of joy and human hope she deemeth vain.
Barren her womb in Spring, and grey with pain
Her face when the green fields flower and bloom.
But, Summer mellowing, she puts on rich robes,
Gold and gemmed purple, glorying in the doom
Of the season's fairness — bright festivities;
Because she deems with cold foreseeing gaze
(Her leaning forehead sunned by Heaven's pure rays)
That the swift weaver falters at his loom,
And Life, the evanescent, flames and dies.

Unto her banquet come bright butterflies,
The mottled grouse, and moths with straining eyes,
And the red fox with leisured gait of gloom;
And will-o'-the-wisps and glowworms light their globes,
The brown elves dance upon the mushroom lobes;
From morn to eve bees hum and snatch the bloom
From the frail heath bells; a harp's wild music knells
Out of the dark woods, down the cavernous dells
Where sweeps the silver of the splashing stream.

And how her flowing contours softly gleam
In Winter when the vales are sodden brown!
She binds her thews with white, Death's triumph gown,
Rejoicing in Earth's naked dark distress,
Her hoar flanks sparkling with loveliness,
Wedded unto the snows and tempests rude,
The frosts and whitenesses of solitude.

Anon she veils her face in cloud and mist,
Kissed unseen by her lover, the vast sky; —
Her grey cheek pressed against the stars, that list
The tremors of that mute immensity,
Whence steal sad twilight sounds, and a song that hovers
About the ears of hearkening minstrelsy.

But what of her scorn of human lovers! —
What of the lure she casts about the feet
Of him who drew the pure maid to her doom
And in the deep glen's night-enfolden gloom
Gave the sad babe its birth, and mocked the sweet
Wild pleadings of impenitent distress,
And changed the mother to a murderess.

The cataract hurtling from the crag, sheer riven,
Washes the dull grey slab that binds to earth
The perishing white limbs of that frail birth.
And the fierce moor stares pitilessly to heaven.

And yet joy's mystery to her is given.
She soars remote 'mid star-hung silences,
Grey vastnesses that round about her cling,
Rock-hewn repose and granite fastnesses,
The blue of dusks burnished with sunset's wing.
And when the Day her beauty doth uncover
Her ways seem kindly to the wandering lover.

Herbert E Palmer

Waymarks of the Elemental

LEA MacNALLY

CLOUDED HILLS

Though you can't see them,
You know that they are there.

Beneath the Herdwick fleece of mist,
You can feel the heave of the hill.

You can sense the tremor of old volcanoes,
Tense with damped-down fire.

Under a white meringue of cumulus,
Or behind the grey rain-break of a winter's day,

You are aware of the pikes straining high above you,
Spiking up to an unseen sky.

Norman Nicholson

DROWNING AMONG MOUNTAINS

Now even the hills are lost to view.
Where yesterday they rose before us, waves
of chiming granite, blood-carnelian, glitter
of a sea of mica lights,
today a colourless mist sequesters all that radiance.

This is a mist we know too well.
Its acid on the tongue, its wicked droplets
gathered in the hair, the lashes of the eyes. How
voices swim from us and drown, and how
its bitter moisture soaks through to the bone.

Slowly and heavily,
in air that seeps between our actions and our thoughts
we clamber through the dripping valleys

whilst somewhere above our heads the summits flash
and call to one another, jewelled and invisible.

Ian Abbot

from SNOWDON

Below this layer of cloud there lies
a dull grey world which cannot see the skies
but perched on top of this lofty ridge
I feel like a Sea Captain on the bridge
My vessel laying becalmed in a fluffy sea
of white cloud and distant visibility.

David Levey

CLOUD

Warm me — I'm colder than the sea,
take me down to the trees — I'm higher than the
    highest cairn,
cover me with summer stones -- I'm damp as moss,
carry me in your lungs, in the clap of your frozen
    hands,
drink me, see me before The Sun.

I'm all gods: a reality!
My form holds all faces and imaginings,
I use sleep and death in my images,
hunch over hills, let slopes brown
with heather and men climb into sudden light.
Breath on a brooch and know my shadow.

Jerry Orpwood

DRIFTING

I watch them,
The rain-clouds drifting from the sea,
Imperceptibly moving nearer,
Shrouding the landscape.

Sometimes I stand in their predestined path,
Here in this fertile valley,
Feel their liquid fall
Upon my upturned face;
Sometimes they pass me by,
And silent, shift along the hills
Like drawn veils dimming women's faces,
Softening the bone-clung loveliness,
The structured elegance;
Shading the harvest's brazen make-up,
Adding allure,
Heightening the mystery.

Margaret Gillies

A SOFT DAY

A soft day, thank God!
A wind from the south
With a honeyed mouth;
A scent of drenching leaves,
Briar and beech and lime,
White elder-flower and thyme
And the soaking grass smells sweet,
Crushed by my two bare feet,
While the rain drips,
Drips, drips, drips from the eaves.

A soft day, thank God!
The hills wear a shroud
Of silver cloud;
The web the spider weaves
Is a glittering net;
The woodland path is wet,
And the soaking earth smells sweet
Under my two bare feet,
And the rain drips,
Drips, drips, drips from the leaves.

Winifred M Letts

RAIN ON DRY GROUND

That is rain on dry ground. We heard it:
We saw the little tempest in the grass,
The panic of anticipation: heard
The uneasy leaves flutter, the air pass
In a wave, the fluster of the vegetation;

Heard the first spatter of drops, the outriders
Larruping on the road, hitting against
The gate of the drought, and shattering
On to the lances of the tottering meadow.
It is rain; it is rain on dry ground.

Rain riding suddenly out of the air,
Battering the bare walls of the sun.
It is falling on to the tongue of the blackbird,
Into the heart of the thrush; the dazed valley
Sings it down. Rain, rain on dry ground!

This is the urgent decision of the day,
The urgent drubbing of earth, the urgent raid
On the dust; downpour over the flaring poppy,
Deluge on the face of noon, the flagellant
Rain drenching across the air. — The day

Flows in the ditch; bubble and twisting twig
And the sodden morning swirl along together
Under the crying hedge. And where the sun
Ran on the scythes, the rain runs down
The obliterated field, the blunted crop.

    The rain stops.
    The air is sprung with green.
    The intercepted drops
    Fall at their leisure; and between
    The threading runnels on the slopes
    The snail drags his caution into the sun.

Christopher Fry

GREAT MOUNTAINS LOVE GREAT STORMS

Great mountains love great storms,
 and lesser hills long rain.
They reach their arms in riotous ridge forms
to hail cloud-comrades from the drenching plain:
their gorges drain the upward rush of thunder;
 their torrents, speeding under,
pour back the lees to breed cloud-riot again.

Great mountains hold harsh truth,
 and lesser heights long trust.
The warring crests make comrades of our youth,
burnish our manhood, rasp our spirit-rust:
kind hills bend for our age a gentler shoulder;
 staying our hearts, grown older,
with hope new-fashioned from our faltering dust.

Geoffrey Winthrop Young

WIND ON THE FACE

I battled against the wind today
 In a lonely, moorland place;
Angrily over the hills it drave
 Arrows of rain into my face --
Like a scourge of grace.

A J Brown

WIND IN THE DUSK

The wind feels hard enough tonight
To crack the stars, and bring them down;
The wildly waving trees are bright
With spindrift from the driving moon.

All round the mountain peaks are curled
Thin wispy trails of foaming cloud.
The wind is hooting at the world,
Or hissing like an angry crowd.

I think I saw a little star
Entangled in a knotty tree,
As trembling fishes often are
In nets that drag them from the sea.

The winding tempest lifts and dips
Between the earth and sparkling skies:
It catches on my hair and lips:
It splashes in my hair and eyes.

Round, down and up the whirlwinds roar;
Each roughly to the other cries ...
Wind, overturn the goblet, pour
On me the everlasting skies!

Harold Monro

WIND

Windy, he shouts,
as if it weren't always
in these hungry uplands:
wind
combing the bent
finding the crack in the wall
the hole in the coat:
wind
blowing out the flame in the heart
and the hill men
to the far world's end.

Bob Harris

WIND

This house has been far out at sea all night,
The woods crashing through darkness, the booming hills,
Winds stampeding the fields under the window
Floundering black astride and blinding wet

Till day rose; then under an orange sky
The hills had new places, and wind wielded
Blade-like, luminous black and emerald,
Flexing like the lens of a mad eye.

At noon I scaled along the house-side as far as
The coal-house door. I dared once to look up —
Through the brunt wind that dented the balls of my eyes
The tent of the hills drummed and strained its guyrope,

The fields quivering, the skyline a grimace,
At any second to bang and vanish with a flap:
The wind flung a magpie away and a black-
Back gull bent like an iron bar slowly. The house

Rang like some fine green goblet in the note
That any second would shatter it. Now deep
In chairs, in front of the great fire, we grip
Our hearts and cannot entertain book, thought,

Or each other. We watch the fire blazing,
And feel the roots of the house move, but sit on,
Seeing the window tremble to come in,
Hearing the stones cry out under the horizons.

Ted Hughes

THE BIG WIND

The big wind trundled our pail, a
                    clanging bell
Through the four crofts,
Broke the clean circles of wave and
                    gull,
Laid the high hay in drifts,
Beat down the stones of the dead,
Drove the *Beagle* aground,
Whirled up Merran's petticoats round
                    her head,
And set three hen-houses (cockerels raging aloft)
                    on the crested Sound.

The kestrel stood unmoving over the hill.

George Mackay Brown

THE WIND

What does the wind say on the hill
When yellow comes the daffodil
And the willow wren begins
His little song among the whins.

What does the wind say on the ben
When the roses bloom again
And in the grey ark of the gloaming
Woodcocks croak and doves are homing.

What does the wind say on the tops
When hairy forearms stook the crops
And when red the sunsets die
And skeins of wild geese cross the sky.

What does the wind say on the height
When close and rigg and park are white
When middens smoke within the yard
And tractor ruts are iron hard.

Syd Scroggie

BLIZZARD

'What is it like up here in snow?'
we wondered, shivering at dusk
on the boggy plateau. Answerless,
we stared along the ruts
of an obscure track. There was
the hint of a wind. Our thoughts
momentarily touched a sleeping fear.

That fear has woken up tonight
with a white scream. Even the valley
suffer's the storm's answer
that we so lightly sought —
the truth from the heights
come shrieking down in darkness
to batter at our safety.

In the morning, when the wind drops,
we will climb again, perhaps,
and in the high white silence find
another answer growing from the first.
Because that was, this is — sun, sun and snow,
and all tracks gone but those
our seeking footsteps make upon the hill.

Ruth Bidgood

AT THE LAKE'S END

At the lake's end,
at the meeting of the waters,
at the gathering of the small streams' tithes,
what unimaginable power and swiftness
hurls, wrestles and tears the white river,
which here does not sing as on the hillside,
but roars and rages its way down
cursing under the doublearched bridge and over
precipitous leaps and downcut pebbled bed.

Water the softest element after air,
has sculptured fantastic forms
out of the strewn boulders, frost fractured long since
and brought life down like landlocked meteors
in winter rages past, till now
all rough and rawedged fragments are smoothed.

Water and the pull of the earth's far centre
have played the artist, moulded these
fantasies in stone, gothic and barbarous,
but water the artist has so many lifetimes!

Frederic Vanson

MOUNTAIN BURN IN WINTER

Often I've rested by this lonely stream
   And listened, with the sun-drenched hills around,
Until its whisper lulled me to a dream,
   Its quiet singing there the only sound.

Urged ever by the distant valley's call
   It seemed upon its journey to rejoice;
Ripple and rapid, tiny linn and fall
   Joined in the song with individual voice.

Now ice has laid its spell on song and speed,
   Wavelet and fall and eddy prisoned fast,
Music made captive waiting to be freed,
   When spring comes laughing to the hills at last!

W K Holmes

THE DOOR

Wildhilled, kestrelcharted,
the clear fallwater
follows a lonely threadvalley.

Leaden skies sponge this earth
cold in its waiting.
The slate door stands alone.

David Goddard

MOUNTAIN BURN

I am the mountain burn. I go
Where only hill-folk know;
Pitter-patter, splash and spatter,
Goblin laughter, elfin chatter!
I am a chain of silver under the moon;
A spell that breaks too soon;
Lost voices chuckling across the peat,
Or faery feet
Echoing where the dancing harebells blow.

The silent places know me. Trees,
Stately and cool,
Gaze at their green reflections where I flow
Into some shadowy pool.
I am a ribbon of light,
A flash of blinding-white
Foam where the pale sun lingers
Over the heathery waste.
And still my long green fingers
Probe with a surgeon's skill the perilous grey
Slopes of the ferny gorge, to carve away
Granite and stone and bleached bone
To suit my changeling taste.
I am brilliant as the stars, and timeless;
Sad as the Earth, and strong
As mortal love. And through the long
Enchanted hours of sun and showers
I charm the hills with endless, rhymeless
Cadences of song.

And the dry reeds and rushes
Tremble and sigh,
Quiver and shake,
When the night-wind hushes
With lullaby
The dreams that die, the hearts that break —
And only I am left awake . . .

Brenda G Macrow

THE WHITE CASCADE

What happy mortal sees that mountain now,
The white cascade that's shining on its brow;

The white cascade that's both a bird and star,
That has a ten mile voice and shines as far?

Though I may never leave this land again,
Yet every spring my mind must cross the main

To hear and see that water-bird and star
That on the mountain sings, and shines so far.

W H Davies

THE STREAM'S SONG

Make way, make way,
You thwarting stones;
Room for my play,
Serious ones.

Do you fear,
O rocks and boulders,
To feel my laughter
On your grave shoulders?

Do you not know
My joy at length
Will all wear out
Your solemn strength?

You will not for ever
Cumber my play;
With joy and a song
I clear my way.

Your faith of rock
Shall yield to me,
And be carried away
By the song of my glee.

Crumble, crumble,
Voiceless things;
No faith can last
That never sings.

For the last hour
To joy belongs;
The steadfast perish,
But not the songs.

Yet for a while
Thwart me, O boulders.
I need for laughter
Your serious shoulders.

And when my singing
Has razed you quite,
I shall have lost
Half my delight.

Lascelles Abercrombie

BECK

Not the beck only,
Not just the water
The stones flow also,
Slow
As continental drift,
As the growth of coral,
As the climb
Of a stalagmite.
Motionless to the eye,
Wide cataracts of rock
Pour off the fellside,
Throw up a spume
Of gravel and scree
To eddy and sink
In the blink of a lifetime.
The water abrades,
Erodes; dissolves
Limestones and chlorides;
Organizes its haulage --
Every drop loaded
With a millionth of a milligramme of fell.
The falling water
Hangs steady as stone;
But the solid rock
Is a whirlpool of commotion,
As the fluid strata
Crest the curl of time,
And top-heavy boulders
Tip over headlong,
An inch in a thousand years.
A Niagara of chock-stones,
Bucketing from the crags,
Spouts down the gullies.
Slates and sandstone
Flake and deliquesce,
And in a grey
Alluvial sweat
Ingleborough and Helvellyn
Waste daily away.
The pith of the pikes
Oozes to the marshes,
Slides along the sykes,

Trickles through ditch and dub,
Enters the endless
Chain of water,
The pull of earth's centre —
An irresistible momentum,
Never to be reversed,
Never to be halted,
Till the tallest fell
Runs level with the lowland,
And scree lies flat as shingle,
And every valley is exalted,
Every mountain and hill
Flows slow.

Norman Nicholson

WATERFALLS

Always in that valley in Wales I hear the noise
  Of waters falling.
          There is a clump of trees
    We climbed for nuts; and high in the trees the boys
     Lost in the rookery's cries
      Would cross, and branches cracking under their knees

Would break, and make in the winter wood new gaps.
  The leafmould covering the ground was almost black,
    But speckled and striped were the nuts we threw in our caps,
     Milked from split shells and cups,
      Secret as chestnuts when they are tipped from a sack,

Glossy and new.
          Always in that valley in Wales
I hear that sound, those voices. They keep fresh
  What ripens, falls, drops into darkness, fails,
    Gone when dawn shines on scales,
     And glides from village memory, slips through the mesh,

And is not, when we come again.
                    I look:
Voices are under the bridge, and that voice calls,
  Now late, and answers;
                        then, as the light twigs break
    Back, there is only the brook
      Reminding the stones where, under a breath, it falls.

Vernon Watkins

WORDSWORTH

The barren mountains were his theme,
Nature the force that made him strong.
This day died one who, like a stone,
Altered the course of English song.

A hundred years! The waters still
Murmur the truth he bent to glean
Where bird and sunset, copse and hill
Composed the grave, harmonious scene.

The humble and unknown became
His oracles. Infirm old age
Matching obscurity to fame
Taught, like a child, the listening sage.

About his melancholy mind
Thundered the waterfalls. How few
Have left on water, light and wind
So calm a print of all he knew.

How cold the waters, yet how clear:
How grave the voice, how fine the thread
That quickening the returning year
Restores his landscape and his dead!

Vernon Watkins

MOUNTAIN POOL

Sunshine spills over
the highest ridge,
falls full face
on this transparent sheet
of water that lies
on a bed of white gravel
cold as the snow it once was.

Where the crystal drops
feed the pool, bubbles
become observatory domes
catching reflections
of space and cloud
with the black earthly
boundaries of soft peat
for their horizons.

Some water beetles glide
across the pool
on floats of mountain air
and cast four-leafed-clover
shadows on the gravel bed,
for they are the harbingers
of spring in this fortunate
and calm terrain.

Charles Senior

SILENCE

Mist creeps over the moor,
Drifting slow;
Hiding behind its curtained door
The world I know.

No sound of beast or bird,
No wind to shake the leaf,
No pulse, no heartbeat stirred,
No joy, no grief.

Time waits on the edge of the hill,
Stopped; caught in a little death.
The formless, vapid world hangs still,
Holding its breath.

Mist, like a winding sheet,
Wraps moor and fen.
Far off I hear a new lamb bleat.
Time starts again.

Nora Halstead

I HAVE LEARNT

I have learnt to be still
when the mist changes course
and the way is lost in silence
of the mountain cold.
I listen, and look, small as a dust speck
on huge loneliness of the chapel floor,
until the sun puts a finger through blurred windows
around all the prayers.

Beautiful that gleam of light
when the mist moves,
and one step forward I can see
before I must hold still again,
and wait.

Odette Tchernine

THE MOORS

Here nature is barely sketched out
    All is a threadbare mat of grass,
    Brutal rock, the dark-wet gash
    Of peat, the call of peewit and lark's far shout —
A place where under thin stretched sky
A man may walk and wonder how he'll die.

    Here where the savaged or mis-born
    Lamb rots by a shedding burn
    Or the wild crow dies in the sun
Is the graveyard of aestheticism.
Moors are not for the squeamish or lonely
They are the playground of the solitary.

    Theirs is a proud drabness of flint and stone
    Where grass is tough as wire
    And the winded rocks ache like old bones.
Deserted they do not invite much growth:
Man and history would pass them by the while;
Yet in legend and question they're strangely fertile.

William Oxley

MOORS THRENODY

No living creature moves, only the skies'
Slow turbulence, the slanting rain that shakes
In sudden gusts and flurries as it rakes
The stubborn grass; no sound except the sighs
Of wind and ceaseless hissing of the rain;
No colour, only varied tones of grey
Against the slate the lowering skies display;
The weather and the landscape speak a pain
That we, not they, must for a while sustain
Until this season break and see, alone,
Close in the foreground the single hunk of stone,
Bleak cenotaph, and one which bears no name.

Vernon Scannell

285

THE SIGNPOST

It's high above a blue, dark lake,
   With a far, far view of the sea,
It's nothing much . . . just a rotten stake,
   The trunk of an old, dead tree;
It boasts no more than a single sign,
   And weather has washed that clean,
   . . . A smudge of paint, the ghost of a line,
   There's all of the name that's been.
It stands alone on a mountain top
   On a heather and bracken heath.
Above there's naught where the mountains stop,
   . . . Blue sky and blue lake beneath.
It's watched the wild moor fifty year,
   And many a sun's gone down,
And some went bright, and some went drear,
   And some with a golden crown;
It's seen grey dawn, and it's seen black night,
   Parched heat and wizening cold,
It's seen cloud-shadows chasing the light,
   And sheep driven into the fold,
Travellers a few, and dogs and men,
   Or a fox in the still white snow.
It's heard the east wind scouring the glen
   And the north wind whistling low.
It's known dull thunder rumble away,
   Lightning break over the plain,
White moons in the night, a sun by day,
   Or the long grey wash of the rain;
And many a shadow's lengthened out,
   And the crops came rich or poor,
For it's fifty year or there about
   The signpost's stood on the moor.

H J P Sturton

ABOVE LLYN OGWEN

High over the subdued colours of Caernarvonshire
From heights which leave the farm
Like a child's toy, complete with scattered sheep
The size of a comma,
This holly, sculptured by the abrasive winds
Leans away from the west, its leaves
Green as Christmas.
Its roots grope beneath the crevices
Of a great boulder, whose cleavage
Gave opportunity for its rooting here,
Where small trees are rare as snowdrops in July
And stunted bushes are a mile apart.

Behind it the massive stone is split asunder
As if by a giant axeblow, yet no steel
Shattered this rock, only water seeping, seeping,
Deep into crack and hairline, finding
Each hidden capillary, till on some bitter midnight
It froze into a micaed ice and burst
These tons of rock apart like a muffled bomb.

These gentle, harmless-seeming things,
The seeking water and the rooting seed
Have power to shatter and cleave
Where lightnings fail and tempests howl in vain.

Frederic Vanson

ROOTS

Hard rocks that quarrymen must blast apart,
fine stone for houses,
slate for roof and path,
yield
suddenly to the chisel,
suddenly
yield to the hammer-blow
with sharpness,
noise.

But
unperceived
they take their shapes
slowly from work of water,
wind's swish.
By the slow
and silent pulsing of the seed's
insistent root
the invaded cleft of rock
is finally
riven.

Frances Marshall

ROCK

I am rock.
I waited for a million years in hot darkness
Before the roaring ice gouged and ripped me into the light.
I lay for a million years, warmed by the sun, washed by the rain
And polished by the frost.
One cold crisp morning I was picked up by a spinner from
    Colne.
He placed me on the cairn at the summit of Wetherlam.
He sat there for a long time, eating his bacon sandwiches
Gazing at the grey, green, gold, blue shining hills,
The stony, smooth, spiky, rounded, blue shining hills,
Then he went away and was killed with hundreds of other
    white,
Black, brown, and yellow men,
Shivering, stinking, and crying,
For the possession of a tennis-court at Kohima.
I was kicked and scattered by a vandal from Bootle
Who came up with the Warden and a party
For the improvement of their character
But he was blind to the grey, green, gold, blue shining hills
And heard only the obscenities nudging and cackling in his
    skull
And his sickness and loneliness spasmed and jerked into his
    boots.
I was picked up by a fitter from Leigh, who went to
Night-school for lapidary.

I spent a year in a big wooden box,
With agates from Botswana, crystals from Idwal,
And conglomerates from Savoy.
But the fitter's wife left him
(She was tired of his snoring, his sweaty feet, and the
Eternal trundling of his polisher under her bed) and she
Emptied the big wooden box into the canal.
It is foul and dark here, beneath two centuries of man's slime,
Amongst rotting cats, and cans, and condoms, far from the
    blue shining hills.
But I am rock
And I can wait a million years.

Tom Bowker

ROCK

Sing of the rock once molten,
Now in silence.
Grass grows not, nor tree,
But rock
      Lives ...

      Slowly ...
Slowly the granite mass
Thinks down year-avenues
Knowing
      slowly
           the centuries
Seeing the years as seconds, —
          sands —

      Their poetry
      The poetry
Of slow fire kindling,
Of rocks red-hot
        and white-flaming
      Their music of slow beginnings
        And slow lives,
      Long crystal symphonies —

Alive for a million years
Consciousness stretched back
                Like a road.

Sing of the slow rocks
Cooling to consciousness
                Fire in their veins
                        And flame in their beginnings.
Sing of the slow rocks.

                                Keith Battarbee

HIGHLAND GEOLOGY

Did she tremble when she made you,
Your rocky frozen shoulders,
The black, bleak backs and flanks of you,
Slowly heaved up and thrown in great plateaux of high rock,
And as slowly borne down,
Burrowed and riven and worn into the valleys and sea,
As slowly worn down,
Cracked by ice,
Rung by hail,
Stripped by meltwater,
Scattering your scanty patches of fertility about the edges of
    you.

Did the earth tremble to create such desolate beauty,
Harrowing and hard on the soul of man,
For she would have known that your bare and frozen flanks
Would break the backs of men,
That your bitter soil would wring the salt from them
And the harvests slake your thirst, their pride.

                                Denis Rixson

STONES LIE . . .

Stones lie inert, of course.
They turn in profligate rain

So slightly.
You observe their smoothness, their edges

But do not see their moving.
They take their time —

Quartz time: flint time, time of bloodstone,
Time for landscapes to settle,

As though they were immobile,
As though their stones lay unmoved,

Aglow with rain, glowing
With the spendthrift rain . . .

You'd call them inscrutable — you haven't changed!
Unchanging, they gleam like stones,

Turn their absent eye
Not at all.

Christopher Pilling

SEMANTICS

More than anything else
Outcrop rock can't stand graffiti:
All those words, huge, scrawled, over her granite face,
Those clean cuts making such dirty words.

Yet she is helpless
To control herself.

Already her writing is fixed on the wall.

We call it
Erosion.

Roger Elkin

291

HIGHLAND PEBBLES

At the mouth of the Spey
I collected pebbles
carried from the hills
and tumbled
so they were ready to mount
with only half a week
of the cerium oxide.
They look well on the skin
of the right girl.

I wonder if she can guess
the million years
she carries at her neck?

On An Teallach
the red sandstone
is embedded with pebbles too
and here and there
they litter the ground
like a spilled bag of sweets.
These too were tumbled
(but at creation's dawn),
carried beyond all rivers
to an ocean floor.

The sea then heaved up
to form great hills
and from the disintegration
of those mountains
the quartz pips were pushed aside
from the pudding rock.
They too tumble well
and, mounted, make
delicate jewellery.

When I placed one of them
on her neck, my gentle kiss
had double wonder:
of her, and this.

Hamish Brown

YOU ROCK, YOU HEAVINESS

You rock, you heaviness a man can clasp,
You steady buttress-block for hold,
You, frozen roughly to the touch:
Yet what can you?

Can you stand over me, suffused
And treading lightly for my love?
Or when I yearn for you, can you
Recover? Or, can you seem best?

Oh, you can be for praises for my grasp:
If thin's the heart you can be cold,
Or if resolved, you too can such.
Can'st add to me?

Look how the wind is treading, fleet
Along the lake. She ripples down
The mountain waters of the heart,
Crossing, re-crossing on the breast.

Menlove Edwards

CONSORTIUM OF STONES

The stones you have gathered, of diverse shapes,
Chosen from sea strand, lake strand, mountain gully:
Lay them all out on a basalt slab together
But allow intervals for light and air,
These being human souls; and reject any
With crumpled calceous edges and no feature
That awakes loving correspondence.

Start at this pair: blue flint, grey ironstone,
Which you ring around with close affinities
In every changeless colour, hatched, patched, plain —
Curve always answering curve; and angle, angle.

Gaps there may be, which next year or the next
Will fill to a marvel: never jog Time's arm,
Only narrow your eyes when you walk about

Lest they miss what is missing. The agreed intent
Of each consortium, whether of seven stones,
Or of nineteen, or thirty-three, or more,
Must be a circle, with firm edges outward,
Each various element aware of the sun.

Robert Graves

STILL LIFE

Outcrop stone is miserly

With the wind. Hoarding its nothings,
Letting wind run through its fingers,
It pretends to be dead of lack.
Even its grimace is empty,
Warted with quartz pebbles from the sea's womb.

It thinks it pays no rent,
Expansive in the sun's summerly reckoning.
Under rain, it gleams exultation blackly
As if receiving interest.
Similarly, it bears the snow well.

Wakeful and missing little and landmarking
The fly-like dance of the planets,
The landscape moving in sleep,
It expects to be in at the finish.
Being ignorant of this other, this harebell,

That trembles, as under threats of death,
In the summer turf's heat-rise,
And in which — filling veins
Any known name of blue would bruise
Out of existence — sleeps, recovering,

The maker of the sea.

Ted Hughes

UNDER THE STARS

Under the stars
In the space of night
I walked the mountain tops
And knew the wind.
The stillness of the dark
Was mine
And the silence of the snow.
Mine were the frosted wind ferns
On the crouching rocks
And the glitter of their veins.
Mine was the creaking snow,
The mist like rime
And the crinkled gleam of the burns.
Mine too, the blue shadows
The grey, cold glint of ice
And the peace of the moonswept hills.

Anne B Murray

from MIRACLES OF NATURE

Now, it is winter
And the red stags are running
Over snowy hills,
Scenting us on the north wind.

So our life has been,
Step by step, notching
The hard, slippery mountain-side;
Ecstatic release —
Down the glistening slopes on ski;
Or battling blizzards,
Steering clear of rocks, boulders,
'Schussing' down to the Sheiling.

Without you, I would not have
Known this life, where the white hare
Lollops over the thick snow,
Or seen the ice-encrusted,
Rainbow-coloured jewels
On grasses and flowers,

Ballet of the red-furred weasel,
Frozen lochs with painted ferns;
Swans, flying through swelling clouds
To distant, sun-warmed lands,
Or heard curlews cry;
Nor seen my small son
Join us on his minute skis,
Initiated into
These miracles of nature.

Marjorie Firsoff

AN ANTLER FOUND ON RANNOCH MOOR

The crumbling bank of peat
   collapsed
Beneath my hobnailed feet,
     Revealing part of one remaining root.
How had a root contrived
   to live
Where nothing else survived?

I cracked the shrouding shell
   of turf
That formed a claustral cell,
     Exposing that which time could not transmute;
The antler of a stag lay bare,
   unaltered
Since he faltered there.

Tentative touch upon this souvenir
   confirmed
That more than bone lay buried here,
     I peered through mist descending on my route,
And saw gaunt ghosts of wolves in grey,
   pass quickly,
Clinging to their prey.

Quietly, I left that place of slow decay,
   knowing
The last wolf was not killed at Darnaway.

Thomas Ronald Smith

296

THE DEER

Quiet are the deer on the hills,
Hidden deep in tussock and heather.
Under the bracken cover
The small calves, secret, lie
Still as the grey rocks scattered
On the mountain.
Overhead the watching eagle
Challenges.
The old hind lifts her head
And barks a warning;
Stamps a hoof.
Her tail is a danger sign,
White flash on the hillside.
The herd runs, hinds and calves together.
The eagle returns to his eyrie.
Briefly, the calves are safe.
Brown necks arch to graze.
Little ones play tag and chase,
And race
In the rare sunshine.
Clouds mask the summer sky;
Rain falls, wetting sleek hides.
Quiet are the deer on the hills,
Hidden in tussock and heather.

Joyce Stranger

HUNTED

The wind on this bright sky-washed day
tears words from my mouth, tossing them
soundless after heedless red-coat children
who bounce over the dry turf of the hill.

Suddenly, ears caught, startled
from its shelter in reedy hollow
out of wind — 'Look, Daddy, look!' —
the brown hare comes erect,

leaps the stream, angles left and right
through gorse and bracken, and steeples sharply
up the hillside, big-footed. He pauses
once (no dog at his heels bites

or snarls) looking back upon his hapless
round-eyed hunters. I can see
his muscles tremble, heart thumping
at ribs, his death in our footfall.

Ken Morrice

THE FOX

Near the mountain's summit, when the bells
of valley churches called all godly men,
and when the bright, still unspent sun of summer
called to the mountain, then — just then —
the silent movement of his thoughtless foot
pathed his rare beauty to our startled eye;
we did not move and did not wish to move,
frozen awhile, like a stone trinity
we stood, as with half-finished, careless stride
sudden he also stopped, the steady light
of the two eyes above the waiting paw
upon us. Then, without haste or fright,
over the ridge his ruddiness moved on,
and like a shooting star had come and gone.

R Williams Parry

THE FOX

On the way we saw the red larch woods
Blurring the mountains above Llwyn Onn,
Two hills, one rising, intensely warm with colour,
One flying free and horizontal from the plane of symmetry.

Those foxwood reds were still warm in the brain
When we walked from Blaen Cwrt across the fields
To the south side of the hill, under the oak wood,
Where the ewes shelter to give birth to their lambs.

The floor of the wood glimmered with white bones;
Little, silver skulls eyed us darkly, and the lambs
Leapt away round the hill. The blood of birth
And life stained the pale bones of the past.

Violence brushed our faces when we found
The vixen hanging from a tree. She was shot.
Her beautiful head thrown back, her life stiffened,
Her milk dry, her fertility frozen. The reds grew cold.

Gillian Clarke

THE SHREW, GLEN KINGLASS

Over a white sepulchre of snow
I saw, instinct with anger, go
the compact atom of a shrew:
its sharp face pointed in the mind's direction,
its scuttering feet made no impression
on snow's blank, bland complexion.
The passionate velvet of its fur, I sing,
the only life I saw on that white morning,
a furious Lazarus of Spring.

J L A Madden

HIGHLAND LANDSCAPE

Here, there is beauty every sense can share
Against the moving back-cloth of the sky;
The murmur of the stream, the scented air,
The various enchantments for the eye.
About my feet the moor is yellow-starred
With tormentil, the friendliest of flowers;
Above, the mighty peak that stands on guard
Forms and dissolves between the passing showers.
Wherever near or far the eye may dwell,
All things contribute to a sense of fitness
So integral, it would be hard to tell
Which of them bears the more impressive witness —
The splendid sweep of the enclosing hill,
The neat perfection of the tormentil.

Douglas J Fraser

ASPHODEL

Best of hill flowers
Is the regal asphodel
That ends our summer
By catching stars, setting them
On wands among the moors.
They burn brightly, gold
And yellow shoots of fire
Which leave dry parchment prayers
Stark on the stalks of winter.
Only when the new-minted stars
Are gathered from translucent skies
Of blue summer
Can the pale princes burn;
For one month sceptres stud the moor —
And asphodel is king.

Hamish Brown

AUGUST COTTONGRASS

Just one mass in the enclosed field
That makes it whiter than the fleece of sheep
For which the walls were piled.

Sheeting over the boggy ground
Each year sees them sewing civilization's shroud,
Sees it ever-growing.

To them it's simply a question
Of replacing one texture with another
Cotton for wool.

Excepting the fact that cottongrass
Will never be tamed,
Nor cropped, nor sheared, nor bought,
Nor bleached, nor combed, nor sold,
Nor ever owned,
Nor ever killed.

Roger Elkin

FERN

Here is the fern's frond, unfurling a gesture,
Like a conductor whose music will now be pause
And the one note of silence
To which the whole earth dances gravely.

The mouse's ear unfurls its trust,
The spider takes up her bequest,
And the retina
Reins the creation with a bridle of water.

And, among them, the fern
Dances gravely, like the plume
Of a warrior returning, under the low hills,

Into his own kingdom.

Ted Hughes

THE MOUNTAIN ASH

My eye perceives reality
which glows like love upon this tree,
in golden leaves and crimson
blood-encrusted
beads: now upon
this tree read the mystery
of fruit and resurrection.
See mingled in one jewellery
the living and the dead.

Eric Nixon

THIS AFTERNOON I LAY UPON A HILL

This afternoon I lay upon a hill
to hear a lark, to watch him lifted by
the liquid ripple of his song, until
I lost him in the dazzling depth of sky:

still so intent I listened that the bird
seemed all alone with his immense desire:
only his voice I heard, although he heard
his thousand brothers over all the shire.

But if the poet keep as great a height
as he can breathe the subtle air, and call
with his best power and sweetness through the day,

Not even the echoes will answer. And by night
nothing troubles the quiet, nothing at all
save a chained mastiff howling, miles away.

William Bell

THE CURLEWS OF BLAEN RHYMNI

The curlews of Blaen Rhymni are calling in the night
And all the hills are magical because the moon is bright,
And I walk alone, and listen, along the mountain way
To curlew calling curlew in hollows far away.

And the crying of the curlew makes more sad and strange
    and fair
The moon above the moorland and the clear midnight air
And the mountain breeze is laden with some echoes that
    must be
The echoes of a music beyond humanity.

And curlew calls to curlew, and I remember as I go
The merrier sounds and echoes out of seasons long ago,
When the nights were full of laughter and all the days were
    bright
And the heart too young to listen to the curlew in the night.

Idris Davies

HAWES TO SEDBERGH

Hay's strewn 'neath the fells,
    Misty rain is falling.
Beck to torrent swells,
    Curlew stills its calling.
Cloud on summit dwells,
Lambs hug dry-stone walling.

Pennine border's past,
    Beauty's re-appearing.
Trees are dripping fast,
    Sullen sky is clearing.
Gloom can never last
    When curlew plaint's in hearing.

H E W Selby

EAGLE

The weather came down from Nevis,
A schiltrom of snow spearmen
Marching across the glen.
We, high on a bare Mamore,
Braced for the blast when
He, above us, slanted into a
Slot of cold air.
Aquila chrysaetos
Poised in his perfection.
For a moment he stopped our world.
Slammed shut all emotion save
Praise to the eagle.
And we did,
Joyfully with eyes and lips.
Then he was gone
Riding easy the teeth of the gale.
Full sail set and rigging singing
He slid round a lee crag.
Gone and away.
But etched on our minds
Forever.

Tom Bowker

THE LLIWEDD RAVEN

From those grey cliffs, streaked with the rain of hills,
Bare of all verdure save where, here and there,
A tuft of heather grows within the slits
Of riven stone, the raven, strong of wing,
Beats the soft mist, but cannot find a way
To let the sunlight in — nore does he care;
The mists, the clouds, the rain, are a barred door
Against intruders on his sombre home.

E H Young

CHOUGHS

I follow you downhill to the edge
My feet taking as naturally as yours
To a sideways tread, finding footholds
Easily in the turf, accustomed
As we are to a sloping country.

The cliffs buttress the bay's curve to the north
And here drop sheer and sudden to the sea.
The choughs plummet from sight then ride
The updraught of the cliffs' mild yellow
Light, fold, fall with closed wings from the sky.

At the last moment as in unison they turn
A ripcord of the wind is pulled in time.
He gives her food and the saliva
Of his red mouth, draws her black feathers, sweet
As shining grass across his bill.

Rare birds that pair for life. There they go
Divebombing the marbled wave a yard
Above the spray. Wings flick open
A stoop away
From the drawn teeth of the sea.

Gillian Clarke

MAGPIE IN WINTER

The snow was almost gone,
most of it washed away by heavy rain,
gobbed into bulging watercourses;

it was leaving piebald rock
and sheep changed back
from sallow-grey to white again.

His plumage matched the mountain
as if snow, melting on his wing,
released him from frozen stillness.

Clyde Holmes

THE BLACKCOCK

We had passed through the lost valley
Yellow-gold with Autumn,
Coming eventually to the dark hill:
Here the rough witch-broom heather
Had faded, not into insipid paleness
But to something that gave
An over-all feel of black-purple.
He was waiting for us
Standing on a rotten fencepost
In an ebony elegance,
Shining silk-feathered in the sun.
He seemed as curious about us
As we about him
Moving only to turn his head
Showing us the metallic blue of his face.
Proud fellow, he sensed our admiration.
Behind him, in the camouflage-scrub,
His wives lurked in purdah;
They too were curious about the strangers —
One shy head after another bobbing up
To have a look;
It was obvious that they
Were in awe of him
As much as we were.

Margaret Gillies

GROUSE-BUTTS

Where all the lines embrace and lie down,
Roofless hovels of turf, tapped by harebells,
Weather humbler.

In a world bare of men
They are soothing as ruins
Where the stones roam again free.

But inside each one, under sods, nests
Of spent cartridge-cases
Are acrid with life.
Those dead-looking fumaroles are forts.

Monkish cells, communal, strung-out, solitary,
The front-line emplacements of a war nearly religious —
Dedicated to the worship
Of costly, beautiful guns.

A religion too arcane
For the grouse who grew up to trust their kingdom
And its practical landmarks.

I see a hill beyond a hill beyond a hill
Cries the hen-bird, with imperious eyes,
To her bottle-necked brood.

I see a day beyond a day beyond a day beyond a day
Cries the cock.

Too late, heads high and wings low
They curve in from heaven —
With a crash they pitch through stained glass
And drop on to a cold altar

Two hundred miles away.

Ted Hughes

THE OWL

Downhill I came, hungry and yet not starved;
Cold, yet had heat within me that was proof
Against the North wind; tired, yet so that rest
Had seemed the sweetest thing under a roof.

Then at the inn I had food, fire, and rest,
Knowing how hungry, cold, and tired was I.
All of the night was quite barred out except
An owl's cry, a most melancholy cry

Shaken out long and clear upon the hill,
No merry note, nor cause of merriment,
But one telling me plain what I escaped
And others could not, that night, as in I went.

And salted was my food, and my repose,
Salted and sobered, too, by the bird's voice
Speaking for all who lay under the stars,
Soldiers and poor, unable to rejoice.

Edward Thomas

WILD GEESE

Wisp of twisting smoke-grey cloud
Flying high against the wind —
Like a ragged chiffon scarf
Blowing on the distant hills —
A tangled skein of geese,
Ranging freely through the sky,
Leaving me a stranger,
Standing at a moorland gate,
Then pacing out my earthbound way
Back along the lochside.

Until with scarce a sound,
A sudden flock of great white geese
Fan close above my head,
And skim and settle on the loch,
Not very far away —
But I am still a stranger.
They are of the air and water;
I of earth, and not much fire.

Ivor W Highley

from WAUCHOPE

A mocking cuckoo cobbles from the glen
And from the hills
Where sheep kneel and gather to silence.
Day in great pilgrimage
Turns his sleepless eyes on the valley,
Leaving with lucent steps and lone
Village and fold.

The low light lies
Fantastic gold on the green. The ruins
Colour and quiver and fade like mirage of the wild.
In the shadow the cuckoo mocks on:

And over my heart that is bleeding and breaking,
Breaking like clots of earth
When the sun and the stars are dead.

T S Cairncross

CUCKOO

Cuckoo! Cuckoo!
What a bloody bird they be;
From mountain top to mealy sea
The very nasty apogee
Of mean summer's monotony.

Anon

ONE KIND OF DIPPER

there he bobs, the bouncy ham,
spotlit, on that plinth of rock,
reeling off his patter-songs
above a squeezed accordion shadow

getting the royal bird
from hissing wave
and windy, pelting spray
but quite oblivious

bowing finally to what he thinks
celestial backing
(more likely
a duck's arse)

then off again
whistle stop
same routine
another rock

I mean,
how in Astaire's sainted name
d'you get like that,
so daft-impervious

and with the gall to give us
the barmy showoff
yet another
— look for it, wait for it —
bill-topping
show stopping
unbearable
ENCORE!

Geoffrey Holloway

from WATER OUZEL

But best I remember the water-ouzel I watched
All of a summer day, in far Glen Lee;
Enchanted, I hid in the heather behind a rock
And saw my dipper fly through the vertical splash
Of the Falls of Unich, emerging to sing again
And bob on his whitened stone below the Falls.

Often, often, in later years, when harassed by the welter
Of modern life, the trappings of civilization,
I recall the ouzel's charm of song, the ripple of water,
The bird's devotion to his own particular stream,
(As mine to the Esk) and I tackle again my desk of duties,
And am refreshed.

Helen Cruickshank

MOVEMENTS

Lark drives invisible pitons in the air
And hauls itself up the face of space.
Mouse stops being comma and clockworks on the floor.
Cats spill from walls. Swans undulate through clouds.
Eel drills through darkness its malignant face.

Fox, smouldering through the heather bushes, bursts
A bomb of grouse. A speck of air grows thick
And is a hornet. When a gannet dives
It's a white anchor falling. And when it lands
Umbrella heron becomes walking-stick.

I think these movements and become them, here,
In this room's stillness, none of them about,
And relish them all — until I think of where,
Thrashed by a crook, the cursive adder writes
Quick V's and Q's in the dust and rubs them out.

Norman MacCaig

ROCKY ACRES

This is a wild land, country of my choice,
With harsh craggy mountain, moor ample and bare.
Seldom in these acres is heard any voice
But voice of cold water that runs here and there
Through rocks and lank heather growing without care.
No mice in the heath run, no song-birds fly
For fear of the buzzard that floats in the sky.

He soars and he hovers, rocking on his wings,
He scans his wide parish with a sharp eye,
He catches the trembling of small hidden things,
He tears them in pieces, dropping them from the sky;
Tenderness and pity the heart will deny,
Where life is but nourished by water and rock —
A hardy adventure, full of fear and shock.

Time has never journeyed to this lost land,
Crakeberry and heather bloom out of date,
The rocks jut, the streams flow singing on either hand,
Careless if the season be early or late,
The skies wander overhead, now blue, now slate;
Winter would be known by his cutting snow
If June did not borrow his armour also.

Yet this is my country, beloved by me best,
The first land that rose from Chaos and the Flood,
Nursing no valleys for comfort and rest,
Trampled by no shod hooves, bought with no blood.
Sempiternal country whose barrows have stood
Stronghold for demigods when on earth they go,
Terror for fat burghers on far plains below.

Robert Graves

from NEIGHBOURS

I live by the face of steep hills,
nor is there any majesty of nature
that I may not justly claim for neighbour;
not the high clouds of heaven itself
are too haughty for my company,
nor shy moss too humble;
for of all of these,
whether stars above or flowers below
may it not be said that I know them lovingly
and that we are creatures of the same great maker?
Therefore as I go my way upon the face of the earth
I yield to no man, but move equal with all things,
being indeed of the same line as Sirius,
and brother to the rose.

J H B Peel

Fells of Lakeland

GEOFFREY BERRY

'I WILL GO BACK'

I will go back to the hills again
That are sisters to the sea,
The bare hills, the brown hills,
That stand eternally,
And their strength shall be my strength
And their joy my joy shall be.

I will go back to the hills again
To the hills I knew of old,
To the fells that bear the straight larch woods
To keep their farms from cold;
For I know that when the springtime comes
The whin will be breaking gold.

There are no hills like the Wasdale hills
When Spring comes up the dale,
Nor any woods like the larch woods
Where the primroses blow pale;
And the shadows flicker quiet-wise
On the stark ridge of Black Sail.

I have been up and down the world
To the Earth's either end,
And left my heart in a field in France
Beside my truest friend;
And joy goes over, but love endures,
And the hills, unto the end.

I will go back to the hills again
When the day's work is done,
And set my hands against the rocks
Warm with an April sun,
And see the night creep down the fells
And the stars climb one by one.

Anon

TOWARDS EDEN

Raise but an instant your dejected eyes,
And they shall view a virgin paradise,
A green immaculate Eden, undefiled
By fallen man's devices, where the wild
Valleys and fells of Cumberland condense
In compass small more beauties than the sense
Or mind may measure; stark magnificence
Of untamed mountains.

F E Brett Young

NAMING HILLS

All afternoon
I sat on rocks watching the fells
massing on skyline —
a great herd of hills,
heaving huge arcs and flanks,
rounded heads and butting crags,
horning the clouds.

Like animals,
they kept their privacy,
held their own nature,
were just what they were,
tossed sun from steaming scarps,
mottled in shade,

and though,
like animals,
we gave them names,
they did not know
or care, or feel in their
vast unconcern,
that we had named them
Bow Fell or Wetherlam,
Pike of Stickle, Crinkle or Scafell.

They did not speak our tongue,
had names
we did not choose,
had their own slow secret
not for me to tell.

Margaret Pain

DROWNED VALLEY

Now they are gone
and the toil of their loving hands
lies deep and water-worn.
Only silence lingers
in this shadowed dale;
silence, and the wild wind
ruffling the grey water,
searching, restless,
where the steeple used to rise.
Mist fingers the fells,
ousting the sun,
and larks no longer trill;
the ice-cool trickle
of a curlew's call
shivers the air in lamentation
above this alien lake.

Sylvia Oldroyd

HIGH STREET

A blizzard caught me, on High Street.
Slamming the breath tight down my throat,
Flaying my face with ice.
Reeling, storm-drunk, I fled for shelter.
Crouched, shivering, by a black tarn,
My chilled hands jammed between my
    shivering thighs.
Silently, out of the drumlins and the
    swirling snow, came three men
To squat beside me.

The first said his name was Tom,
    a London lad.
In '48 joined the Eagles for a laugh
Though his Old Man belted him and kicked
    him out the door.
In '55, when The Wall was breached and
    all the North aflame,
Tried to make his way south, homewards,
With a Brigante arrow in his gut.
High Street and winter put an end to that.

The second's name was Harry Reay,
    a Furness man.
When his wife cuckolded him, laughing,
He followed a Stanley, to Flodden.
It sickened him, 'twas butcher's work.
Heading home took sick, coughing.
Sold his horse and bow for food, shelter,
    and medicines.
Weak, sick, tried a shortcut.
High Street and winter put an end to that.

The third said he was Jack Dunkeld,
    from Manchester.
Followed Charlie Stuart for a drunken wager.
Was taken, with Towneley's pitiful crew,
    when Carlisle fell.
Sentenced to transportation.
Escaped, took to the hills, starving.
His lungs drenched with six months'
    prison rot.
High Street and winter put an end to that.

Silently they left me.
Into the drumlins and the swirling snow.
As the storm broke a sickle of sunlight
Gleaned High Street bare of cloud.
A mighty fist of earth.
Knuckled with crag and veined with ice.
Hard, implacable, timeless . . .

Tom Bowker

318

ANGLE TARN

The silence where the tarn lay still and lone,
Holding the sky between two grassy shoulders,
Might never have known
Footsteps or voices since the Romans built
That foundering Wall hard by.
No doubt they bathed there happily as I,
And laughed the echoes up, drubbing themselves dry.
So as I splashed, and spilt
Loops of glossy water round the boulders,
I wondered if those strangers in our ground
Heard the hill-doubled sound
And stirred with memory in their bones.
No, those collapsed before their wall of stones.
I might have heard them rattling to their knees
If, as one thinks, the exiled have no ease.
Rather their presence lies about that place
Still as a shadow; the slopes they wakened once
They subtly share with me
Who have my roots in a fell-nourished race.
And for that matter the mountains do not heed
My living tread
More than the old reticence of the dead.

Stanley Snaith

AT THE WATERFALL

Touching the mantle of the empty sky
with a clear sound on a canvas of silence,
the stream flows out of the clouds,

And on a rock, high on Place Fell
a gust of wind sounds
with a noise almost animal.

So much nearer than stillness they speak to me!
I have heard too much silence,
listened too long to the mute sky.

Kathleen Raine

319

HELLVELLYN

On Striding Edge there stands against the sky
An iron cross whose rusted legend spells
Some antique story of a slip whereby
A shepherd met his death amongst the Fells
And lay, long lost, beneath that precipice.
But I was strange to Striding Edge, and now
Recall a time I nothing knew of this
And climbed the ridge alone. I wondered how
A solitary hound which panted past
Should seem so strong on some remembered scent
Which plunged him in the tumbled rocks at last;
And then I stumbled on the monument.
One sentence, red with sunset, seemed to burn:
'HIS DOG HERE DIED, AWAITING HIS RETURN.'

Syd Scroggie

IN THE LAKE DISTRICT

Treading the brown mat of the forest floor
I heard two sturdy knocks, and then one more,
And almost stepped aside to open the door
Or call, 'Come in.' It was a woodpecker.

There was a cliff of ledges and a tall
Cascade's descent, each ledge an interval,
The work of nature; man's — mile on mile of wall,
Each stone so chosen and set as not to fall!

A mist about Helvellyn's lofty head;
Black-faced sheep in bracken; a lake of lead;
The mountain ash's berries turning red,
And I, trying to recall what Wordsworth said.

Basil Dowling

WILLIAM WORDSWORTH

No room for mourning: he's gone out
Into the noisy glen, or stands between the stones
Of the gaunt ridge, or you'll hear his shout
Rolling among the screes, he being a boy again.
He'll never fail nor die
And if they laid his bones
In the wet vaults or iron sarcophagi
Of fame, he'd rise at the first summer rain
And stride across the hills to seek
His rest among the broken lands and clouds.
He was a stormy day, a granite peak
Spearing the sky; and look, about its base
Words flower like crocuses in the hanging woods,
Blank though the dalehead and the bony face.

Sidney Keyes

GRASMERE SONNETS

In a tea-garden overhanging Rotha
On whose clear surface cardboard packages
And other discards take their voyages
To the quiet lake, I wondered what he'd say,
Old mountain-trotter with a nose like Skiddaw
Safely asleep there where the river nudges
Its Coca-Cola can into the sedges,
Were his bleak eye to brood upon our day.
Exultant at the goings-on of nature,
Eavesdropping winds' and waters' talk,
That tough egoist, bathetic as ever,
Overlooks at Town End a macadam car park,
Folkweave booths, postcards, and suburbia,
The desert of our century; he'll not baulk.

He was always fortunate and was given
An enviable present; which he employed
To provide the inanimate with a voice,
A mountain stream giving tongue to a mountain.
For he said that they haunted him like passion,
The air, earth, and water, and light and clouds,

321

With which he would intelligibly rejoice,
At one with their solitary interaction.
But his present is past and has for audience
A torn paper floating on the water,
A smell of tar and coaches: a technological present
Of bodily comfort and abominable fear,
Of no resolution and no independence;
Yet never think that he is not with us here.

The mountain winds pummel Fairfield and Helvellyn,
Scrubbing the hills with a blanket of vapour.
Recognize there the inimical nature
Of those elements beyond our controlling
If any are. Call it a foretelling
Of our victorious and rational slaughter
Of useless creation: his versing nostalgia
For the other lives that we see disappearing.
Let him lie there by Rotha without remark.
Hiding and half disclosing, the veils of rain
Make a Chinese painting of his ashen lake,
Of the slopes where woods deciduously mourn
Another autumn about to overtake
A summer's progress with a bony arm.

There is a cragbound solitary quarter
Hawk's kingdom once, a pass with a tarn
High on its shoulder. Inscribed on a stone
With graveyard letters, a verse to his brother
Says it was here they parted from each other
Where the long difficult track winding down
A bald blank bowl of the hills may be seen
Leading the eye to a distant gleam of water.
After that last goodbye and shake of the hand
A bright imagination flashed and ended;
The one would live on, for forty years becalmed
Among the presences he had commanded —
Those energies in which the other foundered,
Devoured by wind and sea in sight of land.

David Wright

322

KEATS AT BOWNESS

The mist of the early morning clearing gradually
You heard the ubiquitous larksong, felt the fresh
Morning air of the north and, suddenly at Bowness, found
Yourself stopped in your tracks — before you a revelation,
A vision which you supposed even Shelley in far Italy
Could not have bettered. Like Cortez in your poem
You looked on a new vista — before you Windermere,
The silver-edged mountains ranged, and in the lake's midst,
A small, green island. You cried out, 'How can this be?'

After the little hills of the south the grandeur of Wordsworth-
Country seemed unearthly; then, as later by Stock Ghyll
    Force,
You knew the truth of the older poet's telling. You wrote,
'I shall learn poetry here'. The great year followed!

Frederic Vanson

INTIMATIONS OF SALESMANSHIP

A sleety, slaty day,
the lake dim as dusty pewter.
A sleazy, hazy day —
fields sorry as shorn tups,
claustrophobic, huddled trees —
the sacrosanct immortal fells
shagged horsehair sofas on a tip,
too damp to burn, too stale to rot —
and with mist-stuffing spilt over their tops.

Tourist Information Bureau.
W. Wordsworth, Prop.
Some P. R. O. job there, Willie —
all those daffodil handouts,
peep-bo violets,
unquenchable, rainless rainbows!
And the cuckoo voiceover . . . masterly.
I've half a mind to dig you out
and complain. Not that you'd say much.

Geoffrey Holloway

REFLECTION ON LAKE WINDERMERE

Stepping from my car
I caught the morning
in a rare moment
as its bud was opening
early before the sheep
feel fright from men and dogs.

The mountains round Windermere,
with their trees like silent pencils,
lay still in the lake.
A solitary bird hung in the air
and I stood alone and tall
against purples and browns
my head with the peaks.
I wanted to merge with
the years it had seen.
But I knew it would never be
part of me
that a passer-by can only
borrow time.

And the moment was lost
in one drop of water.
Very like a tear,
one drop of rain
shattered the mountain curves,
the rocks melted
in my eyes
and the colours blurred.

Illusion was lost
in a muddy bottom
with twisted twigs
and a broken bottle.

I looked up and saw the mountains
and the trees like silent pencils,
and the roads, cars, houses and walls
which are part of me.
Transient. Defacing.
And the shoulders of granite
heaved and cast their shadow
and things were real again
and i was alone and small.

David Watkin Price

THE THUNDERSTORM

When Coniston Old Man was younger
and his deep-quarried sides were stronger,
Goats may have leapt about Goat's Water:
But why the tarn that looks like its young daughter
Though lying high under the fell
Should be called Blind Tarn, who can tell?

For from Dow Crag, passing it by,
I saw it as a dark presageful eye;
And soon I knew that I was not mistaken
Hearing the thunder the loose echoes waken
About Scafell and Scafell Pike
And feeling the slant raindrops strike.

And when I came to Walna Pass
Hailstones hissing and hopping among the grass,
Beneath a rock I found a hole;
But with sharp crack and tumbling roll on roll
So quick the lightning came and went
The solid rock was like a lighted tent.

Andrew Young

DUNNERDALE

Hold this silence
To the noon city's ear.
Hear how the beck and the lilting gill
Spill their sweet waters like
The proud lives of gods over
And over and over the stones,
Once, always, ever —
To the sea to the sunsucked cloud
To the felltop to the spring
To sing time's only prayer
To the noon city's ear:
Be still and listen.

At the dalehead
As far as man has tilled,
Spring fields that bleat now with the rams'
Autumn delights will soon
Whisper to June of winter
Hay for the beasts stored
With the stars in their courses —
O here to the farm, to the rooted life,
You men of power who can raze
Seasons and cities come,
As far as man has tilled:
Be still and listen.

Patric Dickinson

ON DOW CRAG

The shepherd on the fell,
With his wild expert cry
Like an atavistic owl,
His dog a vicarious eye

And obedient tentacle,
His rhythm and routine
So nearly animal,
Is yet completely man.

A buzzard rounds its noose
Of hunger high above,
Its eye can split a mouse
If but a whisker move.

— So will it live and die;
No gene within the shell
Shall change its timeless eye
On the shepherd, on the fell,

On the boy who sets the foot
Of the future on Dow Crag,
Who assumes the shepherd's lot,
The buzzard in its egg,

Whose view is incomplete
Till he sees small and far
Like a toy at his feet,
Down on the western shore,

The beautiful cooling-towers
Of Calder Hall as strange
As Zimbabwe, as the powers
Of man to suffer change.

Patric Dickinson

ESKDALE GRANITE
(from THE SEVEN ROCKS)

Above the dint of dale,
Meadows and mosses, by the side
Of the cat-backed bridge where trailing waterweed
Swivels now to the sea, now to the fell,
At the pass and check of the round-the-corner tide;
Above the salty mire where yellow flags
Unwrap in the late upland-lambing spring;
Above the collar of crags,
The granite pate breaks bare to the sky
Through a tonsure of bracken and bilberry.
The eyes are hollow pots, the ears

Clustered with carbuncles, and in the evening
The warts of stone glow red as pencil ore
Polished to a jewel, and the bronze brow wears
Green fortitude like verdigris beneath a sleet of years.

Norman Nicholson

HARD KNOTT

Some aching brittle-veined soldier, broken
by the north and his dreams of Dalmatia,
must have seen it as I did, hunching over
the edge of this obdurate eyrie
nailed by Rome to a granite pass,
the mountains of a foreign planet heaving
at black horrendous combes of sky:
looking down through the murk at the valley-floor,
I saw the sun opening momently out
on a green vision, Eskdale
orient with meadows and as far
out of reach as angels
on the Plains of Heaven, or another life.

Rodney Pybus

IMPERIUM

Our feet rustle through dead bracken,
Or ooze by the lakes.
Snow in the clefts, and a distant cataract
Like inlaid silver.
Water, and wind in the hills,
Never out of our ears.
A god broods on the fog-bound summits.
Four more stragglers killed, their weapons stripped,
Stark among sheep-shit.
What we traverse, mark on our maps,
Is Rome.

Humphrey Clucas

CLOUD ON BLACK COMBE

The air clarifies. Rain
Has clocked off for the day.

The wind scolds in from Sligo,
Ripping the calico-grey from a pale sky.
Black Combe holds tight
To its tuft of cloud, but over the three-legged island
All the west is shining.

An hour goes by,
And now the starched collars of the eastern pikes
Streak up into a rinse of blue. Every
Inland fell is glinting;
Black Combe alone still hides
Its bald, bleak forehead, balaclava'd out of sight.

Slick fingers of wind
Tease and fidget at wool-end and wisp,
Picking the mist to bits.
Strings and whiskers
Fray off from the cleft hill's
Bilberried brow, disintegrate, dissolve
Into blue liquidity —
Only a matter of time
Before the white is wholly worried away
And Black Combe starts to earn its name again.

But where, in the west, a tide
Of moist and clear-as-a-vacuum air is piling
High on the corried slopes, a light
Fret and haar of hazy whiteness
Sweats off the cold rock; in a cloudless sky
A cloud emulsifies,
Junkets on sill and dyke.
Wool-end and wisp materialize
Like ectoplasm, are twined
And crocheted to an off-white,
Over-the-lughole hug-me-tight;

And Black Combe's ram's-head, butting at the bright
Turfed and brackeny brine,
Gathers its own wool, plucks shadow out of shine.

What the wind blows away
The wind blows back again.

Norman Nicholson

THE SCREES

The screes are speeding down at perfect pitch
before they tuck themselves in envelopes
Wastwater seals and never means to post.
Clouds snuffle past, fat bridesmaids choked with tears.

The screes are swarming up the cliff to lay
their case in heaven. The water's indigo.
A cormorant, wings unpacked, hung out to dry,
stands phoenix-fixed upon a rock. The screes

are drowning out upon the lake, face up.
It rains stops rains; somewhere a bark. The screes
are deep and thinking one emotion through

like Hegel's avalanche of counterpoint
prodding the Absolute to a day's turn.
Sheep press their starter buttons all night long.

William Scammell

WASDALE HEAD

From Westmorland's Cairn the fields are lush,
Segmented beyond count.
Stretched, tight as a drumskin, between
The rough paws of the trespassing fells.
Every patch of pasture hard-won from the obdurate rock
And held-fast to earth by a net of walls;
Themselves the gleanings of a constant, bitter, harvest
   of stone.
Cemented by blood, sweat, and the essence
Of nights when knotted sinew and aching bone
   repelled the balm of sleep.

From Westmorland's Cairn it makes a pretty picture.
Hercules, flicking sweat from his brow,
Would have considered it a task well done.

Tom Bowker

THE FORCE

At Mrs Tyson's farmhouse, the electricity is pumped
Off her beck-borne wooden wheel outside.
Greased, steady, it spins within
A white torrent, that stretches up the rocks.
At night its force bounds down
And shakes the lighted rooms, shakes the light;
The mountain's force comes towering down to us.

High near its summit the brink is hitched
To an overflowing squally tarn.
It trembles with stored storms
That pulse across the rim to us, as light.

On a gusty day like this the force
Lashes its tail, the sky abounds
With wind-stuffed rinds of cloud that sprout
Clear force, throbbing in squalls off the sea
Where the sun stands poring down at itself
And makes the air grow tall in spurts
Whose crests turn over in the night-wind, foaming. We spin

Like a loose wheel, and throbbing shakes our light
Into winter, and torrents dangle. Sun
pulls up the air in fountains, green shoots, forests
Flinching up at it in spray of branches,
Sends down clear water and the loosened torrent
Down into Mrs Tyson's farmhouse backyard,
That pumps white beams off its crest,
In a stiff breeze lashes its tail down the rocks.

Peter Redgrove

ON SCAFELL

Beyond the last gate, where I made my first halt,
The last of darkness still clung on the rock
Though a ladder of sun leaned on a further mountain.
The valley below was a vellum of mist
For all of August's hung thunder among it.
Glad for rest, I watched — refuting the cold
That carried in the shifting damp of the air —
A buzzard rise slowly over the steaming peat.
Mine, else, the mountain was, whose skylarks
Slept, hidden in the wax and shrub of bilberry.
Beyond the long bog I was to cross, no sheep
Moved in a mesh of black runnels. Water,
The very water was dazed, fumbling, unpurposeful.

Once I had left it behind, the formality
Of standing a moment alone on top of England
Would take an hour, no more. But for the buzzard,
Lazing just within sight on a ledge of wind,
I might have claimed as mine, as won there and then
That total, boundless tundra of solitude
I came before dawn to be on the mountain for.
With his sort of eye I watched him, cairn by cairn,
Rug by rug of shrivelling and emptied carcase.
My shoulders felt how flicking a blunt wing
Sufficed to steady the sun or to turn a rock face;
Fingers warmed as they would had I held him
Shot in all the amazement of his needless beauty.

Once begun, the final pitch, my back to slab
For a mooring against the thrown stacks of gust,
My calves flexed from the nudge of my wondering
Whether any flinching creature could keep there
And not be torn across the insubstantial rock,
Hurled to the grit-faced crags of the wind:
To go on, on into the mountain's shifting now,
On, or back, would have been to ride lightning.
And into the afternoon I kept to a crouch,
A whitened gristle of ravelled fear, mindless
Of wonder, beauty, desire or of solitude,
Being the wind's thing, helpless as the mountain,
A harsh, dry rattle assembling within my craw.

Ted Walker

SCAFELL

Its lump-of-coal outline stood above us, bent
With shaft upturned to much higher clouds
Defeating us but others too
In line; determined to finish us.
On the day they went up I stayed down and read quietly.
We had conferred on Wordsworth and all
The Lake writers for a week, heard talks
On beauty and on fear, the love that as William
Wrote hath terror in it. And we had fell-walked
Helm Crag in Grasmere, Dungeon Ghyll
And the long way round up Dove Crag
And over Fairfield in total mist.
We got quite lost up there and trusted
A friend with a whistle, map and compass,
A woman of all kinds of tough experience
And two stone-faced Americans, working at their image.
Should we try the big one? No question.
Studies to do, a touch of boredom at the idea
Of a day in the sky, and terror at sheer height ...
At school when I was ten they enticed me
Out on a ledge four stories up and only two feet wide.
It was there for embellishment. Scared
Of fear I clambered out and found my spaces.

Cliffs rounding their slippery sheep-cropped grass
Concavely; vertical rock but with a tree
Or broken ledge a few feet down;
A hundred-foot descent but angled away;
None of these troubled. It was the sheer, the absolute of fall
That Scafell shaped, holding in its two hands
And gently juggling and never looking down.
Prudent and sensible (and there are other names)
I did Helvellyn and Castle Crag but not Scafell.
The man from Dallas who shared the room
Came back that evening and sat before
His sacrarium of lotions, after-shaves, creams,
As stern as all the week. He stroked his chin
Asking if I had read, had a fruitful day.
He'd done Scafell and got the girl he wanted,
'It was easy,' he said. 'You just go up,
Keep away from the crags
And the lunatic climbers on the vertical face.
And yet it's weird, on top ... To go up isn't enough.
You want to *be* it ... be it with grass and goats
And rocks, standing in the sun forever.'
We sat there with our bottled intentions.
Our plans, our gravity, our fall.

J P Ward

SCAFELL PIKE

Look
Along the well
Of the street,
Between the gasworks and the neat
Sparrow-stepped gable
Of the Catholic chapel,
High
Above tilt and crook
Of the tumbledown
Roofs of the town —
Scafell Pike,
The tallest hill in England.

How small it seems,
So far away,
No more than a notch
On the plate-glass window of the sky!
Watch
A puff of kitchen smoke
Block out peak and pinnacle
Rock-pie of volcanic lava
Half a mile thick
Scotched out
At the click of an eye.

Look again
In five hundred, a thousand or ten
Thousand years:
A ruin where
The chapel was; brown
Rubble and scrub and cinders where
The gasworks used to be;
No roofs, no town,
Maybe no men;
But yonder where a lather-rinse of cloud pours down
The spiked wall of the sky-line, see,
Scafell Pike
Still there.

Norman Nicholson

ON GLARAMARA: 1947

Midnight, and the pale snow
  Crisp underfoot,
A frost-encircled moon
  On Glaramara.

Stone country cannot suffer
  Your loss or mine;
The valley guards its sorrow
  At this New Year.

And every wintry angel
Looks to the hills
Whose frozen comfort stays,
Endures, compels.

A country of stone dreams
The ghost of a hill,
A frozen tarn, the still
Echo of bells,

Bells in the midnight valley
Frosty stars,
Blencathra, Gable, ghostly Helvellyn,
And this New Year.

Michael Roberts

LANGDALE: NIGHTFALL JANUARY 4th

Dark are the shrouded hills, and vague, and the rain,
as the wind changes,
halts, and clouds over the fells
drift, and the Pleiades drown.

The hooded fells are uncertain, the track to the tarn
is lost, the fields are in flood,
and at six the lane is in darkness,
the beck is a ghost.

Night, and the day wasted, waiting,
watching, lethargic:
clouds and star-clusters are shapeless;
lamplight, dim starlight, floodland,

and fellscape, vaguely forgotten. And the wind
changes; the sky is alert:
crag, sheepfold and cairn
rise; and the mist is swept over the fells,

And the seven stars of Orion,
star-points driven home,
are nails in a buckler, or splinters
of light in the mind.

The touch of the track is a landmark,
stone underfoot,
the clouds and star-clusters are islands,
and water leaps down in the ghyll.

Michael Roberts

ROSSETT GHYLL

As I toiled, weary, down the apron of scree
From Hanging Knotts, the twin Pikes, weatherworn
Like old ships' figureheads, were streaked with snow,
And the valley lay forsaken as a deaf face.

Glossy as a chestnut from the peats, the ghyll
Ran, dangled over stones, made snowflower pools
In mossy troughs; breaking and healing; bearing down
To the valley's cold hearth the lost gleam of day.

That hour I had found in the mountain's collar bone
A sheet of tarn sky-watched among rushes,
Of such a leaden depth that I stared
Not recognizing the face drowned in its weeds.

But this live water, hurrying beside me, hid
No secrets, had no history, was fresh as morning's
Dew; gave winter a madrigal innocence;
Uttered flowers, nesting birds, an earth young again.

Stanley Snaith

THE LANGDALES

These last cutting weeks
have stained rocks.

Bracken has dissolved
to blood —

its ribs are crusts
fed to waiting winds

which go berserk
and like predatory birds

delving flesh
uproot and toss about.

The leeching done
fingers fall,

pale lips seal mouths.
But eyes up

find all is still
in pastel shades

soft as down.

David Watkin Price

STORM OVER LANGDALE

From what stable in or out of water
drive these horses renounced by the sea,
climbing the long horizons and the fells,
falling in vaulting tears on the sodden moor?

Through what eye, Stickle with its gloom of pitch,
gulls with their doom, days that have watched the gale,
rocks that have cut the clouds, fluted
with the wind the cantata of storm?

With what announced and widespread violence
these horses have they galloped the rakes,
their hooves bannered the streams, made lino-cuts
of tarns, climbed without ropes Hell Corner?

Over the Terrace, over the frown of Crinkle
atonal wind and cumulus have driven,
folding the mountain ash, dashing the stream to diamonds.
In what cave, or under leaning crag to hide?

Where can we hide in this steeple-chasing fury,
where from the mist and bitter wind
take our nailed boots, and watered limbs,
behind what wall, before what fire of welcome wood?

Eric Nixon

PIKE O'STICKLE

tchek tchek tchek

Grey sky, boulder and scree
and below the scree
one spire of gorse
that a stonechat tops

eyeing the axemen
as they pick out
tuff from slate
to chip and shape;

they in skins,
he, pert braggart,
in a black cap
and a new shirt;

eggs in the nest
crack
and the chicks
scrabble and gape.

Summer
follows on summer,
gorse pods pop
in the heat,

and the men
of Langdale
knowing the bird
for what it is

listen,
and name it,
and name this:
Pike o'Stickle.

Neil Curry

LITTLE LANGDALE

Swans on the tarn
move with the weather,
rain, wind or sun,
drifting together.

Evening: cross over
the mountain ridge,
down by the river
to the slate bridge,

up to the stone
cottage. We play
cards, and fortune
smiles on us equally.

I would like words to be
clean as this life,
free as the water,
strong as the earth.

Peter Jay

AT EASEDALE

At Easedale Tarn, in the hills,
You would think the west wind couldn't get out,
  by the way
The lonely locking hills
Stand down to the water, side by side — but the day
Comes only once in years that you'd find
No wind laughing out on a sudden behind
The hills, at Easedale Tarn.
And the rain . . .
It's the wettest rain that ever
Rained on a man or tumbled a baby river
Trickling down from the hill
Into a roaring spate at Sour Milk Ghyll.
It's the softest and the loveliest
Of all the rain so ready to hand
In Westmorland,
Where winds come quick and laughing out of the west.

Hester Marshall

DIRECTIONS OF THE WIND

On writhing contours whipped by Winter's flail
Mad crow map makers and mindless sparrows
Stamp misdirections as printed arrows
On charts of snow embossed by dinting hail.
The eyeless winds will disregard such Braille
On cold unfolded sheets. They steer through shadows
Of clouds that turn from tarns to shroud the narrows
Of Windy Gap, then swirl down Borrowdale.
No shrilling whistle-signals of distress
Affect the winds, nor calculated pacing
Of timed and measured ways through wilderness,
Nor pointing needle housed in compass casing.
O ride on winds that navigate by guess
And scrap your earthbound map, for Time is racing!

S Russell Jones

GREAT GABLE

The finest mountains stand across the valley.
The one to be climbed offers tides of blood
Testing weak muscles, and the quick flow
Of adrenalin faced by rock and scree.

Where once Norse Odin lived against the sky,
The torn cloth poppies in the summit's wind
Mark fallen Fell men, Flanders dead,
Bones in the foreign mud, souls on a dry

Mountain, whose valley lacks the earth
For burials; yet whose farmers once
Bled energy in shifting stones
To clear a place for birth.

Shirley Toulson

GREAT GABLE, 2949 FEET ABOVE FLANDERS

When Britain bowed her head and held her breath
Beneath a breeze-blown canopy of cloud
And counted in her soul her sons of death,
Bloody with battle, to their country vowed;
While pulse beats ticked the silent seconds by,
As brass bands held their tongues and flags lay furled,
When red wreaths wept with many an unheard cry
And thoughts spanned lands and peoples of the world;
While patterned prayers were printed on the mind,
When pomp and pride and glory gained each door
And pledges of remembrance sailed the wind
As stark November seared the scars of war,
        Then, on a storm-still mountain top I stood
        And on a simple plaque shed poppy blood.

Joanne M Weeks

GREAT GABLE 1940

We stood on the summit.
No debris then or shouts
Of triumphant youths,
Just silence,
Range on range of snow-capped peaks
And the distant sea, frozen-waved.
Two ravens perched near,
Watchful, disdainful of crumbs —
The war and Christmas feasts
Light years away.

Kate Lindsay

HELL'S GATE

It's called Hell's Gate where Great Gable
Plunges down in carmine scree
Through rock pillars to Wastwater
And the heartbeat of the sea.
Once I'd only to remember
That sheer scree-shoot and the wind
Making silences more silent
To become both deaf and blind
To the beast roar of a city
Where I earned my daily bread:
Pillar Rock, Gimmer and Scafell,
Pavey Ark and its wreathed head
Plunged like ships of storm to leeward
From the pavement where I stood.
Somehow being with those creatures
Made of shale and turf and stone
More than other kinds of loving
Seemed to foster my life-line;
I could trace it working upwards
Through the snake path, thin and fine,
That a route is on a mountain,
And through heather and rain shine
Feel, when I had reached a summit
More than what had been was mine —
All life born by one forefinger
Locked into a nick of stone.

343

Though Scafell now and Great Gable
Are quite near a Butlin's camp,
They can hardly be diminished
By the crowds that roar and stamp
Over Styehead to Wastwater
Since their dangers are their own.
Like the Eagle Ridge which offers
Consolation to no one
But within my mind forever
Shapes the route I travel on.
I remember, I remember,
Winding up the slender edge
Whose worn holds cannot be cheated —
Nice to think one cannot dodge —
Hell's Gate in the flank of Gable
And how still the carmine scree
Plunges down towards Wastwater
And the heart-beat of the sea.

Thomas Blackburn

HELL GATE

'The grey of the mist is very blinding to me;
the dew of the grass is bitter on my tongue;
roughness of rock pricks sharp under my finger — '
one man alone, fallen, a doll unstrung.

'I have woken at night and all around is darkened.
There is no gentle mist, beyond this stone,
Nor here bright jewelled dew on the grass tops
that melted against the rock when the pale sun shone.

'I am not I if these are not as I knew them.
A body is here, thoughts hustle it through Hell's Gate;
Beyond — straight rocks rise black, silent in judgment.
They are the same, but not as I saw them yet.

'I have woken, surely, like a child that is frightened
and asks where he is, but silence answers, not sound,
judges and hears, nor is there hope of easing,
not till he sleeps again, and sense is drowned.

'But there is no sleep. O there'll be no more sleeping!
These limbs once past the gate, I wake to the dead
and will never sleep, nor the wild rain stop beating
coldly on a cold stone that is its bed.

'Is it damnation, that loved things go to coldness,
that the sheet of despair veils them with "nevermore"?
that the dear remembered eyes, once bright with gladness,
welcome no more, will be never turning more?

'Is it not hell, that where I looked for comfort,
sound and colour are gone, the shapes remain?
I see the once beloved; old memories flicker:
each thought of joy brings the more hated pain.

'Out then out of the gate, and into darkness!
My hands are not hands that feel, my ears cannot hear,
or I would catch a harmony after sighing,
or I would touch, not cringe at a touch, for fear.

'I shall go out, my old place sodden in the rain,
not to return. The gates are closed again'.

Wilfrid Noyce

JANUARY CLIMB ON HAYCOCK, ENNERDALE

Still ascending into cloud, our path dissolves
in snow and, off the map
where this terrain was codified in clear signs,
definite contours,
we find it hard to visualise the tracks
cartographers located.

We scale one peak to find another peak above it
and then another
luring us higher into the blur. Our footprints
stagger along in our wake
turning to landscape, landscape to snow.
Wet rocks teethe
out of the whiteness, breath comes quicker,
all we can hear
is our own quietness that seems to create
the mountain by climbing.

Is there a boundary where the snow is cloud?
Is the summit a rock
or a cone-shaped hole in the sky? The mist is more
substantial than the ground.
Monochrome drains off what little warmth
we've lugged this far.

Our only bearing now is the footprints
coming to meet us
when we turn back on ourselves. Beyond signs,
beyond contours, our next
step might hurl us into a blackness of ice
or wild colours. We turn
back; imagination is afraid to climb
peaks it has created.

Cal Clothier

HIGH LORTON

Force-fed with rain and wind, the hanging fells
plump like an orange in the sun. Small sails
of grass draw down young skittering sheep. The larger
becks paw at root and rockface, stalk the nearest river.
A path winds up beneath funereal pines
whose branches nail down all the winds
and takes you to a drop: there in a space
populous with unlikely trees
bolt upright on tall rock, or clawing
at the cliff, lush weeds, strange groupings
and grotesques of stone and wood stand gaping
at the Force, that leaps the sopping air
as though all pleasure lay in waiting there
and sheers down to a pool, then, darkening, spills
on down the slope. The heart dies with that fall;
eyes rush to the bone-white edge, play back
the epic instant when, arching rock
the long ecstatic plumes fan out and fall
plucking the sunlight with them. Rich, rank
and gloomy, the operatic falls bank

fresh deposits hourly, spent in the blink
of an eyelid. A green vaulted chasm
shifts all the mysteries of this orgasm
down to the lakes, which on a clear day show
the tops mutely trembling. They do it slow.

William Scammell

SCARF GAP, BUTTERMERE

There is no need to describe the track; a pencil
Drawn diagonally across a slate
Would be more precise than words. The stone walls
Lay ladders of grey against the green; the green
Glissades into the lake.
This pass is known, defined and understood
Not by the eyes but by the feet,
The feet of men and sheep that tread it: the young
Teacher from Cleator Moor, pushing a bike
With a burnish of poetry on the rims;
The girl who is soon to bear a foreigner's child;
The lad who leaves the pit shafts of the Solway
To grope for a brighter fire than coal.
These, in the clang and shuffle of the world,
Are shunted along strange, disordered rails,
To crash on viaducts or into buffers
Or hide in sidings where nightshade trails on the lines.
That world they rejected once, perhaps once only,
And scrambled up the screes of the slithering moment
To seek a combe unquarried yet by change,
Where memory, returning with the wheatear,
Could find the name scratched on the same stone.
Therefore to them this dale, this pass,
This double queue of hills, High Stile and Melbreak,
Robinson, Grassmoor and Hobcarton Fell,
(Themselves the wrack and backwash
Of the geological tides) seem now
More lasting memorial than the rubble of cities —
A track that the wild herdwicks still will tread
Long years after the makers of tracks are dead.

Norman Nicholson

THE DEER, STONETHWAITE

By a frozen stile by a frozen fell
Soft-stepped and steady-eyed
The hoofed shadows glide
Through the ice-cold
Wood to a mossed beck side.
Sharp senses attune to the cold-crack air,
Sharp eyes search each
Lair and, satisfied, lower their guard
        to the leafy ground.

Then crashing in juggernaut boots,
The climbers descend the frosted fell;
Through the startled wood
Glad cries ring,
Bounce from tree to tree;
And half-seen shadows, the deer flee.
Frozen leaves, brown thoughts of summer gone,
Lie without sound while the silent deer
        pass on to safer ground.

Irvine Hunt

WATENDLATH

Where a little tarn lay
coiled
about a confusion
of fell and crag,
an aching arc of rainbow
arched its watercolours
across the easel of the sky
and fell
into the sepia bracken
at my feet.

Judith Smallshaw

348

DANDELION CLOCKS

What's the time, dandelion?
One o'clock, two o'clock,
Third summer's come!
What's the time, dandelion?
Time will be, says the child.
Time now, say I.
Time was, says the old man passing by.
We climb Walla Crag's stony path slowly,
Picking the pink stems below the lichened walls and
Scattering a dance of dandelion lace across the fell in
Triumphant trial of the infallible ritual.
Today we reach the summit's weathered pines and
Childhood seeks no further challenges.
What's the time, dandelion?
Time is coming, dreams the child.
Time is now, I reply.
Remember the old man, says Time passing by.
What's the time, dandelion?
One o'clock, two o'clock,
Third summer's gone!

Joanne M Weeks

CASTLERIGG

Permissive Paths and Motorways
(these waymarks of our lemming life)
mean little in the tramp of time —
     I think.
I saw young Castlerigg dance round a jig,
look up to old Skiddaw with his kin —
     and wink.

Hamish Brown

SKIDDAW

sun beats: slatey stones underfoot
repel my dust bloomed boots
unthinking in their wanton wear
of breasty slopes on whose wide track
a regiment of plodders
dumbly rape eroded mountain grass
each step files memories: archivists
of dust: sky: sheep tracks of my mind:
the sad emotive curlews treble:
background for a lonely runner
panting speckled voice harsh with effort
head band turning runs of sweat
down below growls Keswick's maelstrom
Derwentwater glints in softened focus
my being is alone in landscape curved
not part but plodging waifed through holes
in the continuum of hills
up here subjectivism is my philosophy
i am centred in the universe
i should die on my feet becoming part of it

Roy Brown

SKIDDAW

The hills hang huge and high
against the rain,
hewn by absoluteness
when the young world
was heaving in its womb.
Slow struggling ice
sculpted
these nightmare custodians
of the lake
into petrified Lucifers;
ill-omened idols
hanging the hills huge
against the rain.

Judith Smallshaw

SKIDDAW

At the top of it you'll find
A statement of rock and wind,
Lichen gnawing on split slates;
At your back the pretty lakes,
Japanese-garden wooded islands,
Set upon a glass of silence:
And below, on your right hand,
An unspectacular land,
Shelterless and jumbled hills,
Calva and the Caldbeck fells.

Derelict, a shepherd's house
Where air blows ravenous
Among a valley and mountain's
Limbo of undulate lines,
Decomposes, brick by stone,
To original ground.
Smooth backs of mountains, like
Backs of seas about to break,
Wallow from the valleys to
The nowhere to which they go.

Holidayers in summer
Find a light achievement here,
Who plod up a slope of turf,
Eat their sandwiches, and laugh
On the brittle summit slates
Of a still unhuman place.
And sometimes, higher than Skiddaw,
A plane, unfurling a furrow
Of white feathers in a clear
Evening or morning air,
Writes assurance overhead
That blind rock will never read.

A gauze banner of vapour
Hangs over cooling-towers
Far away, over Solway.
Ceramic as vases, they
Articulate form and line.

Monumental to our time,
As authentic a signature
Of their epoch as henge or spire,
Like them, they fix the eye,
Mastering natural beauty:
The plain or coloured spread
Of land, and sea, and mountain-head.

David Wright

BLENCATHRA

What a long time he looked before he saw!

Orange Blencathra slate registered first
upon the retina; cottages
hunched for shelter against a gray outcrop;
and stony lanes that led round the estate —
walks for an old man soon-out-of-breath
adventuring hill's steepness.
                And there was mist
seeping from the west where, in a break, one glimpse
of Derwentwater startled.
                There was also montbretia
along the wall side, and stiff, brown thistles like
ambushed soldiers propped where they had died
in the little field; and orange toadstools,
harbingers of a later season, where he would come
to a world swept clean with snow, simplified
of colour, empty and wide, cold, but keen
with pricking frost; where that autumnal season
would be — among sharper ecstasies —
erased and forgotten then.

All colour is locked in the brown earth
                to what awakening?

Mabel Ferrett

NEAR DOCKWRAY

On the stream's edge,
Motionless as I can be,
Just quietly drawing breath
On the stream's edge.

I am the still one, he is the moving one,
This stream, tho' he hardly speaks.
I can hear the splash of the little trout as it swims
Ceaselessly moving, catching in fleeting glitter
What the hedgerow allows him of the midday sunlight.

How long ago did he make this tiny stream-bed,
This way for himself, from some fell side spring above
To the thirsty hamlet below?
This green hedgerow which sucks up his cool moisture
From roots thrust under his stones is a late comer,
His trimming of rush and fern and buttercups
Is not many year's growth —

On the stream's edge, the mind drifts wondering back,
And reaches no stopping place in its idle thinking.

Margaret Cropper

STORM OVER ULLSWATER

Wind-cuffed, the world's rain-tree shudders: berries, bombs.
Gunboat shadows hurtle like harpoons at the whale-bulk of
    Place Fell —
explode commandos slinging foam-ropes that strike but
    can't belay.
The mist's a creeping smoke-barrage; the reeds a bristle of
    fighting-knives;
sleety bullets lash the shallows; shrapnel bites in the spray.

In a corner of the squall's convulsive eye sits a fleck of
    dabchick —
that rides, curtseys, gay as a dinky toy, as a child, plays
    swings to seesaws.

Ulf's longship. And I wonder what that ram's horned names-
  man of the lake —
with his barbarously cheap ideas of war — would make of
  this . . .
Or of its future: bluer than cobalt, cleaner than hydrogen,
  napalm.

Geoffrey Holloway

FOR GEORGE TREVELYAN'S 80th BIRTHDAY

The Fells speaking:
  We remember this man, there's scarcely one amongst us
  That hasn't felt his quick step running in youth,
  Yet he was most our own as his age drew on,
  And our spacious wisdom became bone of his bone.
  He was of our kind, there was rock and fern in his being,
  Tenderness too, like the little treasures we harbour.
  Snow capped is he at last? but the sky that blesses
  The white topped hills is the blue of our kindest hope.
  We remember this man.

The Farms speaking:
  We remember this man, he was welcome when he came,
  And sat down famishing for a giant's supper.
  He wasn't a stranger to shippon and cobbled yard,
  Or the dignity of solid walls and beams;
  He felt them in his heart, like one of our own:
  We remember this man.

The Streams speaking:
  We remember this man, we leaping turbulent singers,
  We'd make him a lullaby as the dusk drew on,
  And all was hidden but the last white flash
  In the ghyll, and at last all sounds were still but our voices,
  That will never be still, though we shrink from the fierce
    glory
  Of foam and speed, to the softest of soft whispers.
  We've quenched his thirst, and cooled his tired head,
  He knew the chill of us over the naked limbs.
  We remember this man.

354

The Creatures speaking:
> We remember this man, I the wide winged buzzard
> Swinging from peak to peak, and I the herdwick,
> Making my way up the sheep track that he followed;
> And I, the wild fell pony, and I, the calf
> In the dusky hull; and I, the curlew
> Crying my broken note with its throbbing fall;
> And I, the lamb by the hearth in the flagged kitchen:
> He was our friend; he saw us with watchful eyes.
>   We remember this man.
>
> We remember this man, though many springs have gone by,
> And the years that bring their griefs and their sudden
>   glories;
> We think that he often comes and goes amongst us,
> And in his spirit's hoard we have our place:
>   He remembers us all.

Margaret Cropper

THE SHEPHERD

He scans the fell with keen blue eyes
in weather-beaten face,
Yan, tan, pethera, pim ...
A soft command, a gesture, two lithe
dark bodies race,
Yan, tan, pethera, pim ...
And lo! a scrambling woolly horde
with a mild, protesting bleat,
Yan, tan, pethera, pim ...
As if by magic fills the dale and
jostles round his feet.

Vivienne Burgess

SPRING-CLEANING

She's been out putting the fellside to rights:
Those rocks were askew, that sheep track too rough;
A dust for those hollows with feathers a chough
Should never have shed. Adjusting her sights

To a waterfall she has altered its course
And the stones when dry she has smoothed and stacks
In the air's airing cupboard — where the slope lacks
The cover of heather, or rowan, or gorse.

The wind is too wayward and often too wild!
The hail no respecter of tender skins!
The sun will do till grass yellows and thins!
She's stopped wind and hail; the weather's re-styled

So the hills can sport split skirt and beanie.
Scabs of lichen have been treated with salve.
Valley cows are transfixed, each teat has a valve.
Barbed wire has gone: sheep's wool's soft and sheeny

Until the rains. Rain's all right — it washes
And even the mountains need to be cleaned.
The ferns have their heads raised, the swamps must be
    preened.
She has been out in cagoule and galoshes

But not to go for a strenuous climb
For its own sake. She's been on a mission:
Now the fellside must be above suspicion;
The rivulets had better be running on time.

Christopher Pilling

HAIKU: BESIDE THE LAKE

Bowfell, softly round
This autumn dusk, full and firm
Like the breast of time.

Three heraldic deer
In autumn-colour, proper,
On a bracken ground.

The skylark — shameless —
Strips itself note after note
Down to bare music.

Delicately, God
In His most rococo mood
Thought a dragonfly.

Only well-bred airs
Know that she lines her low leaves
With a silver silk.

Nothing tells a tale
So poignant as an old bridge
No one cares to mend.

At the coach-station
Posters offer solitude
At low party-rates.

It would make the hills
Burst into laughter if once
They thought about men.

Harold Morland

DIET

'Nice job you have here, touring the Lakes'.
I nod, tuck back into my social worker's car
— on the back seat liberal castoffs,
jigsaws, walking aids, a spare torch — thinking
from where I sit landscape means people, work.
My Lakeland polaroids aren't of fells like sleeping bulls,
bandoliering sheepwalls, curlew tambourines,
dippers skimming becks that bask like blue snakes,
Wordsworthian ikons, Beatrix Potter dolls,
but what flanks them, that I have to meet:
the child of forty two with the albino lock
grabbing my hands with pumice paws,
grunting, licking me as if I were coned ice cream;
the man whose pyjamas sag, whom cancer's bashing
random as a rookie spuds;
the man who yesterday drank death from a tarn,
letting its picture fill him, wall up the past;
the crone with scorched legs cuddling a stick fire
that one day she'll fall into,
frazzled wits burnt black as toast.

Geoffrey Holloway

HOLIDAY SNAPS

Dawn rain pasting
last night's chip papers
across greasy tarmac.

Landladies crack smiles.
Sullen sauce bottles grumble
breakfast trivia.

Lakeside cafe's scream
'Morning Coffee'. Bedlam at
30p a cup.
From plastic tables
bread, butter and stewed tea
invite dyspepsia.

358

Afternoon crowds
clutch token memories
made in Taiwan.

At halfpast nine
a cinema bottleneck
leaks sticky trippers.

Midnight Performance.
Forty film freaks spatter
from Mick Jagger's mouth.

Above the shops a crane
jabs a derisive finger
at mountain permanence.

Patricia Pogson

NOISES OFF

There goes April. Wordsworth's daffs have blown
their raucous yellow trumpets at the skies.
The land of bed-and-breakfast's lately grown
a crop of grim and gaudy butterflies
anoraked, booted, programmed, setting sail
to tack up all the valleys and the fells.

Great puffball clouds, like Robert Graves's curls,
lather the mountain's cheeks; the becks run on
as mindless and as pretty as the girls
who host the dafter games on television;
and I'm the demon barber who would spring
the whole lot through the trap-door for a gin

and tonic in a Fleet Street bar, two days
in Paris, or a witty love affair
with someone young and new. This summer haze
corrodes one's mind like acid. Everywhere
the engines of the flesh roar into life
and run down logic like a fearful wife

who's nagged us once too often. Brrrrmmm!
for the border — a do-it-yourself noise
indicative of purpose, dreadful harm
to anyone in the way, climax poised
on looped and whirling wheels: the howl and whine
of all five senses throttled on the line.

William Scammell

The Heart has its Feelings

GORDON J GADSBY

SUMMIT CAIRN

We are the kind that climb and, climbing, know
Why man must mount the scree to stand, sleet-stung,
Where cold the first, clear freshets tumbling flow
And, corrie-cradled, hinds bring forth their young:
Why to the cloud-piled crags must upwards go,
Where in the bealach bare, frost-split, moss-hung,
Embed the ribs of dark and crusted snow
Old boulders grey by tilting Titans flung:
And why, aloft, where whistling buzzard flies
Must panting pause and, pausing, hope to see
Far more of magic than mere hope can dare;
Not little loch, not wind-wrenched rowan tree,
But all Time imaged in each instant there
And beauty past all thought beneath the skies.

Syd Scroggie

THE COMPANY OF HILLS

If I could seal
a wish on younger eyes, then it should be
that they should see hills undisturbedly,
solitary, and in their own design.
For I have seen so much can come between
the heart of hills and mine:
record and route, rivalry, quick report,
all the cloud screen
of human witness, dictionaried sport;
and that these rainbows steal
the selfless joy mountains can make us feel,
the single light from summit and sunshine.

If I could seal a hope for younger time,
climbers to come, then it should be for you
to know of only two
verities, yourself and the hill you climb:
only two voices, the mountain's and your own.
Others are but echoes, of the human pride
would make a sounding-board even of a hillside.

Two voices only. And one,
the serene and still,
magical voice of the hill,
speaks only to you, for you alone.

Geoffrey Winthrop Young

AWAY

Where am I? On what map?
What scale is there between
Another map and mine?
What life by mile or thought
Makes scales of being alone —
One thoughtless word and a thousand
Miles of a frown?

Distance; nearness; a map
Well-read can mean escape
Or the longed-for, chosen,
Impossible to have found.
Words are maps, too, of where
We maybe dont want to be
Discovered on dead ground.

Mercator was not unsound
In his projecting a flat
Fantasy of what's round,
Or seems to be — things not
As they are — equator and pole
In lines that can't be true
But serve the compromise.

All maps deceive deceivers.
Perhaps we lovers
Of 'world enough and time'
Use them only to know
Where we are not to go.
Where we are, has no scale
Of all-or-nothing. It is.

Patric Dickinson

LLYN D'UR ARDDU: THE BLACK LAKE

The cliff fangs

above the cwm and barren mountain flanks.
Only the lake
holds back

the monarchy of rock.

A take-it-or-leave-it
lake,
a work of art spitting spray,
stampeding the breeze —
flickering, flaming manes in a wink

yet you stay,
swaying to sleep,
a dreaming mouth, sprinkled with stars.

In Winter you sing,
organpiping icicles
on the silent stones.
Sometimes you sit all day and think blue.

You are a wound
in his side, cupping the moon.

Wreath of streams, colliery of the sky,
in your depths
where the passing birds reflect,

trembling,
I see myself.

Edwin Drummond

THE MOUNTAINS

Sometimes the mountains seem
Like colossal stones
A Titan could lift up, and under them
Plains of cold white grass
Still ready to grow green:

Or, otherwise, when the clouds
Squat like amorphous hens
On the valley bottoms,
You're afraid, if they got up,
Of a cold void addled nothing:

Then the clear tops wear
Their gloves of sunlight and you —
Lost in a human cloud
Among sheep-bones and waterfalls —
Feel a pulse that throbbed
Before blood was: but ours.

Patric Dickinson

UP PATHS WHICH SCRAWL

A hand shakes

causing a slip
of the pen
and the round O
loses its moon
and becomes a question
— a gaping mouth —
hooked by metal
— flesh and steel —
— a pull —
from the page
up paths
which scrawl
across mountains

to bare rocks
wings and sky.

To looking up
and looking down
for an answer.

On such summits
a hand might
caress a moon
and make
a moment whole.

David Watkin Price

BEINN AIRIDH CHARR

There is a colder, clearer substance
on the other side of this ignorance

it is these hills, blazing
with a sanity that leaves thought behind
this light that is
the limit of austerity
and makes words blind

only in the brain, erratically
an icy ecstasy

Kenneth White

THE HILL IS PASSIONLESS

How futile passion in these hills,
How quiet, how still its noise,
The mind's cry as futile, as incongruous,
As houses scattered on the edge of the land,
For the land is longer than men,
And in the end the land resumes.

What time have they for the quick stir of life,
For emotion flickering in a mind.
What time has wind for a storm of purpose,
What time the sea for a tide of love.

Denis Rixson

THE WOUND

I climbed to the crest,
  And, fog-festooned,
The sun lay west
  Like a crimson wound.

Like that wound of mine
  Of which none knew,
For I'd given no sign
  That it pierced me through.

Thomas Hardy

CONFLICT

The half of me is planted in the plain,
Half on the mountain side.
My wounded whole is rooted deep in pain
Of things that must divide.

Once fostered at the valley's breast I fed,
And cradled at the knees
Of hills I slept till wild winds shook my bed,
And tormented my ease.

But one slow-smouldering spark of spirit-seed
Rose on the wind, and grew
In rocky summits where my soul could feed
In space a lifetime through.

And ravished by the sun and storm I live,
Unbound, through light I fly.
Yet I must bow down to my roots and give
The life I own, and die!

Phoebe Hesketh

THIS IS NOT MY COUNTRY

This is not my country, these hills bald
Like the heads of wrinkled brown old men, these lakes
Vapid as daughters sheltered from the world
Hating their placid home and longing
For the stranger wind to come raging through the pass
And lash them to life with terror and love.

No, I repeat, as I climb the slope
And look at the craggy landscape where the soil
Scrapes a living like dirt under the finger nails
And only the hardiest crop, the northern breed,
Has the heart to dance in the air.
No, as I surprise the sheep
Nagged by the wind and tottering always away
From the wind's rancour into a rock's charity
To crop a poorhouse herbage thin as gruel —
No, this is not my country, the stony cell,
The coarse dreary garment, the pulse and water
Of a faith so frail that wine and wildfowl,
Sensual peach and bejewelled silk
Work its downfall in a swift sweet foray.

Faith of that kind, that can only resist
Temptation that is not present, I abhor,
And keep my praise for those whose faith
Is constantly tried and constantly true,
Who are not afraid to confront the richness
Of orchards and farmyards, of arable curved
Like a brown dress on the earth's swollen womb,
Who give and are given so abundantly
They do not need to hoard their meagre possession.

Clifford Dyment

369

THE PILGRIM

I see a girl climbing the mountain
In a red blouse and blue jeans
Rolled up to the middle of her shinbones,
No shoes on her feet meeting the sharp stones,
Climbing among rocks, a smile on her face
Though her mind may be bleeding from old
And new wounds. In time, she accosts the saint
And in the silence a story is told,
A drop is added to the deepening sea
At the top of the mountain before she
Faces down to the world from that brief height.
Below her, for miles around, the fields
Are graves for sheep that never saw the Spring light
In grass kneeling to receive the bones and skulls.

Brendan Kennelly

NOW TO BE WITH YOU
(from THE MAGNETIC MOUNTAIN)

Now to be with you, elate, unshared,
My kestrel joy, O hoverer in wind,
Over the quarry furiously at rest
Chaired on shoulders of shouting wind.

Where's that unique one, wind and wing married,
Aloft in contact of earth and ether?
Feathery my comet, Oh too often
From heav'n harrried by carrion cares?

No searcher may hope to flush that fleet one
Not to be found by gun or glass,
In old habits, last year's hunting-ground,
Whose beat is wind-wide, whose perch a split second.

But surely will meet him, late or soon,
Who turns a corner into new territory;
Spirit mating afresh shall discern him
On the world's noon-top purely poised.

Void are the valleys, in town no trace,
And dumb the sky-dividing hills:
Swift outrider of lumbering earth
Oh hasten hither my kestrel joy!

C Day Lewis

GREATNESS

The mountain profile: seen at dusk
Sharp black on pastel, or through mist
Coherent among shifting chaos.
Human, unquestioning, response to power
Struck by calmness and stability.

But go nearer. Gain acquaintance.
Get to know. Watch and wait.
Probe for weakness. At last, assault.
And you will find that even this
Giant's feet are in and of the mire,
The face is scarred and pitted
And shares fear, and sweat, and joy.

Martyn Berry

THE TURNING

These falling waters gather
together,
leap from the black glistening rock,
giddily
drain down the air.

Suddenly, so savagely
the winds rose,
now they stride from ridge to ridge,
the waves lap
the thirsty stones.

May tomorrow be like this
and always,
and every night that from the
darkness comes,
stars clear, wind clean.

This is our night and in this
candle's light
your flesh transfigured calls, breathing
deepens, flows
secure and sure.

Perhaps here is the turning,
thin traverse,
into the timeless moment
and beyond
love's birth and death.

C E MacCormack

THE HILL

And turning north around the hill,
The flat sea like an adder curled,
And a flat rock amid the sea
That gazes towards the ugly town,
And on the sands, flat and brown,
A thousand naked bodies hurled
Like an army overthrown.

And turning south around the hill,
Fields flowering in the curling waves,
And shooting from the white sea-walls
Like a thousand waterfalls,
Rapturous divers never still.
Motion and gladness. O this hill
Was made to show these cliffs and caves.

So he thought. But he has never
Stood again upon that hill.
He lives far inland by a river
That somewhere else divides these lands,
But where or how he does not know,

Or where the countless pathways go
That turn and turn to reach the sea
On this or that side of the hill,
Or if, arriving, he will be
With the bright divers never still,
Or on the sad dishonoured sands.

Edwin Muir

THE UNATTAINABLE

Climb your incorruptible high mountains,
tell your summits as a rosary,
carve sea-green ice in brittle fountains
a slow staircase to earth.
Incomparable
triumph of muscle and of mind . . .
Count it to me for worth, I am not blind
to proud achievement. Yet I know
the cold and spiritual snow
shall wrap you round as with a shroud
on your last pilgrimage,
and no returning,
before you reach the uttermost high hill
of sunset burning,
and tread the peaks of intimate mirage
with winged and reverent feet.

Marjorie Milsom

THE THIRD MOUNTAIN

There was this mountain
With a roaring Lord at its core
Which spoke,
Which belched forth Laws in its smoke.
We knocked our heads on its granite floor,
said, Yes, Lord, yes,
and went on doing much as we'd done before.

And there was this mountain
Which mocked our strength by standing there.
Just stood
and dared us conquer it if we could.
We barked our shins on its limestone stair,
boasted our manliness
and stuck a Union Jack on top of its icy hair.

But this third mountain
seemed self-enfolded, wild.
So shy
its shoulder shrank even from touch of sky.
No footprint, man's or god's, ever defiled
its mountain-ness.
No path goes there. To this we are reconciled.

Margaret E Rose

AFFINITIES

Mist hangs about the wood in trunk-torn swirls
   the pine trees wait
Across the listening fields a stormcock hurls
   misgivings late
A singing in the leaves as thin flakes sift
   the holly trees
Forerunners of a questing host adrift
   like swarm-lost bees
Till search abruptly ends and all converge
   with dropping flight
The snowflakes rally and slip down to merge
   in deepening white.

374

Nightlong a raging blizzard off the fell
  flurries the snows
Dies with the dark, its handiwork a spell
  Dawn colours rose
All round with blinding light the snow banks burn
  and crystals blaze
On cornices so far outhung they spurn
  their underlays
In wave-break fullness all along each hedge
  out from each wall
Above blue grottoes fretted to the edge
  just like a shawl.

What wizardry is this which can transform
  so fittingly
Or is this peace engendered from the storm
  unwittingly?

A river torrent scarifies its bed
  and swills the sand
Discards it idly on some island head
  a port unplanned
The grains embroiled for miles in whirlpool race
  here come to rest
Receding waters lay each one in place
  to shape and crest
A long, long ridge: and Beauty there will shine
  beneath the sun
Does ebbing backwash finish by design
  the spate-begun?

Beauty is harmony and rhythm, alike
  to us akin
The snowdrift and the sandbank merely strike
  a chord within
Which, from a bane of tempest or of flood
  we scarce can thole,
Assurance gives of what there is of good
  in human soul
And in the rush of water madly flailed
  or snowflakes swirled
We glimpse the primal chaos that prevailed
  to make the world.

Kenneth Milburn

COLD HANDS

Hacking down the bracken
that was fern when a love
lived, cold hands fend off broken
branches and dreams, cleave

a clean track through the guilt
and putrefaction left
by a year's passing. Felt
less than guessed, the fresh-sloughed

pelt and carcass of some small
and fleeting fellow-soul
slither and creak, crumble
underfoot. Crows cackle

blackly over skeleton
elms, peck the last sliver
of warmth from the bones
of once and forever.

Higher up, heather glows
somehow knowingly, waits
as patiently for heroes
as for cowards, invites

any or all to climb
towards whatever calls.
Darkness falls. An owl claims
the first of a long night's kills.

Michael Daugherty

FIRES

Firelight: the quiet heart of a little room
Where the lamp burns low and the shadows hover.
Out of the night are we come, where the gathered gloom
Hangs softly now that the wild hill rain is over,
And all that moves — a star or two — moves slowly;
Great clouds plod to the slouch of the wind their drover.

In from the great processional of space,
From the tramp of stars in their careless crossing
Of gulf on infinite gulf, from the foaming race
Where the wind caught at the corries, and the old tossing
Of the fire-tormented rock in the ridge of mountains
Seemed to awake anew in the clouds' new tossing —

In from the cold blown dark: from flame to flame —
From the hidden flame of cosmic motion
That roars through all the worlds and will not tame,
Driving the stars on the crest of its own commotion,
To the little leaping flame that our own hands kindled:
In, as the boats come in from the width of ocean.

Narrow the room is, shut from infinities.
Only the new-lit fire is keeping
Hint of the ancient fire ere the first of days.
And we three talk awhile to the spell of its leaping,
And are silent awhile and talk again and are silent;
And an older fire than the hearth-fire wakes from sleeping —

The fire that smouldering deep in the heart of man
Lies unfelt and forgotten under
Our surface ways, till a swift wind rise and fan
The covered heat to a blaze that snaps asunder
The strange restraints of life for a soaring moment;
And we lift unquiet eyes and stare in wonder

At the infinite reaches the tottering flames reveal,
Watching the high defences crumble
And the walls of our self-seclusion gape and reel,
Till with heart-beat loud as a toppling rampart's grumble
Out from our comforting selves to the ungirt spaces
One with we know not what of desire, we stumble.

Nan Shepherd

LOST COUNTRY

Two mountain streams that swiftly pass
Thro' dark and hilly lands,
By secret names I named you, as
You slipped between my hands.

Footpath with the wondrous way
Of spreading sparse and sweet,
Even on a winter's day,
Wild thyme for my feet,

That climbed and climbed as if to find,
High on the moorland's lift,
One aged solitary tree
Swept by the stormy drift:

Cold moorland, vext by winds' alarms
Lost footpath, naked streams,
To you I'm stretching out my arms,
Country of my dreams.

Marion Angus

RETURN (1919)

Steadfast and stern, as in those days of gold
   When they befriended an unwandered lad
With lonely lovingness, before he sold
   For worldy lore the treasure that he had,
Steadfast and stern, the mountains wait for him.
   Their summer barrenness of ridge and range
Buried in wintry softness, and their grim
   Beauty of outline heightened by the change.
And I shall feel again as I draw nigh
   A burning throb within my empty heart,
And know the utter meanness of the lie
   That came from learning's lip and made us part.
Ashamed, yet wild for welcome, I shall throw
My faithless self upon their warmth of snow.

T H Parry-Williams

SONG IN A VALLEY

The mountain like a seer his face has covered
With misty cloak, he will not be entreated,
But hides himself for strange communing.
No man may know whether his ancient lovers
In ghostly pleasure haunt the clinging mist,
Or whether God Himself, as in old times,
Walks on the heights, in faithful cloud concealed
And to His noble servant
Confirms the strength of rock, the purity
Of his white waters flowing to the plain.

Margaret Cropper

GUILT

The mountains are an icelike intercession
in the sand landscape of abstract penance
to forget all else is to remember them,
wander in the blindness of blizzards, stand,
a water droplet on the under side of a leaf.

While in the world, the leaf stirs
and all water is scattered far
as the ends of the sky. Silence
belongs only at the distance of stars.
Behind, above, beyond, cold mountains stir.

Robert Calder

MANX DREAMPOEM

Up in the wild-
cat, pine-dark hills
live lonely souls
who shun a world

that shames a man
for being poor,
honest, simple
in the way he

dresses and smiles.
Uncivilized,
unsure, they hide
among goldcrests

and legends, know
of waterfalls
and sparrow-hawks,
streams and warlocks,

dreams and clifftops
and more, perhaps,
than doomed poets
about living

close to the edge:
their lives their art,
needing no words
to say as much,

as smartly, of
such myths as love,
such wounds as once
upon a time.

Michael Daugherty

THE GOAT PATHS

The crooked paths go every way
    Upon the hill — they wind about
    Through the heather in and out
Of the quiet sunniness.
And there the goats, day after day,
    Stray in sunny quietness,
Cropping here and cropping there,
    As they pause and turn and pass,
Now a bit of heather spray,
    Now a mouthful of the grass.
In the deeper sunniness,
    In the place where nothing stirs,
Quietly in quietness,
    In the quiet of the furze,
For a time they come and lie
Staring on the roving sky.
If you approach they run away,
    They leap and stare, away they bound,
    With a sudden angry sound,
To the sunny quietude;
    Crouching down where nothing stirs
    In the silence of the furze,
Crouching down again to brood
    In the sunny solitude.

If I were as wise as they
    I would stray apart and brood,
I would beat a hidden way
Through the quiet heather spray
    To a sunny solitude;
And should you come I'd run away,
    I would make an angry sound,
    I would stare and turn and bound
To the deeper quietude,
    To the place where nothing stirs
    In the silence of the furze
In that airy quietness
    I would think as long as they;

Through the quiet sunniness
 I would stray away to brood
By a hidden beaten way
 In a sunny solitude.
I would think until I found
 Something I can never find,
Something lying on the ground,
 In the bottom of my mind.

James Stephens

ON THE PLATEAU

This is your hour in time: remember it.
It will not come again. Rehearse it well
And cherish it against the days to come
When you may go no more upon the hills.

Here is the sullen mystery of rock,
The heart-break stubborn stillness of the hills,
The diamond-dazzle treachery of snow.

Here dwells the death-wish, under the smooth snow
 . . . Only to lie down
Lie down for ever in the sheet-white snow,
For ever, to lie down alone . . .

This is your hour in time, in which you know
That it is possible to be yourself and free
From sweetly overwhelming tides of love
For friends who walk the valleys there below . . .

This is your virgin hour, to crystallise
And keep for ever safe from seeking hands.

Eilidh Nisbet

UNLESS YOU CHANGE
AND BECOME LIKE CHILDREN ...

Looking at the slides
   of the Lake District
I take them all for granted
   knowing I've been here
and climbed there before.

Dappled by cloud and sun,
   the tired old fells
are wounded with worn tracks
   like varicose veins
between their buttressed thighs.

Water in plenty empties
   from rain-laden skies
through spurting ghylls
   to tranquil tarns
and majestic lakes.

Only the winter brings relief
   as snow and ice
protect the heights
   from all but the few
with whom they have affinity.

Complacency was startled
   by the gasp of sheer delight
from the youthful audience
   at sunset over Buttermere
turning my hardness to sadness.

Charles Povey

THE TARN

When the world's tumult rages round
As thunderstorms on hill and hill;
When earth cries out against her wound,
Heart, be still:

Silent and still beneath the strife
Of lightning, and the tempest-sweep
Which breaks the surface of your life
But not the deep.

William Soutar

VIEW FROM MOUNTAIN

When through the parting mist,
That the sun's warm gold mouth had kissed,
The hills beneath me came to view
With lochans gleaming here and there,
It was not like the earth I knew;
Another world was shining through,
As though that earth had worn so thin
I saw the living spirit within,
Its beauty almost pain to bear
Waking in me the thought,
If heaven by act of death were brought
Nearer than now, might I not die
Slain by my own immortality?

Andrew Young

MOORLAND NIGHT

My face is wet against the grass — the moorland grass is wet —
My eyes are shut against the grass, against my lips there are the
    little blades,
        Over my head the curlews call,
    And now there is the night wind in my hair;
My heart is against the grass and the sweet earth; — it has gone
    still, at last.
        It does not want to beat any more,
          And why should it beat?
        This is the end of the journey;
          The Thing is found.
        This is the end of all the roads —
    Over the grass there is the night-dew
And the wind that drives up from the sea along the moorland
    road;
        I hear a curlew start out from the heath
        And fly off, calling through the dusk,
          The wild, long, rippling call.
        The Thing is found and I am quiet with the earth.
Perhaps the earth will hold it, or the wind, or that bird's cry,
But it is not for long in any life I know. This cannot stay,
Not now, not yet, not in a dying world, with me, for very long.
        I leave it here:
        And one day the wet grass may give it back —
        One day the quiet earth may give it back —
      The calling birds may give it back as they go by —
To some one walking on the moor who starves for love and will
    not know
        Who gave it to all these to give away;
        Or, if I come and ask for it again,
          Oh! then, to me.

Charlotte Mew

THE MOOR

It was like a church to me.
I entered it on soft foot,
Breath held like a cap in the hand.
It was quiet.
What God was there made himself felt,
Not listened to, in clean colours
That brought a moistening of the eye,
In movement of the wind over grass.

There were no prayers said. But stillness
Of the heart's passions — that was praise
Enough; and the mind's cession
Of its kingdom. I walked on,
Simple and poor, while the air crumbled
And broke on me generously as bread.

R S Thomas

Scottish Bens and Glens

HAMISH McINNES

MULL OF GALLOWAY

In the morning before the mist thickened
I saw the distant peaks of Man and Mourne
framing Moyle's silvered glass.

Later, the creeping fog smelt at the cliff.
The horns roared out a dragon challenge;
a giant answered from the Irish shore.

I meditated on the sad land's extremity.

Returning home at dusk, my isolation came
not from the brown moorland or the flat machair
but that I seemed to travel without mark
towards other headlands more extreme than this.

William Neill

HILLS

1
One heat worn day
we climbed an old existence,
leapt a hundred million years
of stone and recognised — close to the sun —
the source of burns that stay alive in heat:
held in the height, Loch Enoch.

Dog and I drank in a sense:
this is a moment in our moving.

2
Were you not made
in their strata of time,
do you not share the markings?

Under centuries, the old north bedrock
of ourselves, the Lewis and the Moine,
the changed and changing.
God made molecules, not men
or mountains. We are their linking,
their coincidence.

3

In the turning time we need their names,
Mulwharchar, Merrick,
relict energy.
The hills are louring
syllables of strength.

The winter waiting.
Earth force concentrated into root.
Naked standing stones
and cairns;
grass humps that lined
the military road;
march dykes of the former Machars,
Mochrum Fell, Barhullion.
On every hill top, marks of man
who shifts the stones,
like words, and sets them
to his will.

Robin Munro

SUNSET

Along the Ettrick hills a splendour wakes
    Of red and purple; dark the shadows run
On Ruberslaw, but see! the Dunion takes
    The golden sword-thrust of the setting sun!

The evening sky one rolling cloudbank fills,
    Wrought in strange phantasy of tower and tree,
Mocking the ramparts of our Border hills,
    Dwarfing their battlements of majesty.

A snowstorm drifting down the Bowmont vale
    A little hour ago made Cheviot white,
And left him glistening in his silver mail,
    The day's last champion in the lists with night.

Will H Ogilvie

WINTER NUDE

Three white breasts tip the clouds,
Heave extravagantly in the sky,
Mother-earth overdetermined, supernumerary.

A startled grouse as I climb
Whirs from bosom safety.
On scree-edge limping hare
Stops to shiver and listen. I follow
His snowtracks panting, smoking air,
Stop, turn, snap on skis
And print soft wrinkles on the belly
Swelling white and curved below.

Flurry of snow darkens the sun.
I edge into the quick night
Of her breasts and lilipute across a torso
Sculpted in the primitive manner —
White, vast, distorted.

Along the hill-road lights
Bead bright, circling her navel;
And distantly a jewelled garter of icy river
Twists around the limb of Eildon.

Ken Morrice

ABOVE GLENCORSE

In the lee of a stunted pine, we pour
Coffee from a thermos, adding whisky
To keep out the chill. Perched here
It is impossible to escape from history.

Vigorous on the summit of Castlelaw
Scott would tell of the Covenanters
Joyless on the sward below.
Earlier, startled worshippers

Watched a highland soldiery swagger
Towards Holyrood; the Young Pretender,
Unaware of Derby, impending Culloden,
Flicking at flies with a blotched cane.

Breathing deeply, the air keen,
I keep thinking of Stevenson
Longing for home. How soon,
In some Samoa of our own,

Will we sense the grim-visaged visitor come
And, peering through time,
Wonder when next we will, like Cromwell's
Men, 'eate biskett and cheese on Pentland Hills'?

Stewart Conn

FROM THE OCHILS TO THE JURA

I well might envy you those wilder peaks
That have inspired you in a foreign land,
With the great sombre forests whence they spring,
The warm pine-scented ways which call you on —
You've come to love them, and they welcome you
As an initiate who has ears to hear
The song of silence, and the gift to share
With such as I the beauty many miss.
You love the untamed places, but I know
Your first love, that you never will escape.
How could a man forget these grassy heights,
Autumn-bronzed bracken, the uplifted miles,
The wonder of the vision from their tops,
The lark-so-woven sunshine, the lone call
Of Ochil whaups, the little dancing burns?
I know what love lies deepest in your heart!

W K Holmes

COLOURS

Hills mean colours, or
so it seems, as
memory clings to the
shreds of dreams long
after the walker returns.

Torridon was grey and
Jura was blue, Glen
Lyon was gold of a
saffron hue and Glen
Feshie a chalk-like white.

Balquhidder was brown and
Skye was black and the
Trossachs glowed red with
a mist-shrouded sun
that slowly died and bled.

But the Ochils are
green, of every shade,
moss and emerald, lime
and jade, lichen and ferns,
grasses and rock, birch
and rowan, hazel and oak.

They'll all change a little as
the seasons move, but green,
green, above all, is the
colour of love.

Rennie McOwan

ON THE SIDLAWS

The dead heather is dull
  On the hillside under me;
  There is a dead queen bee
On the grass, and a rabbit's skull.

I will go down again
  Into the valley woods,
  And watch the hundred moods
Of trees in sun and rain.

And I shall linger and wait
  For the unawaited things,
  Be it only the sound of wings,
Or a cobweb on a gate.

Or by a woodland pond
  A blue kingfisher flash,
  Or a soot-budded ash
In flower, and the sky beyond.

Or lamb's wool tufted white
  On the barbs of a wire fence,
  Till birch leaves fall like pence
In the dull autumn light.

William Montgomerie

TWO GENERATIONS ON GOATFELL

Huge, grey granite boulders strewn around
Where I stand with my girl and boy,
Glad that there's such a view for us to enjoy
But wondering too,
As the wind blows steadily up from the Sound,
How it must seem to them — all of it strange and new.

Down in the bay the steamers ply like toys,
Much as they must have done
Thirty-odd years ago when first I won
To the very top,
A boy among other girls and boys,
Happily unconcerned that time will never stop.

Now that I look on the view as an old friend,
What is my loss, or gain?
Certain things have been taken, some remain
And memory
Adds a dimension in the end
That time, for all its power, can never take away.

Douglas J Fraser

WATER COLOUR, GLEN SANNOX

The water curtsies, then glides down the granite
Boiler slabs of Glen Sannox, unfurls
Little white flags as it falls captive to the slope,
Loses its grip on them and on its vitality,
Paints itself on the broad rock and hardens
To a fine ceramic glaze — almost: the slanting sun
And the never-quite-smooth-ness of the burn's bed
There offering subtle reminders about movement
Deceptive as a picture.

The silence only just yields to the water.

Containing this throwaway moment — Cir Mhor
And Castel Abhail. Cut on the bone of ice
They serrate an artlessly blue sky. The sun
Administers sudden slashes of white and black
To the crag's north face. A thousand feet of rock.
A still summer evening.
                    Something like a smile
Informs rock, air, sun, water as they compose
Themselves now to have their likeness done —
Lies that will please us snug by our winter fires.

George Macadam

395

OVER FROM JURA

Birth has a raw cry among those hills
and a lamb's life is an uncut cord
as water is ripped from the ice
like a scythe through harsh hay.

The snow on the Paps is hard like sheets
stitched with bone and coarse thread.
The green moss on the low farm wall
is sinister at night and unlucky to touch.

The island across the Sound sprawls
like a woman in a bath and the earth
underfoot heaves like a trampoline
as the dawn haar ripples up the loch.
The girl whose hair was like the sunlight
has gone into the far north country
with her skin rubbed soft with flax
and her eyes as grey as March fog.

The wind cauterised by the seasons,
rattles the skulls of moles on the wire
and the land does not ease its grip
which we have suffered with ecstasy.

Michael Sharp

ON DUMGOYNE

We stood upon the summit of Dumgoyne
When morn was young, the shepherd lad and I,
Beneath we saw the Blane with Endrick join
In that fair Strath where happy hamlets lie.
Ben Lomond reared his rugged head on high,
Whence wisps of cloud trailed upwards one by one.
The loch, blue, island-studded, held the eye,
A Queen that flaunted jewels in the sun.
So beautiful, ethereal, scarce real,
So fairylike a landscape it did seem
No world of actual being, but ideal,
A world of wonder and a world of dream.

But, when the joy in me for beauty spoke,
The shepherd lad but muttered, 'Aye it's pretty',
Then turned and gazed towards a smudge of smoke
Blotting the south where lay the great grey city.
He gazed, he sighed, hilltops to him were real.
That smudge of smoke — ah! that was his ideal.

W D Cocker

A VIEW OF LOCH LOMOND

Mountains open their hinged reflections on the loch,
shape and reshape themselves, grow squat or tall,
are bent by shakes of light. We never find
the same place twice; which is why picture postcards
that claim to lay the constant on the table
(the camera cannot lie) are popular;
what trotting tourists hoped to purchase for the shelf;
the image they'd retain, if they were able.

But landscape's an evasion of itself.

Maurice Lindsay

LOCH LOMOND

Scoops a handful of water from Loch Lomond,
holds it between cupped palms, looks, drinks
through sun dried lips.
It must have magical properties, he says
as he scoops again and looks again
and drinks again, and again and again.
Such beautiful water (he confuses landscape
with liquid, the eyes' sights with the mouth's taste)
must have magical properties, he says again
and drinks half the Loch before he sees
that the mountains are mocking
and he urgently needs to pee.

Giles Gordon

397

INVERBEG

Sliced with shade and scarred with snow
A mountain breaks like Mosaic rock
And through the lilt of mist there flow
Restless rivers of pebble, pocked
And speckled, where moss and centuries grow.

Tree, married to cloud as stem is to feather,
Branches and straddles the convex of sky.
Death is aflame in the bracken where heather
Rears semaphore smoke into high
Blue messenger fire through soundless weather.

Below, like bees, the ivies swarm,
Cast in leaping veins, their trunk, a crippled
Animal of thighs pounced from loch-water, storms
The slated shores of the past into ripples
Interpreting man's fretted cuneiform.

J F Hendry

REST AND BE THANKFUL

Rest And Be Thankful, on the lichened stone.

At mid-day on the summit of the pass
We stretched ourselves upon the humming grass.
Our legs were numb. The hill-wind dried our sweat.
At first we were too tired to speak, but soon
One of us stirred, looked round:
                                    'What is this place?'
His voice was meagre in the mountain air.
'Who cut the words upon that weathered stone?'

Slowly we moved, some sitting up, some standing.
We scanned the long slope we had put behind us,
The valley we were shortly to descend.
The first was full of sun, but bare; the other
Strewn with great dripping boulders, dense with brush,
And dark where the mist crept up a mile away.
On either side the mountains bared their teeth,
Black, broken, splintered, to the empty sky.

We did not know the name of any hill.

'What is this place?' we asked of one another —
And realised that no-one knew his neighbour.
'Where are we?'
     'Who are you?'
          'Why are we here?'
'How did we come?'

      So question answered question.
Fear snapped its jaws. Each knew his neighbour's panic
Run like a caged beast up and down the ridge
And come back cowed.

      And while we struggled there
Out of a dream into another dream,
The myrtle-scented wind sang in our teeth.

We had no order other than the silent
Rest and Be Thankful on the lichened stone.

Iain Hamilton

HILLS BY LOCH LONG

They wear their sackcloth lichen next the skin,
they've seen too much, too long to need to speak
or break emotion open to the sky.

A pride in stubbornness; their heads still high,
obduracy, their endurance is elemental;
they clutch their ragged bracken round their knees,

their grey skin shows, they wear their slippered screes
without excuse. These hills are solely age:
progenitors of vanished landscapes.

The twitch of rain or varicose of ice, each shapes
another wilderness of age. Their puckered flesh
is hard with life; their tears are stone,

their faces rock, how harder then the bone.
Consider their death; they their own graveyard,
outlasting each fabulous life, each skeleton.

J L A Madden

GLEN ORCHY

Sunday, late summer, 1968:
Mull and Iona behind me and eleven days
Of Highland brightness — Loch Awe electro-plated,
Ben Cruachan chiselled and faceted like cut-glass
In a cubic clarity of air; the River of Orchy,
Subterranean almost, glittering below
Hollowed and pendant shelves of sandy stone.
And everywhere down crag and brae, a tumbling
And cataract of yellowing green, birch and rowan,
Leaf and berry and the churned froth of heather.

                                                                Then,
Passing through the village at the foot of the glen,
I stop at a shop with newspapers for sale
And take one, glancing for the cricket scores —
When, like a snapped spring, a familiar name
Headlines clean at me: 'Millom Ironworks
To Close in Four Weeks Time'.

                                            And now,
Whenever I remember Glen Orchy,
I see the stretch of light, the waterfalling seasons,
And ten thousand years of after-Ice-Age weathering
Crash on an Arras Wood of smokeless furnace chimneys,
And, blundering among the dead trunks, five hundred men
At one stroke out of work.

Norman Nicholson

IN MEMORIAM, DUNCAN BAN MACINTYRE

When they took away his hills
Fair Duncan of the Songs
became Grey Duncan of the doggerel.

When the hill passes were closed to him,
the Misty Corrie and Glenorchy
of the green grass knowes,
they gave him a tricorn, a halberd
and hodden grey breeches for the Sabbath day.

The prototype of Hielant Polisman
he sat off-duty in their dingy howffs
in Canongate ingle-neuks
fisting a brandy-glass that the young spirits filled,
delighted to send a Highland poet up
to shout in Gaelic from remembered bens.

Why yes your honour I'll write a verse for you
sa Ghaidhlig a dhuine is traigh na galla ort
and here's your very good health, sir.

'*Would I were striding on Buachaill Eite
and the snow above my kneecaps
while every denizen of dull Dunedin
followed without a shoe between them.*'

Fair Duncan of the Songs,
Grey Duncan of the doggerel,
the fate of all bards
when time takes the hill from them.

William Neill

RANNOCH MOOR

In the gilded frame of memory
a youthful traverse made
midge-free and bog-forgotten
in golden sunlight and silver mist
when the old Caledon forest creaked below
and shivered under the Orchy-Rannoch railway track.
Decades later, oozing through the moor
while the deer stood and looked
unmoved by the plodding dolt
pale of face and bright of kilt
heading for King's House from Rannoch
in the late October twilight.
Recalled ascent of Schiehallion
and now Meall a' Bhuiridh on a marigold horizon,
just the sense of merely being
drove damp tiredness into night.

Roland Gant

RANNOCH

Rannoch in June, Loch Tulla blue
beside white sand,   heather
rusted in the sun,

Rannoch of Scotland where the pine
jags from the bog the fist
shuts sharp on memory, the summer hawk

decides,
dips down beyond Loch Ericht.

G J F Dutton

GLEN ETIVE HEATWAVE

I remember . . .
Bemused sun-hazed senses registering
And paying homage to colours,
Caught in the mind and held,
To be produced again in the dark wet streets
Of some gray-cold city day.

I remember . . .
Our hot and breathless climb,
As we looked down on shimmering green
And blue and golden treasures
Of ancient woods, and far peaks and lonely lochs
Whose permanence tugs at the heart.

I remember . . .
The sun, fiery and relentless,
Driving the deer to shady hollows
And the burns to silence, and the thick,
Luxuriant clusters of bracken
Holding a somnolent heat.

I remember . . .
That special day of warm, dry grass
And rock, and the cool shock
Of water in translucent pools, and
The memory of a grail reached
By joyous fools.

Rennie McOwan

WINTER NIGHT, GLENCOE

The hills lie
White on the sky
Moon cold and still.
And I
Spraying frost
From the bound, gagged grass
Listen for life.

But sound is lost
Held
Fastened to ice.
Stars move
In themselves
In the sky
Throwing sparks
To fire smothered snow
Blazing below
While I
Ringing night
From the close barred earth
Search for keys
Listen for life.

Anne B Murray

ON ANOCH EGADH

The blizzard of the upper air which roars
sedition on these peaks unites them all,
Bidean and Buchaille and the white Mamores
forget their titles underneath that fall,

even this cairn, which once was stone on stone,
trembles no more before the leavening weather;
adversity has like an armour grown;
the crystals of the fog bind him together.

We do not care, although the storm blow colder,
because that ranting breath will join us by
a bond more strong and more elastic than

the nylon rope that's coiled upon my shoulder,
and in the fellowship of peak and sky
enroll the cold and lonely mind of man.

William Bell

CLIMBING IN GLENCOE

The sun became a small round moon
And the scared rocks grew pale and weak
As mist surged up the col, and soon
So thickly everywhere it tossed
That though I reached the peak
With height and depth both lost
It might as well have been a plain;
Yet when, groping my way again,
On to the scree I stept
It went with me, and as I swept
Down its loose rumbling course
Balanced I rode it like a circus horse.

Andrew Young

BELOW AONACH DUBH

five-eighths moon
detaches itself
from Aonach Dubh
as we leave the Clachaig
& brew midnight coffee.

nearing the solstice,
we have again come north
to feel closer to
this strange time
of long light & wide days.

below the black bulk
of the landscape
we talk quietly,
high on beer
& the northern summer,
before bedding down.

as we wait for sleep,
listening to
the soft movement
of cotton tent walls,
a single gull
screams across the night.

Kevin Borman

LOCH LINNHE

Here in mountainous Morven
I stand upon this bouldered beach
Rich red, dark grey, beige,
Whorled and banded,
Sea-shelled, weed-tangled
And yet more deeply coloured
Where tide's pull
Has left it wet:
Under my feet
A seething, salty world,
Crabs in camouflage,
Stone sucking starfish,
Slippery sea slugs
Living out a watery existence
In semi-darkness:
I lift my eyes and look
Across your waters
Silent, sun-sparkled,
See the massive lower halves of mountains
The tops so lost in cloud
That I can only guess
At what is hidden.

Margaret Gillies

C. I. C. DEPARTURE

At six we stood coldly on the snow,
wondered why
we'd left our bunks, the comfort of the hut,
for an icy sky.
    Within?
        Warm walls of wood,
sleep, blanket-deep, dream-drugged —
lazy delight . . .

but we cramponed off before the stars
burned out of the northern light.
    Ahead?
        A new route of our wanting, wanting, lay.
Its price our early exodus,
our joy in matching day.

Hamish Brown

ROUTE

we made a route on last night's mountain.
from the ruin picked out
a single buttress, set it,
twelve hours' rock and ice,

white from the ruck of the dark.
can now look back and trace it,
drifting star to star
across the cold lumber,

committed, all construction over.
can enter the hut and close the door;
beside the fire
rejoin the peace of transience.

G J F Dutton

THE BOAR OF BADENOCH
AND THE SOW OF ATHOLL

Few have seen the King Selkie and few the grand
Sweep of the wings as the Queen Swan comes to land,
In the long light days of summer when
    florrish is sweet on the bough,
Seeking their island mates between the machair and plough.
But none saw the Boar of Badenoch cover his sow.

Away on the skerry the Selkie nurses his dream,
Far from her shining bridal the Swan has flown.
And the Boar of Badenoch couches, still and alone,
Weighted, the ridge of his bristles,
    with scree and heather and stream
For his sow has eaten her pigs and turned into stone.

Naomi Mitchison

CHANGE AND IMMUTABILITY

When I went up to Clova glen
And I was in my 'teens
And got there on a bicycle
And lived on bread and beans.
And covered twenty miles or so
And got up Dreish and Mayar
The May month oystercatcher flights
Were madly piping there.

When I went up to Clova glen
And I was fifty-five,
And lived on wine and caviare
And had a car to drive.
And managed half a dozen miles
And halfway up the hill
The May month oystercatcher flights
Were madly piping still.

Syd Scroggie

408

THE SIGNPOST

Snowflakes dance on the night;
   A single star
Glows with a wide blue light
   On Lochnagar.

Through snow-fields trails the Dee;
   At the wind's breath
An ermine-clad spruce-tree
   Spits snow beneath.

White-armed at the roadside
   Wails a signpost,
'To-night the world has died
   And left its ghost.'

Andrew Young

BRAEMAR RIVERSIDE

The setting sun
On treeless hills,
And corries slowly filling up with evening.

Where the water ripples over sand,
A trout above his shadow
Waiting for a dancing midge to fall.

A curlew in a meadow by the river
Whistling to his echo from the crag.

A breeze that leaves the grass astir,
Like a multitude of people in the streets
Talking of calamity.

William Montgomerie

THE LAIRIG GHRU

Is this the Lairig then, this halcyon way?
Thick terror should by rights possess the soul,
Madness by night, uneasy haste by day
To slip the skinny clutch of loitering troll.
Where is the storm that shrieks, the silent snow
Sifting that ruck of melancholy bone
There where the Grey Man's monstrous footfalls go
And reeling warlocks ring the Tailors' stone?
This is that impish genii the sun
And his the hand and his the shimmering brain
And his the laughter when the wheel was spun.
This is some other age, some other land
And we by noonday's mirage pilgrims twain
Upon the golden road to Samarkand.

Syd Scroggie

CLOUDS ON THE CAIRNGORMS

They come to life in cloud, the old Blue Hills:
In hooded shapes that brood above the storm —
That move and melt and change and queerly flow;
That grow and gather, lift themselves, reveal
A profile proud, a young upcurving breast,
A shoulder set against the arch of heaven.
And climbers on Macdhui hear strange feet
Crunching behind them, while a floating voice
Laughs gustily across the hidden glens . . .

Now Fear, with folded wings, sits beckoning
Upon the edge of chasms. Crags fall sheer
To smoking hollows filled with shapeless gloom,
And phantom peaks loom watchful in the mist.
Yet hill-men lift their eyes and feel as gods,
Until the veil is lifted, and they see,
With new awareness of remembered things,
The Blue Hills lying naked in the sun,
Their faces all ashine with recent rain.

Brenda G Macrow

410

LOCH MORLICH

on a spit of sand, a pine on tiptoe, enough
space under the roots for a man to walk through:
they're like a rusted grab abandoned by workmen
decades ago, somehow the tree's still alive

in a wide clearing, a floor of roots to walk over,
no growth in the triangles of dry sand:
the ravel can never be unpicked, the loops all
uneven like a child's first attempt at weaving

in a fertile corner, with earth and junipers,
a giant pine on its side, almost as white as quartz:
it should be in a museum with metal rods
supporting its bones and learned estimates of its age

in the shallows, a stump (surely older still)
with two moulded roots sticking up like horns:
something has been retreating or advancing so
long and stubbornly only the gesture remains

Robin Fulton

MARCH, LOCH DUNTELCHAIG

By feeling heat, and watching light
fall smoothly over stone and snow
flanks of low hills, I can extract
Summer from the windless sun
behind a South rock. It is the first
of another season. Tourists drone
their cars like bees along the loch,
stirring dust like Summer's up.
But from a higher stance I look
beyond the loch, where Affric hills
rise hidden from the road; and cold,
and firmly cased in Winter still.

Philip Coxon

MOOLA: A LAMENT FOR THE LAND

The land is empty now:
only the roofless homes of the former folk remain,
        bleak heaps of stones.
Rowans grow where, praying, folk smoored their peats.
No need now for the cruisie's glow,
        or the kind hospitality.
The hosts have gone, and gone with them
          the songs.
Smoked out from their green glens
men wept, caged like cattle, carried in carts,
        their families following,
put off the land for ever for the coming
        of the sheep.
Unlettered folk, their songs once floated free,
        never pinioned on paper
        lest the unfeeling eye see . . .
Their craft was art;
each chore a song,
each song the rhythm of a people's life.
Low black thatched dwellings, thick-set walls
housed in those days the wandering Christ, welcomed
with him the foster-mother, blithe singing Bride.
Each Gael then fed, healed and blessed kindred
        and wayfarer,
took ware of elements, of omen and faery.

Few folk remain, fewer have the language.
Exhaust fumes summer long blacken silent glens.
Oil flows. Magnates pipe their profits southwards.
Sell Gaeldom, pre-packed in tartan wrapping.
        Now bed-and-board is pricey.
      Brigit with her Fosterling,
      Mary, Virgin of the ringlets,
        Christ himself
      and Colum kindly
        can't afford to stay.

Jenny Robertson

TALLYMAN

It must be easily
the hottest day so far this year.
Along the crest of the Glendryan Hills
the grass snaps under my feet.
If it were dark the rocks would glow.

I see the flies and hear them
before I see the sheep they quarrel over.
A cloud of bluebottles
thick enough to cast a shadow.
When she moves off at my approach
they rev up and follow.

Maggots, of course. You could scoop them
off her back in handfuls.
Small carnivorous worms with non-stop appetites,
they worry her to death.
The flies wait for the bones.

Sheep die unnoticed as a rule.
I was lucky to come across this one.
They go apart when their time comes
but without knowing why. They die instinctively.

I fan myself with my notebook.
It was cooler after all at sea level.
A stray bluebottle
follows me persistently all the way down.

Alasdair Maclean

RHUM

Rhum is like a great mother
Standing westwards on the sea
Calling silently to her children East and West.
Silent, beautiful, motionless;
Mysterious, beckoning from distant years
Rising out of the depths in her strong firm form.

And Hallival and Askival and Ainshval are her breasts
And the soft hills by Kinloch are her belly,
And she feeds the clouds with her firm paps,
And milky-white they fleece around her,
And sometimes she is covered by them in their grey rain
   of love
As she immerses herself in her children
And in the moist caresses of her lovers.

Denis Rixson

MYSTIC ISLES

Across a crimson glow, the gull wings its way
Towards the ragged rims of islands,
Whose misty peaks beckon us to follow.

To Rhum, Eigg and distant Mull, where sleek otters play
In shallow pools, and oystercatchers rise from golden sands
Cast in tidal ebb and flow.

On timeless shores, nature's hand wields the brush
To burnish magic tints on lichened ledge,
where raven soars, and seals bask in rising light.

In absence, memory returns to mystic isles,
And going back, as if in ancient pledge,
The heart fills with music of delight.

Ian Strachan

AT CORUISK

1
Think of it: a honeymoon at the foot
Of the Cuillin, and not once to see them
For mist — till in the last day we broached
From Elgol the seven crowned kings.

So intense the experience: not summers only,
But years, cramming one afternoon —
Thus keenly the glimpse awaited.
Nor had been envisaged such blueness:

Ice-crests mirrored in Coruisk, blue
Upon blue, as we followed
The path home. The moon crescent.
The sky, powdered flint.

2
Tempting to see these things
As manifestations of the mind
Significant through ourselves,
Which precede and succeed our notice.

For all that, the shadows are real.
They darken or illumine, at will;
Are points from which
To examine ourselves. But watch

How you go: yonder are scurrs
Would cut you down; nearer
To hand, rusty bracken,
Peat-holes where you'd cramp and drown.

3
So we get to know landscape,
And each other, better;
Our breathing filling the air
With each lap tackled. We learn

That the end of the road is seldom
A given point; that bridges exist
Too narrow to be crossed
More than two abreast.

Yet remains the fear, when
We look round, that two figures
Not dissimilar to ourselves should appear
Transparent, then vanish altogether.

Stewart Conn

ROCK APES

For centuries the Cuillin waited,
A svelte beast padding the veldt of the west
Hungry for a name.
In the end men came to play their game,
Aping ancestry, climbing and screaming,
Beating their breasts . . .

Rock struck when they came
With claws sharp from gabbro imaginings;
But the same bare men return,
And return and return,
Stalking the hardest mountains of the mind
(Ice-clean and basalt-smooth)
And wanting them untamed.

Hamish Brown

MIST ON CIOCH SLAB

We are imprisoned . . .
Around us damp grey walls,
Walls of insinuating dampness
Dimming the light, curtailing vision and freedom
                                                of the eye,
And permeating the mind with the chill of
                                        indefinable isolation.
Imprisoned on a rooftop,
A restricted radius, a tilted circle of grey rock,
Wet with the seeping water of recent rains,
Bounded by creeping greyness
And the vagueness of indeterminate shapes.
Darker forms loom above . . . and disappear,
Like strange ships on a moonless night,
As the faint wind rises and dies, rustling the curtain;
But nothing else . . .
And, like blind men, more acutely now we hear
The drip, drip, drip from unguessed walls above,
The rain-born stream tinkling down the unseen gully,
And the far, faint moan of the sea.

416

Once there was another world, and other men,
A vision of a green glen
Spreading below us to a gull-white bay,
Black-beetle boats on a sunlit sea,
And blue islands . . .
It is a dream-world! Only the veil remains;
Only the rope and the rock are real.

Colin Shone

END OF A DAY IN SKYE

Evening is curled round my tent like a flame.
Outside, in its still centre
I watch the rocks burn red
And feel where my hands have touched and climbed
In the day long sun.
Beneath them now the grass is cool;
Lingering cool on the fingers' rawness.
Before me the sea gathers sound from the hills' silence
And slides molten smooth and slow
Out of the burnished sky
Out of the night,
The waves flare white on the splashed, broken shore
Of my bird still island.
Nothing is required of me now
But to watch the flames die
And to see the torn sky turn green behind the Cuillin.
The hills grow black and near my arms' reach.
Out of the sway of wild flowers
I turn to the tent
And the coiled rope
And the coolness.
My limbs rest on turf
And there is only night now —
Night
And the Black Cuillin waiting.

Anne B Murray

CREAG DALLAIG

Expectation and hope are changed,
and there is not much hope;
the sun on the snow of Creag Dallaig,
there is no sense in her speech;
she says nothing at all
but that she is,
and she has said that before,
and left my head perplexed.

My heart is on the ridge
and half of it down,
and my head climbs and falls
and hangs on a narrow shelf,
and my feet have no support
but my heart, which is getting blunt,
and the brain has no foothold
to lower a rope to my heart.

Sorley Maclean

GLEN DESSARRY

I have been here before I feel
Like a wind that circles a hill
And in its own self catches peace —
A memory stilled.

Could an ancestor reach a hand
To take mine, by the old march cairn,
Just as last summer quietly gone
I led my own bairn?

These hills hint no fear of their past.
They are 'home', as to ling, or deer;
But when I look past my son's sons,
It is then I fear.

Hamish Brown

OVERTAKEN BY MIST

Like lightning on the mountain-slope
The stalker's path zigzagged,
And climbing it with steps that lagged
I often raised my eyes in hope
To where Scour Ouran's head was bare;
But mist that gathered from nowhere
With a bright darkness filled the air,
Until, both earth and heaven gone,
Never was man or angel so alone.

Andrew Young

ACHNASHELLACH

Achnashellach is a tweed-scented weave of trees:
Some willows that send catkins stalking spring,
Some alders trying the waters with timid toes,
Some holly, bloodied with holding together ancient crags,
And larches which have the decency to blush this autumn
At the pressing bulk of the green serge
Of pines
Or spruce.
They patiently clothe the hard quartz and gritty sandstone,
Retailing a soft, green summertime.

Here forestry actually dresses the naked hills tastefully,
A couturier's touch on the normal Highland casualness.
High above the trees it may be winter ermine still,
with frozen features on grim faces:
Fuar Tholl,
Moruisg,
But below lies Golden Valley, slippered in moss,
Sequined with little waters, grown opulent with trees.
Achnashellach is all trees!
A tree wardrobe for the smart hills' wives,
Piling ring on ring, fur on fur,
In priceless abandon. It both shocks
And thrills as this rich firm robes
The bare fleshiness of our prim minds.

Hamish Brown

419

THE MUNRO BAGGER

On the hills above the Coulin Forest the air baked.
From a clear pool, on a green col, I drink two hats of water;
Pulling the third around my ears.
High, above the shattered face of Sgorr Ruadh,
An eagle wheels slowly.
Oh bird how I envy you
Planing the thermals with insolent skill,
Garnering Munros by the gross.
With the measured beats of your wings
You slice across the airless bowl of Torridon
And I lose you in the pinnacles of Liathach.
Slathered in sweat, my hat crisp upon my head again,
I turn to the treadmill.
With a feathery flick you traversed from Liath Mhor to Maol
    Chean-dearg,
Huffing and puffing I take a little longer.
You grace the hills, I grease them.
What a ridiculous waste of energy
To gain three ticks in a daft book.
But there's more to it than that.
On an English winter night
When I crackle the map across the table,
Dreaming of unclimbed heights,
Falls from the folds a fine dust,
Old peat, heather and grass.
And I take a sybaritic sniff
Of this dessicated Highland snuff,
And across the screen of my closed eyes pass —
The sandstone towers of Liathach,
The Black Carls of Beinn Eighe,
The green silvered swell of Slioch
And an eagle
Turning slowly in Torridonian thermals . . .

Tom Bowker

AT DIABAIG, WESTER ROSS

long days continue.
the sun over Cancer.
evening , from the tent
      white cloud
      grey loch
      white orchid
      black peat
      white bird.
at eleven
dusk filters in
& slopes darken.
at two
dawn filters in.
we sleep through
such cool hours.
      Old Norse
      'diup vik'
      'deep bay'
      Diabaig.
we wake & look out.
the raw landscape throws us
back   to the dragon prows
up   to the quartzite summits
in   to ourselves.

Kevin Borman

ON BEN WYVIS

I left the straight grey road behind
And followed for two miles or more a crooked glen,
Past falls and rock-pools, coursing to and fro;
Stream waters do not take the shortest way
To where they want to go; not like the roads,
Laid down by men and burdened with their loads;
Hard, new, furrows on the ancient wrinkled land.

The stream flowed down, a rivulet of sweat,
Fresh water salt with sediments of thought,
Borne down from that dark rugged brow above.
I walked against the flow, it did not hinder;
It lent me stones to step on, helped me forward,
Easier than the clogging path 'longside,
That zigzagged here and there amid the heather.

And so I gained six hundred feet of height,
Then left the glen and climbed through rock and scree,
But soon high on that face I paused and stood,
And climbed no more, but followed with my eyes
Up where the broken path was lost in cloud.
The top was covered that day, as were the heads
Of all the other hills around, as if in solemn conclave.

A chill breeze blew and wreaths wrapped round the slopes,
The glooming mists unsettled, then
Slowly round those high rock-towers swirled again.
I wondered what lay up there and how far,
But did not dare intrude upon that restless brooding;
And so I turned and went down, like the stream,
In deference to the gravity above.

Ivor W Highley

COMING SOUTH FROM LOCH LURGAIN

morning: Stac Polly is a total wreck, more
total than the puny wreck of a metropolis,
near the rock a human voice breaks open
like toy thunder, the silence snaps shut on it

evening: from the right distance we can see
the Summer Isles levitate above the water
and Cul Beag bright and transparent as a lace
curtain, if we were closer it would ripple in our breath

Robin Fulton

ACHILTIBUIE

The miraculous panorama of the mountains
Invests this bare arena; Quinag and Ben More of Assynt,
Suilven and Canisp, Coulmore, Coulbeg, Stac Polly
Hollow the earth in a vast palm.
Blue waters by the score, sea loch and tarns by the hundred
Lilt or wink at the immaculate sky.
Down through the brown peat-acres
Sour with reed and rush, beflagged with bog-cotton,
The sea burnished as brass, bright as glass
Glitters away to the Summer Isles that float
Black and bland, buoyantly immaterial
Beyond the edge of accessibility
In the Western sea.

White houses front the shore.
Voices of children borne from the schoolhouse
Across the still air lend the belief
That here men still achieve the daily realities
That earth has not abandoned all to sky and sea,
Shuddering in the grip of a conspiracy of mountains.
A buzzard soaring, hump-shouldered raven upon a rock
Proclaim the tenure earth's frail copyhold provides
Upon the tenuous transparency this place has now.
Pity drifts on the face of the moor: it is with you
Here, it will remain, enchain you. Go,
Look to the west and see tomorrow's sun
Set on the ocean's rim,
The twilight greying and the isles grow dim.

Kenneth Wood

CLIMBING SUILVEN

I nod and nod to my own shadow and thrust
A mountain down and down.
Between my feet a loch shines in the brown,
Its silver paper crinkled and edged with rust.
My lungs say No;
But down and down this treadmill hill must go.

Parishes dwindle. But my parish is
This stone, that tuft, this stone
And the cramped quarters of my flesh and bone.
I claw that tall horizon down to this;
And suddenly
My shadow jumps huge miles away from me.

Norman MacCaig

SUILVEN

It rose dark as a stack of peat
With mountains at its feet,
Till a bright flush of evening swept
And on to its high shoulder leapt
And Suilven, a great ruby, shone;
And though that evening light is dead,
The mountain in my mind burns on,
As though I were the foul toad, said
To bear a precious jewel in his head.

Andrew Young

HILL BEING ORGAN

I once heard
Blunt Suilven throb tremolo and deep down
In an Atlantic gale. I was half-frightened.
Bach would have loved it.

It was as if
A tree were to dance in a Scotch, not Bali way,
Flinging about its field, almost saying Hooch
Like a Scot in a story.

There are other
Differences between me and Bach, but that is one.
He had the advantage, of course; he knew the language
The mountain was speaking.

One thing —
The quirky trebles sounded in the loch below —
I could understand them, agreeably ornamenting
That ferocious ground bass.

A good job, else
I would be frightened of Bach, except when he
Danced like a tree not moving — just imagine
Bach saying Hooch.

Norman MacCaig

ASSYNT 1964: TEN FACETS

Laid
Twelve crofts still lived in, along two miles of road,
No children left, and time demands its toll.
Sans bus, sans power, sans future, the old linger
And blink at Hope across Loch Eriboll.

The Commemorative Spring on the Rhiconich-Durness Road.
There was no road; the Victorians made it.
This well commemorates the feat.
They could not know it merely aided
A population's slow retreat.

Kylesku Ferry, August
The red flag's ripped and drivers curse
While ten-foot waves roar through the caol.
And as the tiny cars reverse
The storm-clouds cover Quinag's smile.

Rubha Coigeach
Eroded walls of red and black
Have stunned the ceaseless sea since time
Swung round upon another tack
And living cells were spawned by slime.

Sandwood
The surf's slow drum-beat on the sand
Buries the rotting timbers deeper.
Beneath scarred cliffs the sailors sleep
With a mermaid for their keeper.

Assynt
Enticing land, where scraped and barren rock
Cups frequent pools where water lilies flower;
Where mountains keep apart and try to shock
By vertical pronouncements of their power.

From Ben Stack
The Lews ride smoothly on the sea;
Arkle's frost-torn hulk squats by.
Lochans, map-coloured in the sun,
Reflect their glacial ancestry.

Loch Clash
The shoal of drifters darned up to the quay
Ensures, you'd think, the locals' daily bread.
Of these tough boats and tougher crews
All bar one came here from Peterhead.

The Warning Notice on the Approach to Suilven
from Lochinver
The wealthy want to make their kill
Without the fuss of shooting you.
So steer clear of this silly hill
Or find *your* guts in ghillie's stew.

From Meall an Fheadain
The Summer Isles sleep in the sun
On a blue bed speckled white.
Stac Pollaidh combs a passing cloud
But cannot stop it taking flight.

Martyn Berry

THE CLEARING OF THE HIGHLANDS

The year that Patrick Sellar came to Strathnaver
black smoke hung along its length
from the homes so lately vacated by his tenants;
too late for one young woman who would not leave,
so perished in the flames, her unborn child within her.
Old men, led out in time, were laid
to die from frost instead of fire.

Some went meekly like the sheep that replaced them
down the road to the barren, rocky coast,
driving their salvaged beasts before them,
oats and barley left for sheep to trample,
potatoes in their lazybeds left to rot.

A lowland jury cleared him later of all charges.

Many were the poor and destitute in Bettyhill,
in Farr, in Tongue, in Golspie and in Helmsdale
who died later from cholera or the famine.

Others, who could survive Atlantic storms
and carve new life from frozen wasteland,
found Canada no more tough than Sutherland;
there are more Gaels in North America
than ever crossed the Minch.

Not only in Strathnaver but in every glen
and by the side of every ben
factors served writs, burnt out, moved on a people
betrayed by the chiefs for whom they had always fought,
but now preferred a four-footed tenantry;

though not named Sellar
only their faces were different.

Seventeen babies died on the Street of Starvation
when six hundred people were cleared from Ulva
and dumped on Mull.

The lairds and Lowland shepherds said
it was for the 'Improvement of the People'

— that vast peasantry
who lost their homes, their hopes
and the inheritance they had thought infinite?

Gerald England

NORTH OF KYLESKU

South, the Summer Isles
sleep in a silver bay
under Suilven and Stac Polly.

Cross on the ferry,
the sild flash their bellies
in the clear green strait.

Abruptly the land is cut
into component parts:
water and metamorphic rock.

There's no compromise:
that was ice-ground,
drowned in a thousand tarns.

Its lord is Poverty.
The wind sacks his domain,
the sea hammers at his gate,

his lodge is a derelict
croft where no bird
shelters in the fallen roof.

Long ago an old song
died in this wilderness
among the rust-red grass.

And yet Fionavon's ruined face
is lit by a wintry sun:
an old man smiling.

John Ward

THE SUTHERLAND HILLS

Stiff they stand like awkward wrecks,
In barren beauty rise aloof,
Mocked by Heaven's regal roof;
Stac Polly and its twisted, tight
Pinnacles, that stretch their necks
Striving for still greater height.
Time's hollow chisel carved them so,
Chipped off a corner, and then scraped
A clumsy gully in its slow
Persuasion of the rock, that shaped
Itself in eccentricity.
Canisp's staid sobriety
Gazes round in drab disdain
Upon these dinosaurs of rock
That, hard, persistent as the plain,
Are with us till the planets flock
Like flies up to the Deity,
Who'll set the luckless lava free.
Will Time then roll up the moor's mat,
And will the wind scrub Suilven flat?

Rayne Mackinnon

QUIET DAYS IN SUTHERLAND

the tides
are opening and closing relentlessly

the hills
year after year are monotonous
shaded now and again by a drifting cloud
or by an occasional autumn with purple shadows

for the curious
there are small hard revelations:
plates of soft shale flake in your fingers
and the whorled fossil is at last unlocked

429

for the lustful
the sudden warm scent of bog-myrtle
pours a voluptuous mirage across the moor

without warning
the days can harden into thin layers
that cling with the pressure of stony ages
and will not be prised apart by the curious
by the lustful or even by the desperate
who carelessly left something small and precious
lying between them while they were still open

Robin Fulton

REMOTE COUNTRY

The way goes snaking upward through the heat.
Out of the carving river's narrow space
Shaken with noise of water, black and white,
You climb at last into a scooped out place
Where nothing moves but wind treading the grass.

All cover's past. Below, the waterfalls
Dig out of sight, like memory. You stare up,
Strange in this trap ringed all about by hills,
To find the one way out, confined and steep,
Watched by whatever eyes look from the top.

When you have crossed the open, reached the height,
It is a brown plateau, cratered and bare,
Low, lumpy hills and black, eroded peat
Stretching as far as light can throw its glare,
No living thing in sight in sky or moor.

Mind finds its way to meet with solitude.
Bear this in mind: the image will not age
Of desert, light and always moving cloud.
It is a vision to exhaust all rage.
Calculate nothing. Leave an empty page.

Sydney Tremayne

430

SCOTIA
i. m. Hugh Mac Diarmid

We have come so far North,
farther than we have ever been
to where gales strip everything
and the names ring guttural
syllables of old Norse:
Thurso, *Scrabster*, *Laxdale*,
names clang like a battle-axe.

Then further West. There beauty
softens, a darkening estuary,
Farr or Borgie or Skerray where
waist high in shallow waters
silent shadows cast at night
to lasso the lazily feeding trout
to gleam upon our hotel plate.

Still farther, mountains gather,
blue peak lifting beyond blue peak,
Ben Loyal and then Ben Hope,
noble, distant as the Twelve Bens
or Brandon; single-tracks on
endless moors, or threading along
the flanks of melancholy lochs.

Loch Loyal and Loch Naver,
where Alpine flowers blossom,
the wilderness's blessing;
as MacDiarmid will proudly remark
in our last, rambling conversation,
'strange, lovely things grow up there,
ecologically, *vairy* inter-resting.'

By such roads, only sheep prosper,
bending to crop the long acre, or
whiten the heather, like bogcotton.
The name of this county, Sutherland,
synonym for burnings, clearance,
the black aura of Castle Dunrobbin,
stone cottages broken, like Auburn.

We are not Thirties aesthetes, leaving
on impulse 'for Cape Wrath tonight'
but fellow Gaels, who have come
as far as the Kyle of Tongue
to see a sister country, Scotland,
or what is left of it, before
Scotia, like Wallia, is plundered.

Along the new motorway, trucks
and trailers strain, an invasion
grinding from England, the Grampians
pushed aside, in search of wealth;
the North Sea's blackening pulse,
the rigs towed from Moray Firth
to prop a fading Imperial strength.

Beyond Tongue, still rises Ben Hope
and that star of mountains, Sulliven,
that beckons to an intent fisherman,
MacCaig, with whom I share a patronym,
His unswerving eye and stylish eye
pierce through flesh to dying bone.
May Scotland always have such fishermen

Nourishing a lonely dream of how
this desolate country might have been!
The rightful arrogance of MacDiarmid's
calling together of Clann Albann,
or the surging lamentations of Maclean,
the sound of his echoing Gaelic
a fierce pibroch crying on the wind.

John Montague

In Lighter Mood

'NAYLOR'

CUMBERLAND ROCKS

O some love rocks for building-stone
   And some love rocks for shade,
And some love rocks because they wonder how the rocks
     are made;
But we just love the rocks themselves
   That stand the test of time —
The high rocks, the great rocks,
The fine upstanding straight rocks,
   The rocks that you can climb.

Now rocks they have a character
   As various as man,
And some will lure you on to leave you sliding if they can;
But we can find the better rock
   And if we can we must —
The sound rock, the sheer rock,
The stand-a-thousand-year rock,
   The rock that you can trust.

O some they go to Switzerland
   And some they go to Spain,
And still they search for greater rocks again and yet again;
But we have found in Cumberland
   The kind of rock we need —
The hard rock, the fast rock,
The stuff-that's-made-to-last rock,
   That we can love indeed.

John C Lyth

MOUNTAIN MEMORIES, 1924

May one of those who normally essay
   The lightest themes of superficial rhymers
Presume, unchecked, to criticise the way
   Of certain mountain-climbers?

I clambered lately to Helvellyn's crest.
   There, if you share my notion of aesthetics
You'll sympathise with the implied request
   In these my homiletics.

Round the full circle when your eyes have gone,
   To mark what scenes the far horizon fringes,
Observe the decorative scheme that on
   Your nearer view impinges.

Chocolate- wrappers, orange-peel, and string;
   Of sandwich-papers, white and brown, say twenty;
A 'Daily Shout'; a mangled chicken-wing:
   Banana-skins in plenty.

I lit a fire and tended it with care.
   I felt a longing that was frankly cruel.
I only wished I had those tourists there
   To serve as extra fuel.

F H J

THE MIDGES

Replete with picnickers' reluctant gore,
But with already appetite for more,
Two midges met upon a warm bald scalp
And, as may mountaineers, raised on an alp
Above concern with mere material things,
Soared after truth on speculation's wings.
'Each midge,' said one, 'will thoughtlessly apply
To what he thinks "himself" the title "I":
The rest are "others", though they're midges who
Use that expression of their selfhood too:

Now, if you're but a concept of my brain,
A midge subjective, and if I, again,
Am one of your illusions, how can we
Debate concerning midge reality?'
'Your metaphysics, sir,' the other said,
'Are definitely far above my head.
I, for my part, am troubled now and then
About these appetizing monsters, men.
Have you reflected how man must be tried
By wonder how his being's justified?
What is his cosmic purpose? From fresh youth
To desiccated age, he misses truth,
To which he might approximate, at least,
On days when we've enjoyed a picnic-feast.
Will not some human sage, enlightened thus,
Cheer him by showing he exists for us —
That, lacking man, no midge-race could survive?'
'At that great truth let's help him to arrive,'
The other answered, and with that the pair
Resumed the banquet pink around them there,
Agile to rise before a slap came down
In futile fury on the tickled crown.

W K Holmes

THE LEADER

The leader, to restore his phlegm,
Designs an artful stratagem,
Aware that, with the rope below,
Should fate disturb the status quo,
Then twice the distance of the rope
He'd drop at speed, without much hope
(Acceleration, unimpaired,
Thirty-two feet per second squared).
He threads his rope through loops of line,
Running belays his anodyne! —
From fear alone; from harm no shield
When there's a deadly flaw concealed,
Producing from this scheme, though shrewd,
An undesired vicissitude.

He slips, and from above is heard
A very rude four-letter word;
Then screams, as he perceives too late
His unpremeditated fate:
The loops were thin, a masquerade
Of safety, and have snapped; betrayed,
He drops spreadeagled through the void,
An unprehensile anthropoid.
But from this lack of commonsense
Results no fatal consequence.
Our ignoramus is not dead:
You see, he landed on his head.

Keith McDonald

STOBINIAN

Mapless into the mist went they,
Mapless into the mist.
We'll just come back, we will, said they,
If the mist gets thick and we lose the way:
Mapless into the mist went they,
Mapless into the mist.

Sprightly on to the snow went they,
Sprightly on to the snow.
Our track we'll follow back, said they,
We shouldn't need a map today —
As mapless into the mist went they,
And sprightly on to the snow.

Torchless into the night went they,
Torchless into the night.
The moon should give us light, said they,
And the mist is bound to clear away —
Ah — mapless into the mist went they,
And torchless into the night.

To seek Stobinian's peak went they
Mapless into the mist.
Now frost-encrusted phantoms grey
For ever more in circles stray:
For mapless into the mist went they,
Mapless, into the mist.

Eilidh Nisbet

OXFORD ACCENT

A Nevis gully choked with ice,
For you, a silent prayer.
They say it makes you hard and tough
For the Himalaya.

It's no go the Lhotse face. It's no go for Hillary.
All we want is the tourist track, and tea at the Distillery.

Hamish MacInnes took a peg,
Banged it in a crevice,
Tried to tell us that it was
The hardest climb on Nevis.

It's no go the etrier. It's no go the piton.
All we want is an easy slab, and a stance to sit your seat on.

Willie Murray 'tween the wars
Forced a route on Buachaille.
The powers that be now think it fit
For anyone to tackle.

It's no go the long run-out. It's no go the clinkers.
Use twenty slings on every pitch, and hide the drop with blinkers.

Dr. Bell when editing
Gave as his opinion,
Moss and slime are good for us
From Suilven to Stobinian.

It's no go the descendeur. It's no go the rappel.
All we want is the quick way off, and a ticket back to Capel.

David Oldman

439

'GENTLE RAIN FROM HEAVEN'

I fret
By Crummock, glum
As clouds are dipping low
And rain is drifting, dripping slow,
But yet
Regret
Is vain. With rain
These Fells were ever fraught —
A cautious thought to set at naught
A bet
That 'Met'
Reports one quotes
Will say 'Set fair to-day'.
Such phrases lead astray, one may
Forget,
So Let
The ONE have fun.
HIS laughter thunders, splits the sky,
But God, I wish Thy wit was dry,
Not Wet!

S Russell Jones

RAIN SPREADING FROM THE WEST

We who dwell among the Mountains
  In the regions of unrest —
Wet we know and wind may trounce us —
Must, oh must you always flounce us
With the B.B.C. Announcer's:
  Rain is spreading from the West?

You who listen in the City
  To the prophets we detest,
Why not cut them down and shorten?
Only one report is certain —
Light the fire, draw the curtain —
  Rain is spreading from the West.

440

How would you feel, when you came in
   Cold and soaking to your vest,
Winter gone, and Summer coming,
Hail upon the windows drumming,
Switched, and heard above the humming:
   Rain is spreading from the West?

Ah, but one thing I shall live for,
   In the hope that once at least,
On some bright and sunny morning,
Hills and valleys Spring adorning,
I may hear this solemn warning:
   Rain is spreading from the East!

John C Lyth

UPON A HILLSIDE

Upon a hill-side
I met an oul fellow,
Sittin' on a dry dike
When the whin was yellow.
There on Slieve-na-Largy
Restin at his ease,
Pullin at his cutty-pipe
As happy as ye please.

On the grass beside him
I tumbled down my pack,
Up again the dry ditch
I leaned my achin back;
Filled my pipe, an lit my pipe
An drew at it wi pleasure,
'A pint in a naggin-glass,'
Sez he, 'is bad measure.'

'What's that ye're talking of,
Oul man?' sez I;
'To think upon this windy hill
Of pints will make me dry.'

'Dry or full, it's naught to me,'
Sez he, 'no harm in thinkin,
But a half-yin in a quart bowl
Is mortal poor drinkin.

'All the wit in life,' sez he,
'I've found is just in knowin
How to fill it to the brim,
But not to overflowir..
Pour your drink to fili your glass,
Neither full nor empty,
Over-scarce will leave ye dry,
An over-full will tempt ye.'

Upon a hill-side
I met an oul fellow,
Sittin in the sunshine,
When the whin was yellow.
Age can talk an youth can hear,
Youth spend an age play miser;
Och, the oul has little sense,
An the young's no wiser.

Richard Rowley

IN MEMORIAM?

In the shadow of the Corner
    high above Llanberis Pass,
A gigantic sort of Boulder
    lies haphazard on the grass.

Hallowed, ancient place of meeting,
    it's a semi-sacred shrine,
Polished by the hands of climbers,
    reverently touched by mine.

(Sheila stayed at Pen-y-Pass —
    do you think I should have told her
That she would have slept no colder
    by the Boulder on the grass?)

Now they want to blast the Boulder,
    want to widen out the road.
Rise, ye ghosts of toothless tigers,
    in defence of your abode.

There's no real cause or reason,
    progress? access? — what a farce!
This is sacrilege and treason —
    leave our Boulder in the Pass!

(For we've slept upon the grass
    in the shadow of the Boulder
    that is older, yes, far older
Than the road along the Pass.)

M A Griffiths

SONG OF AN UNFIT CLIMBER

I've been sick on Beinn Alligin's summit,
I've puked on the slopes of Beinn Eighe
And Slioch is crowned with my vomit
For such is the tribute I pay.

As, retching and wretched, I've stumbled
On Liathach's pinnacled crest,
I've proved, though my body is humbled,
My spirit is up with the best.

The agile and confident tiger
May cover a group of Munros
While planning a route on the Eiger
To spotlight that anything goes.

But who is the keener I question,
The hardened athlete in his prime
Or the man with the failing digestion
Who conquers both it and his climb.

Douglas J Fraser

443

SNOWDONIA

Cader and Snowdon and Lliwedd and Glyder —
    What, after all, are formations like these?
Stratified rocks (if you come to consider)
    Placed at an angle of X-ty degrees!
Why should a person provided with reason
    Batter his bones and endanger his skin,
Trying in vain to revert for a season
    Back to the ways of his simian kin?

Answer, O climber of buttress and gully,
    Writhing in chimneys and wading in snows,
You who have breasted the crags of Cwm Dyli,
    You who have clung to the Parson his Nose,
Looked from the peak to the limitless distance,
    Mountain and sea in the rain and the sun,
Tasted the intimate joy of existence —
    Labour accomplished and victory won:

This be your thought as you turn from the summit,
    Gripping the rock as you gingerly go,
There, where the cliff with the drop of a plummet
    Dips to the scree and the valley below —
Men with a mind on a rational basis
    Walk on a road (as I'm sure that they should);
YOURS are the truly delectable places,
YOURS is a spice of the Ultimate Good!

A D Godley

from THE PEN-Y-PASS SONG

The mountains of youth have all vanished, they say,
    But I know the lie of them still;
Just turn to the right at the end of the day,
    And stop at the top of the hill.
'Tis there you will find it, its beds and its brass
    When Christmas has come to your call:
For the mountains are waiting round dear Pen-y-Pass,
    And the grey sky is over it all.

444

While the wind from Cwm Idwal, Cwm Llydau, Cwm Glas,
  Comes welcoming over the scree:
'Come back, mountain friends, to your Rest on the Pass;
  Come back, mountain climber, to me.'

Our cairns for the bairns of the future may last
  As signs of the climbs of our day;
But we hear the cheer of our friends of the past
  In the dark, as a mark for our way.
Though memory calls us, 'tis memory of joys
  Ere sorrow joined fun in our sack;
And the thoughts that we shared with each other as boys
  Are the thoughts that old Snowdon brings back.

And the wind from Cwm Idwal, Cwm Llydau, Cwm Glas,
  Comes whispering over the scree:
'Come back, mountain friends, to your youth on the pass;
  Come home, mountain climber, to me.'

Geoffrey Winthrop Young

HILLS VARIANT

Green hills, brown hills,
Hills old and grey,
Dim distant purple hills,
Fresh hills of May,
Wet hills of April morn,
Hills of the silver dawn,
Hills of the tempest torn,
    My hills for aye.

Rough hills, smooth hills,
Hills stern and bold,
Wild shaggy rampant hills,
Hills stark and cold,
Quiet hills of silent tarns,
Hills of those soul alarms,
Hills of those peaceful calms,
    My hills to hold.

Hard hills, soft hills,
Hills low and high,
Sky-romping laughing hills,
Hills that defy.
Glad hills of spirit poise,
Hills of those rock decoys,
Hills of a thousand joys,
 My hills, I cry.

Ice hills, snow hills,
Hills cold and bleak,
Light vapoured misty hills,
Hills all a-shriek.
Hills of the blizzard wild,
Hills of the fiends reviled,
Hills yet unreconciled,
 My hills to seek.

Cloud hills, rain hills,
Hills dour and dread,
Bracken-waved, heathered hills,
Hills of the dead.
Hills of a noble height,
Hills of the wild birds flight,
Hills of illumined night,
 My hills to tread.

Bare hills, pine hills,
Hills rent and shorn,
Blue-sky-enhanced hills,
Hills aeon worn.
Stone hills of sweeping scree,
Hills of the boulders free,
Hills of fraternity,
 My hills to swarm.

George Basterfield

THE TRIPPERCOCK

(A very Loose Carol of the Lake District)

'Twas dammot! and the flicksy sails
    Did fly and flimmer o'er the wave;
All toorisd were the Borrodails,
    And the Beercasks outgave.

Beware the Trippercock, my son,
    The glass that flies, the stones that crash;
Beware the Pop-Pop bird, and shun
    The frumious Bottlesmash.

He bound his clinknale sole on foot;
    Longtime the lantic foe he sought;
Then rested well by the Pinnakell,
    And groused awhile in thought.

And as in thought he humpied there,
    The Trippercock, with lingo blue,
Hurled piffling through the scorfie air
    And hurtled as it threw.

One-two! Click-click! and sharp and quick
    The clinknale foot went clitter-clack;
Till, when it swore to chuck no more,
    He went jodumphling back.

And hast thou smit the Trippercock?
    Come to my arms, my plucksome boy!
A safious time, Kerloo, Kerlimb!
    He kaykwalked in his joy.

'Twas dammot! and the flicksy sails
    Did fly and flimmer o'er the wave;
All toorisd were the Borrodails,
    And the Beercasks outgave.

Claude E Benson

HILL-WILLIES

If you're sick of queues of climbers and you think you'll spend a day
In that wild and lonely corner of the mountains far away,
When you reach your private wilderness you'll find it's not the same,
For that wild and lonely corner has been caged and rendered tame:
    It's a modern mountain landscape of the forward-looking kind —
    With the Forestry in the foreground and the Pylons up behind.

Where the moorland once rose purple to the silver of the crags
Parallelograms of ditches cross the mosses and the hags,
And a thousand thousand Christmas-trees the mountainsides adorn
Where the glens once held their revelry of oak and ash and thorn;
    And a rigid rank of giants bars the skyline, black-outlined —
    Just the Forestry in the foreground and the Pylons up behind.

'I am Progress!' shouts the Forest. 'I'm the symbol of Today!
Moors and mountains aren't productive so we've got to make them
    pay!'
'We are Power,' growl the Pylons, 'and you'll have to stand the cost —
Which is Us all over Britain and your clear horizons lost.
    We're afraid you're just not With It if you haven't got resigned
    To the Forestry in the foreground and the Pylons up behind.'

They'll be lost, our lonely places; though the Beauty-Spots will stay
With their disregarded litter-bins and odour of decay —
With some Scheduled Crags for Climbers (pay your fees and book
    your routes)
Where a Government Official checks your slings and krabs and boots.
    For the walkers, metalled footpaths, very carefully designed,
    With the Forestry in the foreground and the Pylons up behind.

And about the year Two Thousand, when our children's children ask
If we tried to save their heritage, and why we failed the task,
We may tell the shameful truth about our fond and foolish creed
Which declares that Power and Money, more than Beauty, is our need.
    They will turn away in pity, as the sighted from the blind,
    Whispering, 'Did they see the murder done, and watched, and
        didn't mind?
    Or did these faltering weaklings grow disheartened and resigned
    To the power-line's swift encroachment and the Forest tractor's
        grind?

They, who had *their* days of freedom — they, who wandered
    unconfined,
Have bequeathed to us a prison, for escape we'll never find
From the Forestry in the foreground and the Pylons up
    behind!

Showell Styles

THE PROBLEM-CLIMBING BORE-O

I am the Mountain Marabout, the world knows not my equal.
If anyone climbs a crack 'all out', I climb its stiffer sequel.
I never have climbed a cliff the way that it's been climbed
    before-O,
I'm that finger-nipping, tooth-hold-gripping, record-pipping
    Paladin,
        The Problem-Climbing Bore-O!
Just say a rock's too steep (Ha-ha!) I floor it with a leap (Ha-ha!)
I'm that highly-knowing, back-and-toeing, trumpet-blowing
    Paladin,
        The Problem-Climbing Bore-O!

I never think the rope's the thing to wear in any danger.
But I drape one arm with a hank of string, to impress a nervous
    stranger.
I drag a novice or two about, till they're numb and dumb and
    sore-O,
I'm that mazy-roping, clutch-the-coping, anteloping Humorist,
        The Problem-Climbing Bore-O!
I pause to make harangues (Ha-ha!) on absolute overhangs
    (Ha-ha!)
I'm that telescoping, stomach-groping, hairsbreadth-hoping
    Optimist,
        The Problem-Climbing Bore-O!

In enterprise of wintry kind, if the hills have any icing,
I lead my party from behind — I find it more enticing;
But if ever my party's on the rocks, 'tis then my turn to score-O,
I'm that boulder-grubbing, Alpine-snubbing, india-rubbing
    Prodigy,
        The Problem-Climbing Bore-O!

'Course, we didn't have fancy gear like that when we started.

IVAN CUMBERPATCH

I look on snow and ice (Ha-ha!) as a senile mountain vice (Ha-ha!)
I'm that slipper-slither, dare-and-dither, hither-thither Prodigy,
    The Problem-Climbing Bore-O!

I know that climbing rocks began when I did — last September;
And I'll form a Club in which every man must be the only
    Member.
It can't be true that that quaint old crew thought much the
    same of yore-O —
That beetle-booting, snowfield-scooting, fossil-looting
    Pentateuch,
    The Ancient Alpine Corps-O!
Oh how could it be true (Ha-ha!) that ever YOU or YOU (Ha-ha!)
Were that record-routing, high-faluting, parachuting Paragon,
    The Problem-Climbing Bore-O!

Geoffrey Winthrop Young

THE CROCK'S APOLOGY

When I started to climb as a very young man,
    Said I to myself, said I,
I'll work on a new and original plan,
    Said I to myself, said I.
I'll never assume that each tourist I meet
Is a leader of fame in the Climbing Elite,
Because he's a pair of nailed boots on his feet,
    Said I to myself, said I.

I'll never throw dust in the Second Man's eyes,
    Said I to myself, said I,
Nor pelt him with rocks of immoderate size,
    Said I to myself, said I.
Nor assume that a novice the size of a horse
Who's striving to climb with no skill and much force
Can be held from above as a matter of course,
    Said I to myself, said I.

Ere I start for the rocks, I will read the book through,
    Said I to myself, said I,
And I'll never lead climbs I'm unable to do,
    Said I to myself, said I.

451

The sport of the mountains I'll never disgrace
By describing a climb with a grin on my face —
When I've taken good care to keep clear of the place,
   Said I to myself, said I.

In other amusements which add to our cheer,
   Said I to myself, said I,
Such as Billiards, or Bowling, or Boxing, or Beer,
   Said I to myself, said I,
Endeavour to emulate him who excels
Against one's enjoyment most certainly tells —
And I fancy the rule might apply to the Fells,
   Said I to myself, said I.

John Hirst

GERIATRIC RHYMES

We're the geriatric mountaineers, the septuagenarians;
All younger climbers we regard as immature barbarians.
In days of yore when we were young climbing was most
   respectable
And all the peaks were virginal — immaculate — delectable;
No pitons scarred the rock face, no beer cans soiled the corries,
No ski lifts reared their ugly heads when we went on our forays
With Sherlock Holmesish head gear and belted Norfolk jackets,
And six foot alpenstocks in hand and boots so full of tackets
That sparks flew out from every rock, igneous or sedimentary.
We talked in their own language to all the landed gent(a)ry;
Their keepers standing cap in hand were everywhere obsequious,
The very deer expressed delight to be on the same peak wi' us!

We had our little quiet jokes but frowned upon vulgarity —
The silence of the lonely hills discouraged cheap hilarity,
And we had come to understand what Wordsworth and what
   Byron meant
In all those lovely poems on the mountainous environment.
Our hearts leapt up at rainbows, and to men of education
There's not the meanest flower that blows but brings its apt
   quotation.

And so we tramped the mountainside and on into the distance,
And sometimes reached a summit — by the line of *least* resistance,
But when rocks above got steepish or the thick mists proved
    bewild'ring
A vision flashed before us of our sorrowing wives and childring —
A vision that inspired us to fresh effort and activity,
And very quickly took us to the foot of the declivity
And home to where our prattling babes received us with felicity,
And the anxious 'Little Woman' wrapped us round in
    domesticity.

And thus we have survived to be the septuagenarians
Compared with whom all younger mountaineers are but
    barbarians
Who fail to show respect to older men of proved ability,
Intelligence and enterprise, discretion — *and* gentility.
But were it not for modesty that borders on humility
We'd tell you tales remembered — and embellished! — in
    tranquillity
Of desperate adventures in the days of our virility,
When Mummery paid tribute to our climbing versatility
And even Whymper envied us our courage and agility;
And — but enough! The world today lacks reverence and civility
And treats our tales — and verses — as the maunderings of senility.

Barclay Fraser

CLIMBING SONG

Sun on the bothy, wind on the grass,
Shadow of cumulus over the pass:
Yawning and scratching and stretching of legs,
Boiling the billy and frying the eggs.

Moon on the loch, a bouldery camp,
Guy-ropes like banjo-strings, matchboxes damp;
The primus is bust, the pricker is bent,
But there's baccy and whisky galore in the tent.

453

An easterly wind, a bedraggling mist,
Rainwater trickling in at the wrist:
Wet to the belly, wet to the bum,
The boots are awash and the fingers are numb.

A furnace of sun, a tropical day,
Drowsy the hills across the way;
Line dangles listlessly over the edge
And the third man's asleep on a heathery ledge.

Dazzling cornice, pink cirrus or two,
Ice-crystals sparkling up in the blue;
One more Gold Flake and the bastard will go
And the fragments are dancing and tinkling below.

Syd Scroggie

A SONG OF THE ULSTER WAY

I took a walk in Ulster,
The Way is long to tell,
I went by Fairy Water
And over Bessy Bell.

By Little Dog and Big Dog,
Lough Formal and Lough Doo,
I followed on the Lakeland Way
Until I reached Belcoo.

I passed the lonely crossroads
At Eshywulligan,
I stopped at Keady Orlitt
And Lough na Blaney Ban.

Past Ballygawley Water
I walked to Aughnacloy,
I went by Legatellidy,
By Maghery and Moy.

By Ramaket and Ballynure
Drumguff and Quiggy Hill,
By Pettigo and Swanlinbar,
Drumlee and Columbecille,

Fardross and Favor Royal,
Moydamlaght and Slenshane,
Benburb and Ballycullen,
Bannfoot and Crabtreelane.

All these were on the Way I went,
Their names spelt out my track,
And still their echo haunts my mind
As I lay down my pack.

Alan Warner

THE JOE BROWN SONG

Many tales are told of climbers bold
Who perished in the snow
But this is a rhyme of the rise to fame
Of a working lad named Joe.
He came from good old Manchester
That quaint, old-fashioned town
And his name became a legend —
The legend of Joe Brown.

We've sung it once, we'll sing it twice
He's the hardest man in the Rock and Ice
He's marvellous — he's fabulous,
He's a wonder man is Joe.

He first laid hand upon a crag
In the year of Forty-nine
He'd nowt but pluck, beginner's luck
And his mother's washing line.
He scaled the gritstone classics
With unprecedented skill —
His fame soon reached the Gwryd,
Likewise the Dungeon Ghyll.

We've sung it once, . . . etc.

In the shadow of Dinas Cromlech
Where luckless leaders fall
The Corner it was towering high
And Joe uncommon small
But his heart was as big as the mountain,
And his nerves were made of steel —
It had to go, or so would Joe,
In a monumental peel.

We've sung it once, . . . etc.

When Evans raised his volunteers
For faraway Nepal
'Twas young Joe Brown that hurried down
To rally to the call
On Mighty Kangchenjunga
His country's banners blow
And the lad that raised the standard
Was known by the name of Joe.

We've sung it once, . . . etc.

In the cold, cold Karakoram
Where crags are five miles high,
The best in France had seen the chance
To pass us on the sly.
You may talk of Keller, Contamine,
Magnone, Paragot,
The man of the hour on the Mustagh Tower
Was known by the name of Joe.

We've sung it once, . . . etc.

With Colonel Hunt on the Russian Front
He paved the Paths of Peace
And helped to bridge the gulf that lay
Between the West and East
That Climbers all might Brothers be
In the Kingdom of the Snow
And the lad who led the Summit Talks
Was known as Comrade Joe.

We've sung it once, . . . etc.

He's like a Human Spider
Clinging to the wall
Suction, Faith and Friction
And nothing else at all
But the secret of his success
Is his most amazing knack
Of hanging from a hand-jam
In an overhanging crack.

>   We've sung it once, . . . etc.

But now Joe Brown has settled down
To raise a family
He's wedded to a local lass
By name of Valerie
But he sometimes takes his exercise
On Cloggy's gentle heights
When he isn't exercising
His matrimonial rights.

>   We've sung it once, . . . etc.

Some say Joe Brown is sinking down
To mediocrity
He even climbs with useless types
Like Dennis Gray and me
He's lost the pace to stay the race
And keep up with the van
And Baron Brown that tragic clown
Is now an also ran.

>   They sung it once let that suffice
>   For the Faded Flower of the Rock & Ice
>   What's he doing? He's canoeing!
>   Old Long gone Hand-Jam Joe.

Thus said Martin Boysen
And young Bas Ingle too
Ranting Allan Austen
And Peter 'Motley' Crew.

When from the outer darkness
A voice like thunder spake
As Baron Brown, with troubled frown
From slumber did awake.

He showed 'em once, he'll show 'em twice
The Grand Old Man of the Rock and Ice
He's marvellous, he's fabulous
He's a Wonder man is Joe.

Tom Patey

THE BALLAD OF IDWAL SLABS

I'll tell you the tale of a climber; a drama of love on the crags;
A story to pluck at your heart-strings, and tear your emotions
to rags.
He was tall, he was fair, he was handsome; John Christopher
Brown was his name;
The Very Severes nearly bored him to tears — and he felt about
girls much the same.

Till one day, while climbing at Ogwen, he fell (just a figure of
speech)
For the President's beautiful daughter, named Mary Jane Smith
— what a peach!
Her figure was slim as Napes Needle, her lips were as red as Red
Wall;
A regular tiger, she'd been up the Eiger North Wall, with no
pitons at all!

Now Mary had several suitors, but never a one would she take,
Though it seemed that she favoured one fellow, a villain named
Reginald Hake;
This Hake was a Cad who used pitons, and wore a long silken
moustarsh,
Which he used, so they say, as an extra belay — but perhaps we
are being too harsh.

John took Mary climbing on Lliwedd, and proposed while on
Mallory's Slab;
It took him three pitches to do it, for he hadn't much gift of
the gab.

458

He said: 'Just belay for a moment — there's a little spike close to
   your knee —
And tell me, fair maid, when you're properly belayed, would
   you care to hitch up with me?'

Said Mary, 'It's only a toss-up between you and Reginald Hake,
And the man I am going to marry must perform some great
   deed for my sake.
I will marry whichever bold climber shall excel at the following
   feat —
To climb headfirst down Hope, with no rubbers or rope,
At our very next climbing-club Meet!'

Now when Mary told the Committee, she had little occasion to
   plead,
For she was as fair as a jug-handle hold at the top of a hundred-
   foot lead.
The Club ratified her proposal, and the President had to agree;
He was fond of his daughter, but felt that she oughter
Get married, between you and me.

There was quite a big crowd for the contest, lined up at the
   foot of the Slabs;
The Mobs came from Bangor in Buses, and the Nobs came from
   Capel in Cabs.
There were Fell and Rock, Climbers', and Rucksack, and the
   Pinnacle Club (in new hats)
And — sight to remember! — an Alpine Club Member, in very
   large crampons and spats!

The weather was fine for a wonder; the rocks were as dry as a
   bone.
Hake arrived with a crowd of his backers, but John Brown strode
   up quite alone;
A rousing cheer greeted the rivals; a coin was produced, and
   they tossed.
'Have I won?' cried John Brown as the penny came down.
'No, you fool!' hissed his rival. 'You've lost!'

So Hake had first go at the contest; he went up by the Ordinary
   Route,
And only the closest observer would have noticed a bulge in
   each boot.

459

Head first he came down the top pitches, applying his moustache
   as a brake;
He didn't relax till he'd passed the Twin Cracks, and the crowd
   shouted, 'Attaboy, Hake!'

At the foot of the Slabs Hake stood sneering, and draining a
   bottle of Scotch;
'Your time was ten seconds,' the President said, consulting the
   Treasurer's watch.
'Now, Brown, if you'd win, you must beat that.' Our hero's
   sang froid was sublime;
He took one look at Mary, and — light as a fairy — ran up to the
   top of the climb.

Now though Hake had made such good going, John wasn't dis-
   couraged a bit,
For that he was the speedier climber even Hake would have had
   to admit.
So, smiling as though for a snapshot, not a hair of his head out
   of place,
Our hero John Brown started wriggling down — but look! what
   a change on his face!

Prepare for a shock, gentle ladies; gentlemen, check the
   blasphemous word;
For the villainy I am to speak of is such as you never have heard!
Reg. Hake had cut holes in the toes of his boots, and filled up
   each boot with soft soap!
*As he slid down the climb, he had covered with slime every
   handhold and foothold on Hope!*

Conceive (if you can) the tense horror that gripped the vast con-
   course below,
When they saw Mary's lover slip downwards like an arrow that's
   shot from a bow!
'He's done for!' gasped twenty score voices. 'Stand from under!'
   roared John from above.
As he shot down the slope, he was steering down Hope — still
   fighting for life and for love!

Like lightning he flew past the Traverse — in a flash he had
   reached the Twin Cracks —
The friction was something terrific — there was smoke coming
   out of his slacks —

He bounced on the shelf at the top of Pitch Two, and bounded
    clean over its edge!
A shout of 'He's gone!' came from all — except one; and that
    one, of course, was our Reg.

But it's not the expected that happens — in this sort of story at
    least;
And just as John thought he was finished, he found that his
    motion had ceased!
His braces (pre-war and elastic) had caught on a small rocky knob,
And so, safe and sound, he came gently to ground, 'mid the
    deafening cheers of the mob!

'Your time was *five* seconds!' the President cried. 'She's yours,
    my boy — take her! You win!'
'My hero!' breathed Mary, and kissed him; while Hake gulped
    a bottle of gin,
And tugged his moustache as he whispered, 'Aha! my advances
    you spurn!
Curse a chap that wins races by using his braces!' and he slunk
    away, ne'er to return.

They were wed at the Church of St. Gabbro; and the Vicar,
    quite carried away,
Did a hand-traverse into his pulpit, and shouted out 'Let us belay!'
John put the ring on Mary's finger — a snap-link it was, made of
    steel,
And they walked to the taxis 'neath an arch of ice-axes, while
    all the bells started to peal.

The Morals we draw from this story are several, I'm happy to say:
It's Virtue that wins in the long run; long silken moustaches
    don't pay;
Keep the head uppermost when you're climbing; if you *must*
    slither, be on a rope;
Steer clear of the places that sell you cheap braces — and the
    fellow that uses Soft Soap!

Showell Styles

THE MANCHESTER RAMBLER

I've been over Snowdon, I've slept up on Crowden,
I've camped by the Wain Stones as well,
I've sunbathed on Kinder, been burned to a cinder,
And many more things I can tell.
 My rucksack has oft been my pillow,
 The heather has oft been my bed,
 And sooner than part from the mountains,
 I think I would rather be dead.

CHORUS:
 I'm a rambler, I'm a rambler from Manchester way,
 I get all my pleasure the hard, moorland way,
 I may be a wage slave on Monday,
 But I am a free man on Sunday.

The day was just ending as I was descending
Through Grindsbrook just by Upper Tor,
When a voice cried, 'Hey, you!', in the way keepers do,
He'd the worst face that ever I saw.
 The things that he said were unpleasant,
 In the teeth of his fury I said:
 'Sooner than part from the mountains,
 I think I would rather be dead.' (chorus)

He called me a louse and said 'Think of the grouse,'
Well, I thought but I still couldn't see,
Why old Kinder Scout and the moors round about
Couldn't take both the poor grouse and me.
 He said, 'All this land is my master's!'
 At that, I stood shaking my head.
 No man has the right to own mountains,
 Any more than the deep ocean bed. (chorus)

I once loved a maid, a spot-welder by trade,
She was fair as the rowan in bloom,
And the bloom of her eye mocked the June moorland sky
And I wooed her from April till June.
 On the day that we should have been married,
 I went for a ramble instead —
 For sooner than part from the mountains,
 I think I would rather be dead. (chorus)

So — I'll walk where I will over mountain and hill
And I'll lie where the bracken is deep,
I belong to the mountains, the clear running fountains
Where the grey rocks rise rugged and steep.
    I've seen the white hare in the gulleys,
    And the curlew fly high overhead.
    And sooner than part from the mountains,
    I think I would rather be dead. (chorus)

Ewan MacColl

THE 700 FOOT VERTICAL CRACK

I'll tell you the tale of a mountain
The same way he told it to me
As I lay on my back in the heather
Fifteen hundred feet over the sea.
'I was born in convulsions synclinal
Some parts of my nature are gneiss
But I suffered a lot from erosion
In the latter post-glacial ice.'

'I can boast of a quite handsome talus
And many admire my scree.
I've a rotten gendarme near my summit
And a cliff that is rated A.P.
My cornices flourish in winter,
I have one quite imposing serac,
But my pride is my as-yet unconquered
Seven-hundred foot vertical crack.'

'You may talk of your Dru or your Grepon
You may talk of the Pic du Midi
Or about the north face of the Eiger
Or the south face of Tonlegee.
They all have their problems, I grant you,
But there's one thing the lot of them lack,
And that is an as-yet unconquered
Seven-hundred foot vertical crack.'

'One day, on my talus, some climbers
Were taking their ease and their lunch.
On their badge was a cloud and a mountain.
They looked quite a respectable bunch
    But then . . . !
My gneiss parts grew quite metamorphosed,
The heather rose up on my back
When I heard one man say to another
"Let's tackle this vertical crack."

'I put all my resources in action,
Sent down for a storm to the lake,
Tied a length of old climbing rope, broken,
In the seventeenth pitch, to a flake,
I stuck in three misleading pitons,
Brought a half gale of wind from the east,
And sent out some gilt invitations
To the ravens to come to a feast.'

'They buried them down in the valley
And over each head it was writ,
On a tombstone I kindly presented,
"Veni, vidi, but the mountain vicit".
So, listen, young fellow-my-laddy,
Here's a message that you can take back —
If you're out for a row or a ruction
Just tackle my vertical crack.
  If you're out for a row or a ruction
  Just tackle my vertical crack.'

Sean de Courcy

THE BOTANIST

Miss Astrea Montensis climbed
With only half her agile mind;
The other half went wandering wide,
Over each moory mountainside,
To spy some hidden, lonely bud
Obscured in cranny, scree or mud.
Full often would she seek for it,
Though long her comrades had to sit
And shiver in the driving rain
While she secured her specimen.
She knew each mountain, path and gap,
Not by its name upon the map,
But by the flora rich and rare
Which she had once collected there.
She never used an aneroid,
But, to judge every height, employed
Her knowledge of the habitat
Of lichens, moss and things like that.
But, though we must admire the skill
That led her on o'er rock and hill,
We must record her tragic tale,
Her botany did not avail.
During the New Year Meet, one day,
A snowstorm chanced to come — and stay.
The Club had asked our botanist
To lead a walk in snow and mist.
She knew the mountain there so well
From staghorn moss to asphodel.
Brightly she said, 'First let us go
To the top where alpine willows grow,
Then visit dear Silene's col,
And then return straight by the knoll
Where grows the little Drossera
Rotund, and Longifolia.'
The route today would no doubt go,
But in those times there still was snow;
The snow was very deep indeed,
It covered every leaf and seed;
The lady could not even see
Where alpine willows ought to be;
Each little plant was buried deep
In drifted snow-fields, wide and steep;

In vain the lady sought to find
Some landmark there to ease her mind,
In vain she scanned each frozen slope;
No flower was there, no leaf, no hope;
Completely lost, in wild despair,
She seized her ice axe then and there,
And strove to dig her way to ground
Where buried landmarks might be found;
But, though she dug with all her might,
The swift-approaching winter night
Closed up this brief and flowery page —
It froze her to a saxifrage.
The moral of this tale is clear;
All those who hold Dame Flora dear
Should not go climbing when the snow
May inconvenience them so;
And certainly should never be
Members of L.S.C.C.

Janet M Smith

SOME CAUTIONARY EPIGRAMS

If bagging all the Munros
Is only a duty one owes
To gods of fitness, God be Witness,
From Highland Hills the fun goes.

A map has many uses we are told,
It traces tracks and marks the bridges,
Defines the contour lines on ridges.
It will unfold, then tightly rolled
Can massacre the bloody midges.

The use of a drill
On rock is depravity.
It takes Climber's Will
To overcome gravity
And no Dentist's skill
To fill in a cavity.

Injections and Dressings
Saved most of his nose.
He counted his blessings —
Six fingers, seven toes.

Across the Styx a Climber is ferried.
The Dead Man wasn't properly buried.

'T-Shirts and Jeans will by now be quite white
So blow on your whistles and flash a bright light',
Said the Leader, then asked, 'Does anyone know
How to follow smooth sandal prints under new snow?

S Russell Jones

SOME LAKELAND LUNACIES

A Short Exercise in Local Pronunciation

'Tis woeful
From Bowfell
To gaze on the tangles
And muddles and wrangles
Of cars in the Langdales;
And awful
From Scafell
To see the hysteric
Processions from Keswick;
Or to breathe the miasma
Of car fumes at Grasmere.

Funny Peculiar
(dedicated to Manchester City Waterworks)

I often think it wonderful
And fabulously queer
To run a tap in Manchester
And bathe in Windermere!

Dialogue

'Don't go so near the edge, Tom,
There's a terrible drop below,
And keep well away from the cornice —
There's nothing so flimsy as snow!'

'Oh, shut up, you cautious old sausage!
I've a very good head, you'll agree,
And I think the snow's firm as a rock, man.
Here I go'. And he went. R.I.P.

468

Lover of Beauty

'How sweetly sound the waters
Pouring down the ghylls!
What majesty and beauty
Enfold these mighty hills!
How wonderful the sunshine
That makes the lakes a-glitter
With silver magic!' So he mused
As over Lakeland he enthused —
Then left behind his litter!

Look Before You Lap!

The sun was hot
So he drank his fill
From the flowing waters
Of Sour Milk Gill.
But little he knew
That out of view
And splitting the rushing stream in two
Were the rotting remains of a Herdwick ewe!

Tongue-Twister

Lisped a spinster when climbing Blencathra
'I'm afraid I am bound for dithathter;
        If I get to the top
        And find I can't thtop
I'll be heading *per ardua ad athtra!*'

Richard Clough

Retrospective

TOM WEIR

THE CLIMB

Leaving the shore, I took the rising road
  Inland, as I had done so many a time.
When, as a stripling, to the top I strode,
  I should have laughed to hear it called a climb.
    Now I was glad, when I had reached the crest,
    To make the view **my** pretext for a rest.

W K Holmes

A MATTER OF TIME

How I would love
to be walking on and on
up the hill
with increased vigour
my face in the sun,
with full strength,
gaining ground.
But I have passed my zenith,
and every step
tails towards the west.

Rupert Strong

BEACONS

There is a hill that stands for me
beyond the sunset and the sea,
    a ladder of light ascending:
when I have crossed the evening ray
and lost my comrade of white day,
    it beckons to me, bending
a mountain-way of wind and rain
to draw my feet from the dark plain: —
Where stars of slumber kindle on its crest,
my hill, the high hill, from wandering to rest.

There is a hope that calls to me
stronger than hills, than sun, than sea, —
    the fire of life still burning
when I resign the light it lent
and welcome darkness, well content;
    leaving to life's discerning
to lift my dreams on timeless wings
and lose me with the dust of things: —
The borrowed gold searched from my passing breath,
my hope, the high hope, to bear my dross to death.

Geoffrey Winthrop Young

CRAG OF CRAVING

Tonight a moon, and a star
Of unusual potency
Break the conventional blur
Of this time-chartered city,
Bringing with them Snowdonia,
My cottage under such sky
And the smell of the mountain night,
Loaded with heather and hay,
Salt water smells from the bright
Disc of Tremadoc Bay.

And it is all waiting there,
Like the other side of a death,
For spring's more clement weather
And then summer; a tapping moth
Outside the window where I sit
Long after embalmed midnight
Seeking the appropriate word
For some wandering soul in limbo
Who does not know death has occurred
But has nowhere but dying to go.

I think of the twin lakes under
The Crag of Craving and their
Uncompromised gesture of splendour,
Their water lapping on scree,
And the sense it gives of some other
Uncircumscribed quality,
To which you and I will come;
It's beyond the Crag of Craving
But I cannot give it a name.

Thomas Blackburn

PERSPECTIVE

Suddenly I remembered how the mountains of home
Would lie under the hunter's or harvest moon
Shellpale and passionless, shadowed like shifting dune
Or desert ribbed and veined by the wind's tide
And plucked into peak and crater at a whim.
I see them still
Shawled in a mist of moonlight; the dark cwm
Splaying the mountainside,
Climbing from fields to the Druids' coven of stones;
Curve and contour of each fold and hill,
Trees storm-sculptured into a frieze of flight,
Valleys a waterfall of shadow.
                    Remembered, remote
Are the dove-breasted hills that ever brood over night,
Becalmed in time, soundless and mindless and mute,
Their beauty piercing the heart, because life's span
But pricks eternity, so frail is man.

Margaret Rhodes

FRAGMENT

I looked into the fire, the hills were there:
there in the distance, mirrored in magic tongues,
summoning my heart, the hills that I remember.
Broad, the bare-breasted, solemn with changing shadow,
still, never variant, where the long sweet sense
whispering low, men are not all of the world,
has once seemed mine. Passions and symphonies stir;
they ask nothing of men, nor would be heard.

Since we live in the cage of ourself, sphere-bound,
they have been lost, beat of those mightier times,
or would be lost, but that one day, long ago,
some few notes crept, pressed their way through a chink
into our cage. There, ghost forms, they wander . . .

Wilfrid Noyce

LAMENT

We met on Cader Idris one December in the snow,
Courted in Snowdonia in two degrees below.
In the north night
It's almost light
In Shetland where, in June,
We saw the snowy owl together on our honeymoon.

At Easter up in Derbyshire you took good care of me,
I was happy in the hills there, but I couldn't drink the tea.
Then came a hike
Up Scafell Pike;
The summer after that
Your rucksack red had arms and legs and wore a knitted hat.

Our children love the mountains, but they'd rather have
    the beach,
We all enjoy a country walk to places they can reach,
Though now I mind
Being left behind,
But I love you and I know
How very much they mean to you, the mountains and
    the snow.

My climbing boots are dusty and my confidence is gone,
I often speak too sharply and you wonder what is wrong,
While at the sink
I sometimes think
Where did that young girl go —
The one you loved because she loved the mountains long ago?

Maureen Jones

BLUE REMEMBERED HILLS

Into my heart an air that kills
   From yon far country blows:
What are those blue remembered hills,
   What spires, what farms are those?

That is the land of lost content,
   I see it shining plain,
The happy highways where I went
   And cannot come again.

A E Housman

UNVISITED

Lonely places I have not seen,
Distant glens I have never viewed,
Islands where I have *almost* been,
Mountain tops where I have not stood;
Down the years you have called to me,
'Come, we are here for you to see.'

Times when the weather drove me back,
Days when the goal proved too remote,
Strayings away from the proper track,
Once when, alas, I missed the boat;
These are the themes that haunt my mind,
Lonely places I did not find.

White shell beaches where sea birds flute,
Secret pools where the burn flows deep,
Soft pine needles beneath the foot,
Towering crags where the eagles sweep;
What have I lost that I might have known?
Wisdom I might have made my own.

Years roll on (I have had my share);
Time has humbling lessons to teach.
Miles seem longer than once they were,
Many goals are beyond my reach.
Lonely places I may not see,
Is it too late you call to me?

Douglas J Fraser

WHEN FIRST

When first I came here I had hope,
Hope for I knew not what. Fast beat
My heart at sight of the tall slope
Of grass and yews, as if my feet

Only by scaling its steps of chalk
Would see something no other hill
Ever disclosed. And now I walk
Down it the last time. Never will

My heart beat so again at sight
Of any hill although as fair
And loftier. For infinite
The change, late unperceived, this year,

The twelfth, suddenly, shows me plain.
Hope now, — not health, nor cheerfulness,
Since they can come and go again,
As often one brief hour witnesses, —

Just hope has gone for ever. Perhaps
I may love other hills yet more
Than this: the future and the maps
Hide something I was waiting for.

One thing I know, that love with chance
And use and time and necessity,
Will grow, and louder the heart's dance
At parting than at meeting be.

Edward Thomas

EXCURSION IN AGE

Sunlight and frost
crack and brace
each wind-raked blade, each combing leaf.
This is the place
that, in his youth, he'd sought.
Now, alone,
shabby, ill-shod,
the opaque blast on head and back
beats like a rod.
In its encompass caught
scoured he is,
bleeding and torn.
This is the world's wind; yet, still in him
may joy be born;
through stubborn neck and thigh
the fires of joy be borne.

Decades ago,
conquering this height
— limbs eagled to the rock's incline
and the sun's light —
earth dipped, sky opened wide.
Young and braced, he stood,
naked and brown,
bone to the tinder, flesh to the flame.

While, below, the town
traded,
he saw spirit
made muscle in flood
earthing, in sap
branching, in blood
quickening; insect, bird, beast, man,
each different; each the same.

But now he is old,
life is all
turning of field and beast and child;
wit to forestall
his burnt-out body's ache;
folly to drown.
Blown, gad-fly-driven,
dissolving flesh
seeking what haven?
Three trees are black, opaque
above the ghyll.
Three masked trees
put death at the wind's turning.
The old man sees
and, stiffly, descends the hill.
Below, the town waits.
                    Fires are burning.

Mabel Ferrett

RESOLVE

When the days come that I must live alone
In my own thoughts, and when my eyes are dimmed
And cannot see the shadows on the hills
Cast by the clouds, and when I cannot hear
The far-off sounds of hurrying streams and sheep,
Then I will turn my mind to those great days
I spent upon the fells, and I will count
Them over one by one, and treasure them
As jewels that no one can take away from me.
Days when I climbed among the lowering clouds
And saw the mist come swirling up like steam;
Its flying streamers passing me so near,
I felt their ghostly fingers on my face.
I will remember seeing through the clouds
Drawn sudden back as curtains at the play,
A distant lake, a valley brightly green,
A glittering torrent down a mountain side,
Just glimp'st before 'twas blotted out again.
Days when the sun was hot on rock and heath,
And I could lie far up upon some ledge,
Hearing below the sad incessant voices of the dales.

And I will dream of little mountain flowers,
The butterwort with slender purple blooms,
The sundew sticky with its catch of flies,
The spongy mosses green and rusty red,
The cotton grasses waving silken plumes
Beside some lonely tarn high in the hills.
I will remember rain and bitter winds,
The feel of clothes drenched by the stinging shower,
Teas at a wayside inn with some good friends,
Hot baths and fires and warmth for tired limbs,
And all the loveliness of home and rest.
And while I think of all those joyous days,
Of all the heights I've gained and hours I've loved,
I will not envy those who take their turn
In tramping manfully in storm or fine
The hills I know for they are part of me;
A heritage of beauty naught can spoil.

Anon

ONCE UPON A TIME

Do you remember from the Glen Doll hut
The eerie bellowing of stags in rut,
A pair of golden eagles at the Sheiling,
Blue sky, white snowfield, soaring, wheeling,
The plovers where the lonely Slugain stood,
That whistled plaintively as plovers should,
The moon from yon stone bothy in Glen Loch
How it was full and had a rainbow broch,
The burn, the bubbling whaup, the puff of breeze
Where Bynack Sheiling was among the trees,
Shrill oystercatcher, snipe and heather linnet
From Lochend bothy door when we were in it,
The smell of wood smoke in the gloaming hour
Around the walls of crumbling Altanour,
The surreptitious squeak of vole or mouse
That broke the silence of Auchearie house,
Do you remember as I always can
From Broad Cairn hut the croak of ptarmigan?

The roofs, the walls, the floors we lay upon
Are gone these many years, completely gone.
What would you give, my friend, your sons, your wife,
Your income or a lease upon your life,
Or every other thing to have again
These smells and sights and sounds from there again.

Syd Scroggie

MEMORIES

Switch-flick,
Back it floods:
Muttering bass — Sibelius Three
Strings meander familiar thematic curve
Circling across towards centre;
And from memory's stream
A message flows —
— Washes me back to Mam Unndalain
That sunny day's stride to Kinlochquoich —
— Zig-zag down to lonely 'nam Breac
Cradled in loving fold of mountain flank.
Boots in rhythmic tread-stamp
Downbeat and upbeat on fine, firm path.
Exultation in blue-skied sunshine,
In nodding asphodel, in deer's strut
And ewe's tail-bob-panic,
In upreared femininity of conquered summit,
In power of firm body and keenness of sense,
In width of space — Sibelian space,
In music, in rhythm, in being there;
And ultimately because I was there, and still am there
Then because
I am here.

James Benson

HOME-MADE MOVIES OF AN OLD MOUNTAINEER

As darkness grips the shaft that drives the wedge
Of light on whitened wall that no one scales,
A shallow ledge stands out like Striding Edge
And Plaster cracks are mountain tracks in Wales.

Then figures form and flicker from the void
Through imitation snowstorm, black and white,
As undulating serpent celluloid
Uncoils and brings my yesterdays to light.

From metal cave a blinking Cyclops eye
Projects a rucksack pile by Chapel Stile,
The Devil's Kitchen heaven, angels high,
Unclouded Youth on shrouded Islay Isle.

A fly alights and traverses the lens,
Its shadow spreads gigantic from the glass.
No shadow darkened days in Highland Glens
Or dulled remembered ways from Pen-y-Pass.

A rasping scrape of nails on soundless stance
And strident silent shout 'Belay O.K.'
In jerking frames the lurking years advance
To show that *now* is five decades away.

The locust years, unfocussed, I forget.
The mechanism stops. An image dies.
No doubt I should stub out my cigarette,
— I find another film before my eyes,

A jumbled film assembled by a fool,
Of Snowdon Horseshoe prints above Loch Ness,
The Glyders gliding on to Ullapool
Along a Langdale lane to loneliness.

S Russell Jones

LISTENING AND LOOKING

What a day that was by the river
That called all time to itself
And beckoned us to dreams.
What re-affirmation of birth that was —
You, seeing sounds by the deep green rock,
And I, upon the pool below,
Hearing the colours of the earth.

T Ll Williams

RETURN

They stretched long arms, —
grey ribs of granite, muscle and joint in grass
clothing the naked bone;
and bright pools shone,
deep as a child's eyes, at the untroubled air,
near covert dimples where the fern beds were.
Clouds stirred, to pass
dragging their shadows over the rough rock face,
past furrowed caves, bright heather, or the rim
of chasms far in space,
calling the old to rest, the young to race.

He stood alone.
He blinked into the sun, blinked at the veil
of light that hung
and masked his sight.
He cried, 'I was your lover once, I raced
and climbed to kiss your foreheads one by one.
By noon and sun
each day, each hour I'd long to hold the crest
of each of you, and count you to my crown.
Years chained my pace.
What comfort have you for this broken man
Who stands alone?'

Wilfrid Noyce

NEARING THE SUMMIT

Under the telescopic July sun
Each detail of the mountain by my house
Seems what a Chinese master has well done
And what an india-rubber could erase.
Yet climb it and you sweat from stone to grass
And grope and grapple every step of the way,
Each moment growing more steep and strenuous,
You only reach the summit by what you pay.

I used to think that life a pageant was,
But now I know that it is an ordeal
And one must grit one's teeth and make no fuss
As one sweats through the stringencies of what's real.
It's something to do with a pliant kind of zest
That still insists that joyfulness is a fact
Though we've no hiding place or lasting rest
And all immediacies such joys restrict.

Knowing this we extend our space and time
Into a careless medium and more free
And postulate that by death we are taking aim
Into a novel kind of ecstasy.
Maybe this grows as the good muscles soften
And we no longer can enjoy the sweet
Taste of success as all the crag routes harden
And we can't love the airs beneath our feet,
Coming towards the summit it is sterner
And what the good will be there I don't know,
Perhaps it will be easier to ask pardon,
I haven't been there but it may be so.

Thomas Blackburn

CONDITIONAL

Beckon some cragsman's paradise from the sky,
Heart-beat slows down, lungs halt their heave,
So to descry, conceive
How it was with me when that sport began:
Muscle and nerve wrought for me by the strain.
Fain as of old I feign that yet I can.

485

Pass by some image of the world's desire,
Eye beam narrows, glance sharpens to discern,
So to attire, adorn
Some visitant from when that hunt began
Whose hardihood now tells me what is vain.
Fain as of old why feign that yet I can?

Butterfly thought, sail gaily through the void,
Seeking your mate, belike — gale-borne astray,
To be destroyed, betray,
Ice-caught, the thoughts from which your life began:
Torn downy wings that will not sail again.
Fain as of old, I feign that yet I can.

I A Richards

THE GHOST

He is the collector of icicles,
left empty-handed,
the journalist
of bird-calls,
the millionaire
of pebbles.

Page after page of snow

will not stop you
finding the footprints
behind you,

as if what you tracked tracked
you,
haunting the snows,
ice-axe in hand.

Edwin Drummond

486

THE ESSENCE

If now my unrelenting words —
though they be poorest art
for there is music and there are mountains
more beautiful than rarest words —
could hound me down
the unthought thought, the form, the essence,
that hidden thing that still remains
beyond the most desired and farthest vision!

Ah what if no veil is rent!
The essence of the trees and hills is left,
the still strange-to-human, morning lighted cwms
where the blood-red rock pours
from the riven mountain-side;
there may my being grow with the climbing trees,
the heaven-rooted flowers and this heart
fill with the lake and the high hills beyond.

C E MacCormack

THE HILLS AT SUNSET

We must turn, wanderer, now,
For the frost-fires burn.
Their wild silver will sear the stones
On the track to the cairn.

Shun the strange and painted sky,
The high lonely fell.
That is only a mirage of meadows
Of asphodel,

Gentians, lilies, violets —
The tenderest flowers.
That is rock, and granite, and chasms
Where the north wind towers.

That plunging, gentian shadow
Is cold, cold as death.
The peaks of lilac will wither
Man and his breath.

We must turn to the deepening vales
From the fire in the skies.
It is only a vision of violets
That has dazzled our eyes.

Diana McLoghlen

A MAN MUST CLIMB

A man must climb his mountain-side of years
And from each conquered height of age or fame
Look down above the precipice of fears,
The bogs of doubt, and see the way he came;
How every venturous mile was rich with gifts,
Streams where he thirsted, scented turf for rest,
And so press on into the mountain rifts
No wanderer, but a long-expected guest,
Until he feels full in his face and free
The summit-wind of high eternity.

Showell Styles

LEVAVI OCULOS

Lord of the sovereign heights — I ask no length
    Of honoured life, no span of gracious days —
Yet while I live I pray you grant me strength
    To follow year by year the old snow ways.

Of those that hearken to the mystic quest
    A score return unscathed, one pays the price —
If I should yield the forfeit for the rest
    I shall not grudge the hills their sacrifice.

But spare me, Lord, the valleys of regret,
    The vain long greeting of forbidden height,
The long, white pass that whispers — Farther yet —
    Mocking the failing strength with lost delight.

Grant me a grave swept by the mountain wind
    Beside the laughter of the snow-fed rills.
Grant I may pass with strength undimmed and find
    The sleep that is more ancient than the hills.

B K

THE MOUNTAINS OF GLAMORGAN

The mountains of Glamorgan
Look down towards the sea:
Their song is clear as any bell
In melodies that sink and swell,
And there they stand to sentinel
A land of mystery.

The mountains of Glamorgan
Grow wondrous in the Spring:
Perhaps our dead folk gather there
To bless their land in song and prayer
For every thicket, nook and lair   ·
Is loud with whispering.

When I have reached my journey's end
And I am dead and free,
I pray that God will let me go
To wander with them to and fro
Along those singing hills I know
That look towards the sea.

A G Prys-Jones

MOUNTAINS

To love without conquest
as I you all my days,
love with a zest
as unquenchable as ways
to fulfilment were barred —

is to be lifted and blessed
truly, for what is gained,
soon palls. But that far crest
never touched, never attained
makes of the mind a sky, starred.

Gregory Blunt

EPILOGUE

These are my riches, that none can take away from me,
    Stored as mountain-grass is stored in the byre;
These shall shine of an evening when Winter befalls me,
    Sitting by the fire.

Mine are the torrents and the timeless hills,
    The rock-face and the heather and the rain,
The summits where the life-wind thrums and thrills,
    And, answering, the glad heart sings again:
The good grey rock that loves a grasping hand,
    The stress of body, and the soul's rebirth
On the tall peaks where gods and men may stand
    Breathless above the kingdoms of the earth:

The drowse of summer on the sunlit crags
    Lulled in the blue and shimmering air of June,
When Time, the lazy mountain-traveller, lags
    To dream with us an endless afternoon:
The ice-wind stealing downward from the crest
    To hush with frost the reedy river's flow,
When all the mountain-land on winter's breast
    Sleeps in the deathly silence of the snow.

490

These are my riches, these and the bright remembering
　　Of ridge and buttress and sky-shouldering spire;
These I shall count, when I am old, of an evening,
　　Sitting by the fire.

Showell Styles

MOUNTAIN VIEW

Can those small hills lying below
Be mountains that some hours ago
I gazed at from beneath?
Can such intense blue be the sea's
Or that long cloud the Hebrides?
Perhaps I prayed well enough
By crawling up on hands and knees
The sharp loose screes,
Sweat dripping on the lichen's scurf,
And now in answer to my prayer
A vision is laid bare;
Or on that ledge, holding my breath,
I may even have slipped past Death.

Andrew Young

I HOLD THE HEIGHTS

I have not lost the magic of long days:
　　I live them, dream them still.
Still am I master of the starry ways,
　　and freeman of the hill.
Shattered my glass, ere half the sands had run, —
I hold the heights, I hold the heights I won.

Mine still the hope that hailed me from each height,
　　mine the unresting flame.
With dreams I charmed each doing to delight;
　　I charm my rest the same.
Severed my skein, ere half the strands were spun, —
I keep the dreams, I keep the dreams I won.

What if I live no more those kingly days?
   their night sleeps with me still.
I dream my feet upon the starry ways;
   my heart rests in the hill.
I may not grudge the little left undone;
I hold the heights, I keep the dreams I won.

Geoffrey Winthrop Young

ALL DAY I HAVE CLIMBED

All day I have climbed by slate and ling.
Now by the low becks' murmuring
I walk in humble quietude;
Till I turn and see the mountain's brood,
Long backs, wild manes, against the sky,
And their steaming flanks: and I triumph, 'I
have laid on your sides my pride's fierce rods:
I have tamed and bitted you, steeds of the gods.'

Edmund Casson

TO THE HILL HAUNTED

You who have scaled the steep
and challenged the gale;
bathed in the burns that leap
from summit to dale —

Watched the low cloud unfurl
o'er the shadowy pass;
sought for the ferns that curl
in the dim crevasse —

You who have loved old tales
by a peat-fire told;
followed forgotten trails
to the realms of gold —

Clung to the pinnacle's crest
in the burning noon;
slept on the mountain's breast
'neath a haloed moon —

You who have walked alone
in the sun or rain
where the long-whitened bone
scatters the plain —

Follow, my comrades, friends,
to the hills we know —
hills where the rainbow ends
at the edge of snow.

Brenda G Macrow

FROM SKYE, EARLY AUTUMN

I hope that Death is a pass
Through the brown-green, blue-brown, blue-grey,
    grey ghost mountains,
With the mists hanging in the vales,
    hiding the hard places;
The calm sheep proving my path;
And the sun shining soft
On the loch I have left.

M L Michal

A WAINWRIGHT

ACKNOWLEDGEMENTS AND INDEX OF AUTHORS

The editors and publisher are grateful to all authors, agents, publishers and other copyright-holders who have given permission to print copyright material. Every effort has been made to trace copyright holders, and where this has proved impossible, and the work has been included in the anthology, it is with apologies and in the hope that such use will be welcomed.

All the poets in the anthology are listed below in alphabetical order. Names of copyright holders etc are added where appropriate, followed by the titles of poems, the titles (in brackets) of books or journals in which the poems have already appeared, then by the page number(s) in this book where the poems are to be found.

500

502

504

505

506

511

ACKNOWLEDGEMENTS (Illustrations)

ALLEN John: photograph of Kinder Downfall in winter conditions (section 8 Hills to the North)

BENNET Donald: picture of winter on the Mamores (section 3 The Seasons Through)

BERRY Geoffrey: picture of Brothers Water in the Lake District (section 10 Fells of Lakeland)

BORD Janet and Colin: picture of Castlerigg Stone Circle near Keswick (section 7 Habitation and Habitat)

BROWN Hamish: photograph of the Ridge of the Reeks from Carrauntoohil in Ireland (section 6 Green Rim of Ireland), and photograph of the Cuillin Ridge in Skye (jacket design)

CLEARE John: photograph of Pete Livesey on 'Dream', Great Zawn, Bosigran (section 5 The Human Animal on the Hill)

CUMBERPATCH Ivan: cartoon (mid-section 13 In Lighter Mood)

GADSBY Gordon J: photograph of Cwm Bychan ii the Rhinogs (section 11 The Heart has its Feelings)

GAYTON Leonard and Marjorie: photograph of the Castle of the Winds, Glyder Fach (section 4 Wales of the West)

GILLESPIE Alex: photograph of the Carn Mor Dearg Arete to Ben Nevis (section 1 The Restless Compulsion)

McINNES Hamish: photograph of Applecross hills from the Bealach nam Bo road (section 12 Scottish Bens and Glens)

MacNALLY Lea: photograph of a golden eagle (section 9 Waymarks of the Elemental)

'NAYLOR': cartoon (section 13 In Lighter Mood)

POUCHER W A: photograph of Cul Beag from Stac Polly (Frontispiece)

RICHARDS Mark: drawing of Cheddar Gorge in the Mendip Hills (section 2 On Southern Slopes)

WAINWRIGHT A: drawing of Pavey Ark in the Lake District (section 14 Retrospective — Endpiece)

WEIR Tom: photograph of the Old Man of Hoy in Orkney (section 14 Retrospective)

514

LIST OF SUBSCRIBERS

The editors and publishers wish to acknowledge the generous subscriptions made by those listed below towards the publication of this anthology.

1	Mrs E G Brown
2	Michael Keats
3	Mrs M Fyvie
4	Rennie McOwan
5	Miss Vi Shannon
6	Keith W S Anderson
7	Dr and Mrs W M Pollok
8	Peter Murray
9	Margaret Griffith
10	Professor and Mrs R J Berry
11	Dr Colin G Scales
12	Berghaus
13	Ernst Sondheimer
14	Geoffrey Berry
15	Charles R Knowles
16	Chislehurst & Sidcup Grammar School
17	E F B Spragge
18	Sam Galbraith
19	J E Gamble
20	John Bourke
21	Derek Bean
22	Christine Mill
23	Bob Dawes
24	W R Swinburn
25	Bank of Scotland
26	Dr T H Steele-Perkins
27	Mike Fry
28	Christopher Main
29	Susan Margaret Baldock
30	Grant Gordon
31	A V L Dowdeswell
32	Mrs Gladys Guthrie
33	University College of North Wales
34	Rev Ronald Monk
35	R E Lambe
36	John Miller
37	A Ian L Maitland
38	Geoff Milburn
39	John Cheesmond
40	Barclay S Fraser

41	Chris FitzHugh
42	J K King
43	Kenneth McVean
44	Maurice Bennett
45	A A Gingell
46	Nigel and Shane Winser
47	Edward and Dorothy Ashburner
48	Islwyn Jones
49	Eskdale Green Outward Bound Mountain School
50	William M Morrison
51	Alpine Club Library
52	K L Davies
53	Roland Gant
54	David M John
55	Jean R Brown
56	P S Mould
57	John George Ashe
58	Adam Baptie
59	George Frederick Harrison
60	R K Harwood
61	Dr N C Craig Sharp
62	Dr Rodney C G Franklin
63	Merrilyn A Iddon
64	Peter G Robins
65	Mairi MacDonald
66	Peter Ward
67	The Earl of Limerick
68	Mrs Edith MacRae
69	William Paton
70	Michael Teal
71	Lt Col P G H Varwell
72	Dr D C Thomas
73	Fiona L M Wild
74	Charles Annand Fraser
75	Martin David
76	Gabriel Dunne
77	The Berry Family

INDEX OF FIRST LINES